BUILDING SUSTAINABLE COMMUNITIES

Spatial policy and labour mobility in post-war Britain

Mike Raco

First published in Great Britain in 2007 by

The Policy Press
University of Bristol
Fourth Floor
Beacon House
Queen's Road
Bristol BS8 1QU
UK

Tel +44 (0)117 331 4054
Fax +44 (0)117 331 4093
e-mail tpp-info@bristol.ac.uk
www.policypress.org.uk

British Library Cataloguing in Publication Data
A catalogue record for this book is available from the British Library.

Library of Congress Cataloging-in-Publication Data
A catalog record for this book has been requested.

ISBN 978 1 86134 743 5 (paperback)
ISBN 978 1 86134 744 2 (hardback)

Mike Raco is Senior Lecturer in Human Geography in the Department of Geography at King's College London.

Cover design by Qube Design Associates, Bristol.
Front cover: photograph supplied by kind permission of Mary Evans Picture Library.
Printed and bound in Great Britain by Hobbs the Printers Ltd, Southampton.

Contents

List of tables, figures and boxes

Tables

Figures

Boxes

Acknowledgements

The research material used in this book is drawn principally from two research projects, one funded by the British Academy (grant award: SG: 40053 'Key Worker Programmes, Changing Modes of Citizenship and Regional Development in Post-war Britain 1945-70') and the other under the Engineering and Physical Sciences Research Council's collaborative research programme on 'Sustainable Urban Brownfield Regeneration: Integrated Management' (grant number: GR/S148809/01).

I would like to express my thanks to a number of people whose comments, thoughts, and suggestions have influenced some of the ideas presented here. In particular, I would like to acknowledge the encouragement and support of Sophie Bowlby, Philip Catney, Allan Cochrane, Tim Dixon, Joe Doak, Ian Gordan, Steven Henderson, Rob Imrie, Martin Jones, Nikos Karadimitriou, Peter Merriman, and two anonymous referees for their thoughtful comments on the original proposal and an earlier draft.

I am also grateful to all those who attended and commented on the seminars I conducted and papers that I presented in relation to the research. Presentations were made in geography departments at the Universities of Aberystwyth, Durham, Hull, King's College London, Manchester, and Reading, and at conferences in London, Denver, and Chicago.

A big thanks also to those who have contributed to the research process. Effective archival work can only be carried out if supported by efficient and dedicated staff. I can safely say that all of the people that I troubled during my visits were extremely helpful and it would have been impossible to undertake the work without them. Thanks also to those who gave up their time to be interviewed and for their honest and revealing insights. I would also like to express my thanks to Jo Morton, Emily Watt, and the rest of the team at The Policy Press. Their hard work and patience with the author have been much appreciated.

And finally, I am also very grateful to my wife Sarah for her ongoing support in putting this book together.

Responsibility for the final product, of course, rests with the author alone.

ONE

Changing times, changing places

Introduction

The coming to power of the Blair government in 1997 promised a new era for the politics and practices of spatial development in the UK. Under the Thatcher and Major administrations inter- and intra-regional inequalities grew inexorably, not only as a consequence of wider economic processes but also as part of a deliberate strategy to promote the economic growth and competitiveness of the South and East of England (see Jones, 1997). The emphasis was on supporting those individuals, businesses, and places that were already seen to be globally competitive and successful and reducing support for those whose citizens were perceived to lack entrepreneurial dynamism and competitiveness. The re-election of a Labour government promised to end these divisions and to bring about greater social cohesion across the UK, albeit in a context where stable and strong economic growth was to remain the number one priority of policy (Blair, 1996). The new agendas were to be delivered by modernised state institutions whose powers, resources, and responsibilities would be devolved to empowered regional and local actors and communities (see Imrie and Raco, 2003). It seemed that 'one nation' politics was firmly back on the political agenda.

And yet, since 1997 the economic geography of the UK has become more, rather than less, divided. In 2004 it remained the most unequal country in the European Union with a staggering 23% of its wealth owned by just 1% of the population (ESRC, 2005).[1] This was reflected in the spatial economy in which divisions between and within regions and cities continued to grow (see Dorling and Rees, 2003). In some areas the demands for housing and property markets have been so low that development sites have remained empty for years at a time, while in other areas costs of living have increased so rapidly that even medium-income groups have been finding it increasingly difficult to purchase a home or sustain anything like an 'acceptable' quality of life. Businesses have been complaining of severe labour shortages in some parts of the country even though concentrations of unemployment and underemployment exist in others. Meanwhile, in some parts of London and the South East there has been a growing fear that the loss of so-called *key workers* (KWs) is beginning to undermine the social fabric of communities and spatial economies. As the gulf between economic rewards and the costs of social reproduction become increasingly wide, so, it is argued, communities and places will become unsustainable. Similar fears have, of course, existed in more deprived communities for decades in a context where work opportunities, rather than workers, have been absent.

It is partly in response to these inequalities that in February 2003 the Labour government launched its new development blueprint for regional planning and spatial policy in the UK – the *Sustainable Communities: Building for the Future* plan. The plan set out a vision to create new communities and reinvigorate existing ones so that they would be able to 'stand the test of time' and 'stand on their own two feet'. At the heart of the new agendas is an emphasis on imagining and constructing 'harmonious' and 'balanced' *sustainable communities* that will become both the objects of policy and the activated subjects through which wider development policy objectives will be brought to fruition. The focus is to be simultaneously on the regional scale, in terms of economic competitiveness, and the local with the creation of thriving and sustainable local communities. In this way, spatial policy could at last bring together the seemingly contradictory policy objectives of promoting economic competitiveness and social cohesion in an increasingly competitive global context.

At the same time other long-standing spatial development issues have re-emerged with a new urgency. For example, the 2000s have witnessed the rise of an increasingly contested *politics of labour mobility and migration* at a variety of scales. On the one hand, the flow of people across regional and national borders is presented by some as a vehicle for overcoming the growing problems of uneven spatial development. Attracting the right types of workers to move to the right places at the right times helps to create more competitive places. Thus, the Labour government has been keen to promote the migration of *knowledge workers* into fast-growing regions of the UK to help local businesses to sustain and enhance their global competitiveness. It has also sought to attract public sector KWs from Less Developed Countries in order to sustain public services, primarily in these areas. On the other hand, however, new barriers have been erected to try to halt the flow of the 'wrong types' of immigrant whose presence would, it is argued, destabilise community harmony and undermine both competitiveness and social cohesion. Ironically, such groups have been blamed by some for fuelling the shortages of housing and public services that exist in fast-growing areas. As we will see, the immigration process has been significantly tightened under the Blair government in an attempt to manage it in the 'best interests' of the UK's development.

And yet, the core elements of these contemporary agendas have strong continuities with earlier rounds of policy that also sought to engineer and create more balanced and harmonious communities. This search for balance has been, and continues to be, presented as a neutral and common-sense policy objective through which development processes can be made more effective and inclusive while benefiting a wider range of people. But, as we shall see, the definition of what constitutes 'a balanced place' is underpinned by power-infused, often normative, visions and imaginations. Later chapters will show that since the end of the Second World War the concept has, in fact, been defined and redefined in different ways as policy-makers have tackled complex questions not only over what *types* of economic development and community-building should be promoted but also *where* and by *whom*. The new emphasis on sustainable communities represents only the latest chapter in a long line of initiatives, projects, and programmes.

Within this dynamic and fast-evolving policy environment long-standing questions over the fundamentals of spatial development in the UK have therefore re-emerged. What role, for example, should spatial policy play in ordering places and communities and with what purpose? Should policy focus more on the construction of so-called 'balanced' places in which there exists a mix of different types of people and communities with different needs and aspirations? If so, how should this be achieved and how do development programmes ensure that in particular places there is a close and functioning relationship between paid employment and the 'right' types of workers? Moreover, at what scales should direct policy interventions take place and who decides where the boundaries between different places, communities, and citizens should be drawn?

Aims of the book

It is in this wider context that this book develops a historically grounded analysis and assessment of the relationships between spatial policy, community development, and labour market-building strategies in post-war Britain. It analyses the complex interrelationships between the politics of labour mobility and migration, modes of citizenship, and state capacities and activities during different eras of regulation. This focus, it will be argued, sheds new light on the ways in which modern states operate, how they seek to govern, and with what results. The central argument will be that within these wider development discourses functioning, balanced places have long represented both *real and imagined constructs* and that their form and character have been subject to reinterpretation and reformulation during different eras of governance and regulation. The creation of a balanced place requires a set of discursive frames of reference and imaginations to be actively created, deployed, and remade and these in turn draw on specific and context-dependent conceptualisations of how spatial economies work and how particular, bounded regions and places could and should be shaped to improve their efficiency and sustainability. The principles enshrined in the sustainable communities agendas of the 2000s represent the latest incarnation of these longer-term concerns.

The book will also argue, both conceptually and empirically, that within these wider development discourses the location and character of different types of *work* and *workers* have been a critical priority for policy-makers and planners. Paid employment is at the interface of the relationships between economic competitiveness and social reproduction. Ensuring that it is distributed in an effective and efficient manner is, and has long been, a core objective of spatial policy programmes. In developing and implementing such strategies, political decisions have to be made over what types of *local labour markets* are necessary for a community or place to function effectively. This, in turn, draws on particular conceptions of how spatial economies operate and what types of work and workers must be *present* in order for a place to be both economically competitive and socially cohesive. It is in light of this desire to order the relationships between employment and workers that we must interpret post-war inter-regional and international *migration* policies. The book will argue that the ordered movement of migrants, in a context of planned community-building programmes, has been directly associated with wider economic development strategies and rationalities. Unregulated movements, conversely, have been perceived as a 'problem' by policy-makers and others at a variety of scales. The politics of migration and the politics of community-building have, therefore, been closely intertwined, with significant social, political, and economic implications.

In order to develop these arguments the analysis will draw on *detailed empirical evidence*, from archives, policy statements, and interviews. In this sense it differs markedly from the growing trend within 'non-representational' human geography in which writing has become increasingly abstract and divorced from the complex, and at times contradictory, realities of policy definition and implementation. It will show how problems and policies came into being, how they became institutionalised and delivered, and how they were subject to contestation and change at a variety of scales. In so doing, it will address four interrelated sets of questions:

- In what senses have programmes that seek to engineer balanced communities and labour markets been important in the construction and implementation of post-war spatial policy agendas? What have their main characteristics been and how and why have they been subject to change?
- What have been the experiences of such policies and programmes? Does the mobilisation and movement of particular workers across boundaries have the capacity to influence the trajectories of spatial development? How effective have such programmes been in enhancing place competitiveness? What does the evidence reveal about the impacts of programmes on different types of workers and citizens?
- What are the relationships between such programmes and changing modes of state regulation? What does their existence and implementation tell us about the changing relationships between citizens and states? Are these programmes inherently divisive or cohesive? Do they encourage the formation of mixed or divided communities?
- In what sense is some type of citizen (and worker) selection programme a necessary ingredient for an effective spatial development strategy? What lessons can be learned for New Labour's spatial policy agendas from earlier policy initiatives? What are the prospects for sustainable communities agendas in the coming decades?

The remainder of the chapter is divided into three sections. The first sets out some of the core themes surrounding the relationships between 'balanced' community-building and spatial policy and highlights the key concepts that will inform the analysis in subsequent chapters. The second section discusses the value of using a historical methodology, before the third briefly signposts the book's principal contents and sums up the book's key points.

Building balanced communities: exploring the rationalities of spatial policy

The promotion of balanced communities in spatial planning discourses is nothing new. Utopian models of urbanism have long incorporated the principles of diverse community-building as evidenced by the Garden City and New Town movements in the early 20th century and the design of post-war New Towns in which it was argued that '*all social classes should be represented*' and their places of residence mixed (The Reith Committee, 1947, paragraphs 22-4; see also Ward, 2004, and Chapter Four of this book). This recurring focus on balanced communities throughout the modern era has been linked to spatial planning's wider concern with *ordering* spaces and places so that the needs of capital accumulation can be integrated and supported by some wider sense of social cohesion, reproduction, and integration (see Law, 1994; Hall, 1998). It is for this reason that the concept of balance carries such intellectual and political capital within the discourses of spatial planning.

Longer-term conceptions of balance have strong echoes in contemporary blueprints for sustainable community planning and design. As Chapter Seven will illustrate, through the 1990s and 2000s the discourse of sustainability has become increasingly significant across Western Europe with its core messages of greater democratisation, a new futurism, and more equitable forms of economic growth (see Meadowcroft, 1999, 2000). These ideas have found expression in what Gordon and Buck (2005) have called New Conventional Wisdoms in which it has become commonplace to argue that some sense of socioeconomic balance and diversity can provide communities and places with a vibrancy and in-built entrepreneurialism that makes them more dynamic and creative and better able to take advantage of new opportunities in a global economy (see, for example, Urban Task Force, 1999, 2005; Florida, 2004). The problems that afflict many cities and regions today are put down to a spatial juxtaposition of failing markets, economic changes, and social exclusion. Their regeneration requires the planning process to 'balance and integrate the social, economic and environmental components of their communit[ies]' (ODPM, 2005, p 1).

And yet, the seemingly inclusive, functional, and motherhood-and-apple-pie concept of 'balance' has multiple meanings and interpretations depending on whether it is conceptualised as a process or as a thing. The *Collins Concise English Dictionary* (1993), for example, describes 'balance' on the one hand as '*a state of equilibrium*' or '*harmony in the parts of a whole'* (pp 93–4). In these terms a balanced place or a sustainable community would be represented as a thing or an end–state, a static self–reproducing and self–contained object. On the other hand, the process of balanc*ing* focuses attention on the activities through which actors may seek '*to arrange so as to become a state of harmony'* (p 94). Balancing is an ongoing activity that reflects and reproduces selective, politically constructed definitions and understandings of what a balanced object or community *should* look like and how it should be constructed. Conceptualising processes of balance in this way opens up multiple interpretations over what the outcomes of spatial planning policy could and should be and how definitiions of balance are shaped through differential power relations between different social groups.

In order to analyse and address these processes this study will draw on four interrelated conceptual themes: (i) dominant imaginations of places and spaces; (ii) mobility–fixity tensions; (iii) citizenship, selectivity, and subjectivity; and (iv) state capacities and practices. Each of these will be briefly discussed here and will form the basis of a deeper conceptual analysis in Chapter Two and the empirically based chapters that follow.

Dominant imaginations of places and spaces

Imaginations of places and spaces play a key role in shaping the contours of any spatial development programme. Within modernist discourses places have often been elided with the static, the ever–present, and unchanging elements of social reality (see Berman, 1982; Massey, 1994, 2004a; Harvey, 1996). They have represented objects to be (re–)imagined, worked on and converted into more efficient spaces through defined policy programmes (see Tuan, 1977; Taylor, 1999). As Massey (2004a) notes, spatial planning has primarily been concerned with how the messiness and chaos of places can be ordered and made into rational spaces or 'how juxtapositions may be regulated, how space might be coded, [and] how the terms of connectivity might be negotiated' (p 151). This, in turn, draws attention to how particular sets of 'problems' and their 'solutions' take on defined forms through frames of thought or, what Foucauldian authors term, 'governmentalities' (see Dean, 1999; Larner and Walters, 2006). In different places these processes of problematisation take on diverse forms and are structured by politically contested conceptions of socioeconomic needs, priorities, objectives, and capacities.

Such processes raise a number of questions that will be examined throughout the book. Who, for example, defines what a balanced place consists of in social and economic terms? What criteria are used in this selection process and what types of understandings of place and space are deployed at different times and with what ends in mind? In relation to contemporary debates, what should be done to create 'sustainable places and communities' and whose needs and requirements should be prioritised in the process? Moreover, what visions and priorities are excluded from these imaginations of places and spaces and through what processes are decisions taken and implemented?

Mobility–fixity tensions

Spatial planning's focus on controlling and shaping places, both now and in the future, requires the construction of particular forms of mobility, or what Cresswell (2001, p 15) defines as 'the process of regulated or controlled movement'. In order to shape and create balanced places and spaces, some types of mobility are essential such as the ordered movement of jobs, housing, businesses, and investment from certain locations to others. And yet, this movement has the potential to destabilise places and may also be difficult to effectively regulate and control. At the same time, spatial policy is also, paradoxically, concerned with creating new forms of *fixity*. An ordered place is imagined in rather static terms as a location where 'unnecessary' and 'unwanted' mobilities are kept to a minimum (see Chapter Two; Cresswell, 2001; Sheller and Urry, 2006). In drawing up spatial policy strategies, questions, therefore, have to be addressed such as: What sorts of mobility and fixity should be encouraged? What sorts of policy measures are most effective? Moreover, should mobility strategies be linked to wider policy objectives, such as those that encourage new forms of economic competitiveness and greater social cohesion? Again, these are questions that will be examined conceptually and empirically in later chapters.

Citizenship, selectivity, and subjectivity

The 'balancing' of places also draws attention to broader questions concerning the form and character of *citizenship* and state–citizen relationships in the planning system. As Turner (2000, p 132) notes, 'citizenship controls access to the scarce resources of society and … [this] allocative function is the basis of a profound conflict in modern societies over citizenship membership criteria'. In defining and creating places, *selective* decisions relating to citizenship have to be taken to determine who should live in a particular place; what their socioeconomic characteristics and capacities should be; what resources should be allocated to different groups; and how these processes of allocation, selection, and community-building should be governed. Spatial policy has explicitly concerned itself with the creation of 'better' citizens and the belief that through a logical and coherent ordering of spaces and places, individuals and communities can be nurtured that can take greater responsibility for their own well-being and socioeconomic reproduction.

However, any place- or community-building strategy involves choices to be made over whose presence is desirable and what such citizens require in order for them to reside and work in a particular place at a particular time. In defining and supporting such 'key' citizens, their needs and aspirations have to be identified and provided for. As later chapters will show, the emphasis on supporting KWs in post-war spatial policy has always been subject to selective judgements over what a KW 'requires' and how their aspirations and expectations can be catered for within balanced or sustainable communities. Similarly, the treatment of non-essential workers has reflected particular conceptions of what their needs, as different types of citizens, consist of.

This differentiation between different citizens does not simply reflect the characteristics of individuals and/or communities. It is also a consequence of the ways in which *citizens are created and recreated* through policy. If, in constructing balanced communities, it is decided that particular forms of entrepreneurialism and active citizenship need to be generated, then policy agendas need not only to identify and mobilise the right types of citizens but also to create them. It is in this respect that spatial policy can be conceptualised as *an active social policy* as citizenship is constructed in and through a range of policy arenas, from education and healthcare, to housing, and of course the availability of employment. Spatial policy gives us insights into how these processes of citizenship-building have been implemented at different times and in different places.

State capacities and practices

In order to implement and deliver any spatial planning agenda, states need to establish and mobilise their resources and capacities of action. Exactly how this is done and with what effects varies from context to context. For example, as later chapters will show, the decades after the Second World War are often characterised as representing an era of state-led, Keynesian governance in which planning and its implementation were directed by elected bodies and their executive, bureaucratic agencies (Cochrane, 1993). In recent decades the notion of state capacities has been broadened to include other groups, citizens, and agencies whose powers and resources can be directed and mobilised in the development and implementation of policy agendas (see Rose, 1999a; Imrie, 2004). States, it is now argued, operate through increasingly complex networks of governance and the concept of state 'capacities' has been subject to change. The continuities and changes that have occurred over time and the effects they have had on the form and character of spatial policy are highly significant and will be the subject of analysis in later chapters.

The possibilities, practices, and limitations of the historical research method

In order to satisfactorily address these themes this study will draw on a historical overview of the policy programmes that have sought to construct balanced places and labour markets since the end of the Second World War and the imaginations and discourses that underpinned their objectives and priorities. Developing a historically oriented analysis of this type raises a series of questions over the value and relevance of historical research. As Chapter Two will argue, the focus of recent writing on how state regulation has changed and how boundaries of citizenship are being reconfigured draws on particular narratives of change over time. Indeed, the whole concept of a sustainable community requires new time frames and imaginations of the future to be deployed, for in Dodgshon's (1999, p 610) terms, 'only time can reveal relations of succession or change, whereas only space can reveal relations of structure or organisation'.

However, there are three principal methodological problems with conducting historical research on the themes covered in a book such as this. First, there is the danger of taking policy programmes from the past and 'reading off' their meanings and significance from the perspectives of contemporary debates. There can be too little attention paid to the ways in which the latter are the products of an ongoing and continuous reinvention and re-articulation of concepts and ideas fostered by policy-makers, academics, public and private sector-sponsored think tanks, and consultants. It is tempting to take loosely defined concepts such as 'sustainability', 'competitiveness', and 'social cohesion' and apply them to policy debates of a different era. Similarly, the concept of community is one that has been articulated by policy-makers in many different guises from contexts as different as healthcare in the UK in the 2000s to colonial/imperial policy of the mid–1950s (see British Colonial Office, 1958; SEATO, 1966; Imrie and Raco, 2003). However, without an adequate *contextualisation* of the ideological and practical circumstances in which such terms were defined and deployed, a simple reading off of earlier policy programmes through a contemporary lens is not only dangerous but misleading.

Second, there is the problem of collecting enough quality evidence to allow meaningful and in-depth analysis to take place. Any assessment of the discourses and practices of policy initiatives requires an interrogation of the historical processes through which policy objectives were identified, prioritised, and implemented. Using a range of archival sources can provide a window on such processes but the evidence will always be partial and selective. While this is always a problem encountered in any social research, the reliance on archives poses particular problems over issues such as confidentiality, what is kept and what is destroyed, and the categorisation of files as 'secret' or unavailable for use by public researchers (see May, 1997). Such issues have become particularly pertinent in the UK with the introduction of the Freedom of Information Act in 2000 and its opening up of key documents relating to debates within government since the early 1970s, although this is still conditional on their sensitivity.

The third problem is one of *narrative* and *hindsight* with the tendency to portray events as moments in a wider story with a clear, linear logic. Narratives are integral to the transfer of knowledge between and within generations (see Giddens, 1995; Hastings, 1999). The ability to 'tell a story' conveys information in a meaningful, logical, and practical way. It can provide a justification for events and decisions taken at specific moments and can become a 'truth' that shapes the ways in which subsequent understandings and interpretations are shaped and understood. Yet narratives can provide a broad-brush approach to what were, in reality, complex and contested ways of thinking and acting. In trying to tell a story, evidence can be included or excluded depending on the wider story that is being portrayed. With historical research this is compounded by the often patchy and restricted nature of the evidence base. For example, in contemporary writing from a broadly regulationist perspective, it is commonplace to highlight the regulatory differences between an era of Keynesian governance in which social and economic problems were characterised by particular understandings of the role of the state and its powers and responsibilities, and a post-Keynesian context in which very different, more laissez-faire modes of regulation have become dominant (see in particular, Brenner and Theodore, 2002; Brenner, 2003). While such a narrative is, as we will see in later chapters, extremely powerful and furthers understanding in many ways, it can become something of a framing device from which policy decisions can be all too easily interpreted as a teleological product of a broader, overarching logic of changing modes of regulation.

Given these significant difficulties, what is the value of historically based research? Is it possible to provide a meaningful historical inflection on contemporary policy debates and processes, such as those that characterise the recent rise of sustainable communities? In addressing such questions I would argue that there are three strong reasons for pursuing research of this kind.

First, any research on policy processes needs to address what Dodgshon (1999) refers to as the 'principle of persistence', that is the extent to which contemporary policy initiatives are developed in existing, and path-dependent, socioeconomic contexts. This persistence may extend to the impacts of earlier rounds of policy that shape and guide the future form and character of development agendas. So, for example, contemporary efforts to transform urban residents into active, entrepreneurial, and dynamic citizens are inherently limited by earlier periods of governance in which active citizens have either been marginalised or ignored (see Raco et al, 2006). Too often, policy initiatives, as we will see in later chapters, are launched with little regard for what went on before, thereby limiting their potential (and actual) effectiveness. In this sense the past is political with processes of remembering selectively used to substantiate particular perspectives. We must be mindful that 'history is meaningful to us only because it forms part of how we code what is around us' (Dodgshon, 1999, p 618) and that 'in domesticating the past we enlist it for present causes' (Lowanthal, 1997, p 15). For example, in relation to British urban policy under New Labour a range of controversial earlier initiatives, such as the Urban Development Corporations, have been selectively re-imagined and re-presented as 'misunderstood' programmes that, in reality, sought to bring about the sustainable urban regeneration of inner-city areas (see Florio and Brownill, 2000). This has been used to justify their recent reintroduction in the Thames Gateway (see Raco, 2005a).

Second, too much contemporary policy, and indeed policy research, is launched as if it were 'new' or different from what has taken place before. A central element of modernity is the ongoing drive towards improvement and betterment, with the consequence that what already exists must be overridden and superseded. Policies are often launched, therefore, in an ahistorical vacuum in which the same debates are played out time and again. For example, the experiences of Community Development Projects in English cities in the 1970s and the evaluations of them that subsequently took place highlighted the key difficulties of attempts to mobilise communities in urban policy design and implementation (see Lawless, 1989). And yet, the return to community during the 1990s and 2000s has been implemented with scant regard to the lessons of the 1970s thereby limiting its effectiveness and potential in the contemporary era (see Imrie and Raco, 2003, for a wider discussion). Presenting a policy or an analysis as new is seen as a necessary prerequisite for it to be legitimate and historical research can play an important part in challenging such notions.

Third, while the collection of historical data has limitations this is true for all types of social research, which is always partial, limited, and fallible (see Sayer, 1992). If archival material is adequately and thoroughly contextualised so that the circumstances in and through which it was produced are acknowledged and worked into the analysis, then it can provide evidence of wider social, political, and economic changes. As discussed above, contemporary interpretations of shifts towards post-Keynesian welfare systems, for instance, require a thorough understanding of what took place in earlier rounds of regulation, and historical analysis can provide this. It can provide a richness and depth of material that enables the development of new insights into taken-for-granted socio-political processes. Without such critical reflection it is all too easy for researchers to be limited by their own 'dominant narratives' and conceptualisations.

The research for this book was conducted over an 18-month period (during 2004-05) and drew upon a range of methods. For the historically based chapters it involved the uncovering, accessing, and analysis of archival documents from a range of government and non-governmental sources. Research was carried out on archives in the locations listed overleaf.

Location	Main sources
The National Archives in Kew, London	Government records, letters, correspondence; ministerial documents and files
The Modern Records Centre, Warwick	CBI and other business representative organisation archives; Trades Union Congress (TUC) archives; individual Trade Union archives
The People's History Centre, Manchester	Labour Party, Trade Union, and Communist Party archives
The Thatcher Foundation, Cambridge	Archives of the career of Mrs Thatcher
National Library of Scotland, Edinburgh	Government records, letters, correspondence; ministerial documents and files
British Library of Political Science, London	Government records, letters, correspondence; ministerial documents and files

In addition to the archival work, interviews were also conducted with policy-makers and planners in a range of organisations including the Office of the Deputy Prime Minister (ODPM), the Department of the Environment, Food and Rural Affairs (DEFRA), Thames Gateway London Partnership, the Trades Union Congress (and other unions), the Home Office, and regional development agencies. The use of semi-structured interviews represented the most effective method for ascertaining and collecting the views and perceptions of those working in the policy fields discussed. It enabled views on current agendas to be explored and analysed and provided the foundation for much of the second half of the book.

Structure of the book

The book is divided into three sections. Part One introduces the study and outlines the key questions and concepts that inform the subsequent analysis. It is followed by two empirically driven parts that engage with the post-war decades of 1945-79 and the period since 1979 respectively. The former is often characterised as the high water mark of the Keynesian Welfare Settlement, and an era in which states saw it as their moral responsibility to reorganise the spatial economy of the UK in ways that would ensure greater social justice and economic efficiency (see, for example, Harvey, 2005). The latter examines post-Thatcher Britain and the ways in which spatial and labour market-building policies have been transformed and restructured. However, it should be noted that one of the primary objectives of the analysis is to highlight the *continuities* as well as the contrasts between these periods. Indeed, one of the key findings will be that the tensions that underlay contemporary spatial policy agendas between economic (competitiveness) agendas and socio-environmental (cohesion-sustainability) concerns were also present in the immediate post-war period. Similarly, the processes and practices of state selection and the persistence of relational conceptions of citizenship have also been evident over time, despite changing social, economic, and political contexts.

The chapters within each part are structured along similar lines to assist with the comparative analysis. Chapters Three and Six concentrate on the fluctuating character of regional policy and the role of labour mobility programmes in building functioning communities and labour markets. The former focuses on labour transfer and KW programmes in the aftermath of the Second World War and the ways in which these were used to encourage the mobility of firms and to foster new 'cultures of entrepreneurialism' in the UK's Development Areas. The latter examines the breakdown of the regional policy settlement since 1979 and the changing conceptions of what constituted essential and non-essential labour. It situates conceptions of labour market structures into the wider context of regional (and urban) competitiveness and entrepreneurial dynamism. It also discusses changes to regional policy under the post-1979 Conservative and Labour governments and the recent rise of the 'sustainable community'.

While these chapters concentrate on policies to support existing areas, Chapters Four and Seven assess policy programmes that have sought to establish and build new communities. Chapter Four looks at the New Town programmes after the Second World War and assesses their definitions of what constituted a balanced and functioning place. In contrast to the large number of studies that have been carried out on the New Towns, this chapter explores, in some detail, the ways in which planners conceptualised the relationships between the spatial distribution of different types of employment and the balanced and functioning communities that they were building. There is an analysis of how essential workers were defined and the programmes that were introduced to facilitate selected forms of labour mobility. Chapter Seven looks at contemporary initiatives to build sustainable communities in the UK and draws out the comparisons and contrasts with the New Town agendas. It focuses, in particular, on conceptualisations over what constitutes a competitive place and whose presence is seen as necessary to the fulfilment of wider spatial policy agendas. It examines the Labour government's definitions of KWs and examines the ways in which spatial policy programmes are being shaped to support such individuals and groups, in the context of a wider construction of sustainable communities.

Whereas these chapters are primarily concerned with inter-regional labour mobility, Chapters Five and Eight broaden the discussion and examine the relationships between international migration and spatial development strategies in the two periods. Policies that focus on building balanced communities and labour markets cannot be understood without an analysis of these wider policies and programmes. As we will see there are direct relationships between the extent to which labour mobility boundaries are made 'selectively permeable' and the economic objectives of spatial policy. These chapters argue that there have been strong continuities in the rationalities of such programmes since the war, despite the changing political and economic contexts within which policy is being implemented. Migration policy has been driven by particular ways of thinking about the relationships between worker mobility and the creation of ordered and balanced places and communities.

Conclusions: spatial policy as an active social policy

Before moving on to a more conceptual discussion of the relationships between spatial policy, labour markets, and 'balanced' community-building, let us summarise the key points made thus far. The core argument of this book is that we need to understand spatial policy and broader conceptions of balanced or sustainable communities as more than just an outcome of rational or technical decision-making processes. Instead, spatial policy must be conceptualised as an *active social policy* that seeks not only to create more competitive places but also to construct new forms of citizenship so that individuals and communities can act as both the subjects and objects of policy (see Cochrane, 1999; Clarke, J., 2005). For a place-based community to be 'in balance' it needs to possess the right types of citizens, possessing the right types of skills and capacities. It also needs to possess some degree of social 'harmony', derived from a healthy labour market and the presence of the right types of citizens and communities. This involves more than just the handing out of resources to enterprises or entrepreneurs. It requires the mobilisation and coordination of a range of policy fields covering areas as diverse as entitlements to housing and the provision of transport infrastructure. It is this integrated nature of spatial policy, lying as it does at the interface between economic production and social consumption, that makes it such an important field of study. Indeed, it could be argued that post-war spatial policy represents a Rosetta Stone through which wider state practices and broader economic, political, and social processes can be translated, interpreted, and analysed.

The chapter has also argued that, in order to conduct such an analysis effectively, policy must be situated in and through the contexts from which it emerged and has evolved. Without an assessment of the continuities, as well as the changes, that have taken place our understanding of contemporary processes is diminished (see Imrie and Raco, 1999). For example, the discussion of post-war KW support policies will shed light on contested changes in conceptualisations of policy – categories such as essential work, knowledge, citizenship, entrepreneurialism, place harmony, and competitiveness. In this sense the book is seeking to push forward debates over spatial policy in new ways and develop new avenues for further research. It examines change as a *process*, rather than a thing.

In addition, the book will argue that there are strong *recursive relationships* between policy imaginations and the practical and grounded changes that have affected both people and places since the 1940s. It will demonstrate that pejorative definitions of policy discourse analysis as being too 'academic' or 'esoteric' and having little or no connection to the realities of 'practice', does not necessarily hold true (see Sayer, 1994; Fuller, 2004, for a wider discussion). For in tracing the contours of spatial policy and the dominant conceptions of communities and labour markets that have underpinned them, the analysis will document the ways in which the latter have shaped, and in turn been shaped by, the former. In short, discourses directly shape policy implementation at the same time as grounded realities, such as deindustrialisation or changes to the global labour force, play an important part in shaping imaginations. The book will, therefore, go beyond a discussion of representations, important though these are, to map out the relationships and connections between political, economic, and social processes.

Note
[1] A report published by the Central Intelligence Agency (2005) uses Gini Index scores to rank socioeconomic inequalities in different countries. A score of 100 equals perfect inequality, a score of 1 equals perfect equality. The figures for the EU in 2004 were: Austria 31; Belgium 28.7; Czech Republic 25.4; Denmark 24.7; Estonia 37; Finland 25.6; France 32.7; Germany 30; Greece 35.4; Hungary 24.4; Ireland 35.9; Italy 27.3; Latvia 32; Lithuania 34; Netherlands 32.6; Poland 31.6; Portugal 35.6; Slovakia 26.3; Slovenia 28.4; Spain 32.5; Sweden 25; *United Kingdom 36.8.*

Part One
Conceptualising spatial policy

Conceptualising sustainable communities: place-making and labour market-building

If one aspect of social life can be said to dominate views of society, it is the organisation of production. Work relations enter virtually all models of social organisation and associated images of man or woman as an actor in and product of structured relationships. (Miller, 1998, p 327)

'I grew up in the thirties with an unemployed father. He didn't riot. He got on his bike and looked for work.' (Norman Tebbit, Conservative Party Conference, 1981)

Introduction

Conceptions of sustainable and balanced communities are premised on the formation and retention of functioning *labour markets*. Labour is a 'commodity' unlike any other in that its regulation, control, and reproduction is an inherently social and political, as well as an economic, process (Jessop, 1990; Harvey, 1994; Jones, 1999). On the one hand, labour power represents a factor of *production* in that it is a core requirement for the accumulation of profit. Workers with the appropriate skills or 'human capital' are a necessary element in the production and delivery of goods and services. On the other hand, the reproduction of embodied workers requires that their social needs and their access to certain forms of *consumption* are adequately met. States need to provide access to a range of services (such as health and education) and commodities (such as housing) in order for citizens to live and work. The absence or presence of different types of labour in particular *places* is, therefore, directly connected with the processes and spatial patterns of economic development.

Drawing on a range of literature this chapter examines the relationships between labour market-building, place imaginations, citizenship, and mobility. It will assess the wider significance of these relationships for processes of sustainable community-building and policy programmes that seek to enhance both the economic competitiveness and social cohesion of places. It will discuss the ways in which the balance of different types of labour and citizens in defined places becomes converted into a 'problem' of government to be addressed through active social policies that define, identify, and mobilise different communities and groups in the wider pursuit of policy objectives. It begins by examining processes of spatial selectivity and the shift from Keynesian to post-Keynesian governance. It then turns to questions of citizenship and identity and links these to broader processes of labour market-building and (dominant) conceptions of essential or key workers (KWs). Finally, the discussion engages with questions of migration and labour mobility before introducing the key issues to be addressed in later chapters.

Spatial selectivity and spatial policy: from Keynesianism to the new regionalism

For many writers, the rationalities and practices of governance and regulation in the UK can be divided into distinct historical periods. In the decades following the Second World War what Brenner (2003) terms a 'strategy of spatial Keynesianism' represented the dominant state strategy for most western countries. Spatial Keynesianism was based upon a strong *national* welfare state and contained within it a 'project of equalizing the distribution of industry, population and infrastructure across national territories' through a conception of 'the entire national economy as an integrated, auto-centric, self-enclosed territorial unit moving along a linear developmental trajectory' (Brenner, 2003, p 207; see also Harvey, 2005). Within a wider one-nation politics of universal citizenship, a strategy of socio-spatial integration was developed by post-war governments with the aim of mobilising support from wider interests to act as partners (see Gamble, 1988; Jessop et al, 1988). As Brenner (2003, p 207) argues, the core aims of Keynesian spatial policy were to tackle uneven development through the de-concentration of population, industry, and infrastructure investment from major urban centres into peripheral areas and the standardisation of economic investments and infrastructure across the national territory. As later chapters will show, a spatially selective labour market policy was also a central feature of this wider state strategy.

Thus, under Keynesianism, while it was the national scale that became the focus of development policy, it was the regions, or Development Areas, that became the key spaces for the policy interventions through which this objective would be mobilised and delivered. Equalising growth between the regions became a core policy objective as the 'problem' of regional development was perceived to result from a lack of spatial *mobility* on the part of capital and labour. As Chapter Three will show, spatial policy was, therefore, designed to facilitate enhanced, directed movement through resettlement programmes and infrastructure investments.

The conventional wisdom is that since the breakdown of the Keynesian settlement in the mid-1970s and the growing internationalism of the global economy the form and character of spatial selectivity, state strategies, and state projects has been transformed so that states now 'strive to differentiate national political-economic space through a re-concentration of economic capacities into strategic urban and regional growth centres' (Brenner, 2003, p 207; see also Tickell and Peck, 2003). These so-called *new regionalist* strategies are underpinned by very different understandings of how spatial economies operate and the policy mechanisms that are necessary for national and regional competitiveness (see Scott, 2005; Lovering, 2006). The discourses of globalisation and global economic competition now dominate political and spatial policy agendas with cities and regions seen as autonomous units whose competitiveness is dependent upon their internal capacities and potentials. Unlike post-war programmes, this new regionalism/localism is a philosophy that downplays the *interrelationships* between successful and unsuccessful spatial economies. Indeed, in its most extreme forms, it calls for the problems of uneven development to be solved through capacity-building programmes in problem places as a response to new contexts of enhanced global territorial competition for mobile investment (see Harvey, 2000).

The consequence of such strategies has been a lower priority given to the direct, large-scale transfers of resources from donor to recipient regions in many countries. Alternative programmes have been developed that on the one hand support already successful places to become even more globally competitive, while on the other identify degenerate places whose internal capacities need to be enhanced through the mobilisation of existing institutions, resources, and communities. In Brenner's (2003, p 207) terms, this involves a new 'glocal developmentalism' in which national economic space has become fragmented into 'distinct urban and regional economies with their own place-specific locational assets, competitive advantages, and development trajectories'. Different types of capital mobility are promoted in which places compete to be selected for investment, placing the onus on places to make themselves attractive. The new regionalist development politics, therefore, promotes 'the re-concentration of industrial growth and infrastructure investment within strategic urban and regional economies' (p 208).

Globalisation and the shifting regulation of western societies

These changes in the philosophies and practices of spatial policy and state regulation are underpinned by new ways of thinking about the factors that drive economic competitiveness. New imaginations and vocabularies have been developed to characterise the emerging 'realities' of economic competition (see Giddens, 2002a; Raco, 2002; Thrift, 2005). Foremost among these has been the emergence of the discourse of the *knowledge-based*, global economy in which competitiveness is said to be determined by the extent of innovation and creativity within a spatial economy. For Jessop (2002a) this change in thinking involves a shift from a Keynesian welfare system to what he terms a Schumpeterian Workfare Postnational Regime. Table 2.1 highlights the core elements of this shift.

These new Schumpeterian agendas, it is argued, are premised upon a reconceptualisation of the relationships between knowledge, competitiveness, and the global economy so that 'the promotion of the knowledge-based economy [becomes the] primary object of economic governance' (Jessop, 2002a, p 272). This primacy accorded to knowledge reflects a broader shift away from a concern with manufacturing industry towards producer, high-skilled services and

Table 2.1: The Schumpeterian Workfare Postnational Regime

Distinctive set of economic policies	Focuses on innovation and competitiveness in open economies, with increasing stress on supply-side
Distinctive set of social policies	Subordinates social policy to an expanded notion of economic policy; downward pressure on the social wage and attack on welfare rights
Primary scale (if any)	Relativisation of scale at expense of national scale. Competition to establish a new primary scale but continued role of national states
Primary means to compensate market failure	Increased role of self-organising governance to correct both for market and state failures. But state gains greater role in the exercise of meta-governance

Source: Jessop (2002a, p 252)

'weightless' forms of development (see Amin et al, 2003). For Jessop (2002a, p 7) such characterisation is inevitable as:

> economic and political relations are so complex that any action oriented towards them requires some discursive simplification ... such discursive simplifications have a key role in their turn in the always tendential constitution and consolidation of the economic, political and other systems, shaping the forms of their institutional separation and subsequent articulation.

In short, discourses and imaginations matter. They play a central part in the identification and definition of the 'problems' that governments face. They also shape the limits of state action by framing the boundaries of state legitimacy and (perceived) effectiveness. Similar points have been made by a range of authors arguing from a more Foucauldian perspective for whom the mobilisation of particular problems of government involves the creation of specific ways of thinking, or governmentalities, about the nature of reality (see, for example, Miller and Rose, 1990; Larner and Walters, 2006).

The shift towards a Schumpeterian workfare state has significant implications for the relationships between capital and labour and the politics and practices of labour market-building. The focus on entrepreneurialism places greater emphasis on the *knowledge-worker* whose presence is a necessary requirement for the development of competitive and efficient economic regions. Perhaps the most influential recent advocate of such ideas is Richard Florida (2004). He argues that the presence (or absence) of a new *Creative Class* of entrepreneurial and dynamic wealth producers plays a critical part in shaping the economic competitiveness of places. This Creative Class consists primarily of young, highly skilled, and increasingly mobile workers whose vitality and creativity facilitate new forms of growth and entrepreneurial dynamism in the places in which they live. In addition, Florida argues, they also play a vital role in generating a sense of community and commonality and encourage the formation of more tolerant, open, and inclusive forms of place politics. Such discourses have been extremely influential, particularly in the anglophone world where national, city, and regional governments have tended to be more sympathetic to the discourses of globalisation and the possibilities and practices that new types of economic activity can bring (see Peck, 2005).

The logical consequence of these new imaginations is that 'social' policy becomes focused on organising 'conditions favourable to the international mobility of technologies, industrial and commercial capital, intellectual property and at least some types of labour-power' (Jessop, 2002a, p 273). The role and purpose of the welfare state is transformed so that instead of existing to support the needs of social reproduction, it becomes a vehicle for the promotion of entrepreneurialism and competitiveness. For example, labour market policies have increasingly focused on the promotion of flexibility and the minimisation of (direct) costs for employers as a vehicle for employment generation and profit accumulation. The objectives of policy become redefined with welfare support restructured towards the promotion of access to the labour market and paid work (see Levitas, 1998). Rather than pooling the risks associated with unemployment, emerging welfare systems, it is argued, adopt:

> a more active approach to labour market policy through a combination of measures to create the conditions for full employability in the labour market and of active preparation of some or all of the unemployed to get them back to work. (Jessop, 2002a, p 154)

The implications and effects of these new ways of thinking are, therefore, profound. They involve particular conceptions of the social and economic 'value' of different workers and citizens. These, in turn, lead to the logical conclusion that in order to promote new forms of competitiveness in particular places, state support should be targeted on those of greatest value. It is their presence or absence that will ultimately determine the economic and social futures of spatial economies. In his stinging criticism of this new Florida-inspired school of thought, Peck (2005) makes the point that what we are witnessing is a new politics of inequality that *ascribes* particular forms of value to particular types of citizens and in so doing institutionalises and reproduces structural divisions between different groups of workers – a theme that is directly explored in later chapters.

Citizenship, selection, and labour markets

Citizenship is a multifaceted concept. In essence, it concerns the interface between states and individuals/communities and the balance of rights and responsibilities on each party. In Britain it has two principal dimensions (see Plant, 1991). On the one hand, it includes the right to civil and political citizenship, such as the right to free speech and freedom from religious persecution. On the other hand, it is intrinsically embedded in broader conceptions of social and welfare rights in which 'as a status [it] confers some rights to resources such as income, health care, social security and education' (p 56). The difficulty is that in general the former does not involve significant resource implications whereas the latter do. Addressing this tension has been at the heart of the contested politics of the welfare state in Britain since 1945 based on questions such as how rights to welfare provision should be assessed. Can there be universal rights in a context of scarce resources? If so, how are these resources to be shared out and how are particular citizens selected for support and assistance? Moreover, what responsibilities and obligations are there on citizens that may entitle them to specific rights and resources and how can states use policy to create the 'right types' of citizens?

In the aftermath of the Second World War the construction of the welfare state went some of the way towards guaranteeing social and welfare rights to all citizens. Indeed, for Ignatieff (1991, p 29) 'the history of the welfare state in the twentieth century can be understood as a struggle to transform the liberty conferred by formal legal rights into the freedom guaranteed by shared social entitlement'. However, the architects of the post-war welfare settlement, such as Beveridge and Attlee, saw that the state had 'only a general duty to provide collective services in the fields of health, education and welfare' (Plant, 1991, p 57), not to guarantee that all individual claims to resources would be met. Given that resource restrictions have always been a key element in welfare state systems, much of the focus of debates since the mid-1960s has been on the relationships between obligations and entitlements. The neo-liberal, post-Keynesian critique of the welfare state was primarily based on a challenge to the principles of the latter. Radical thinkers in the 1970s and 1980s such as Keith Joseph increasingly argued that rights to welfare should be linked more closely to the fulfilment of obligations on the part of recipients (Gamble, 1988). This new philosophy was driven by a core belief that there exist 'different kinds of citizens who are recognised not for what they do or what they have been made into but for what they lack' (Cruikshank, 1999, p 123). Those 'lacking' in responsibility, or what Schneider and Ingram (1997) term 'degenerate communities and citizens', should not be entitled to unconditional state assistance as this would only foster new forms of dependency and stifle individual and collective creativity and innovation (see also Chapter Six).

For many commentators the universalist emphasis of post-war welfarism has, therefore, been undermined and superseded by new processes of state selection and differentiation, some of which were examined above (see also Dean, 1999; Peck and Tickell, 2002; Larner and Craig, 2003). According to Rose (1999a) we are witnessing the creation of new forms of *relational citizenship* that reflect 'as much a capacity to act in relation to the particular circumstances of one's environment, as well as in relation to others, as it is a 'right' conferred by the state' (p 99). This new 'citizenship of capacity' becomes something to be earned, to be legitimated, and to be conferred on to individuals or groups as a reflection of their relational socioeconomic position and the extent to which they have proved their value by being good active citizens. As Rose (1999b) notes, 'this transformation from citizenship as possession to citizenship as capacity is embodied in the image of the active and entrepreneurial citizen who seeks to maximise his or her lifestyle through acts of choice, linked not so much into a homogeneous social field as into overlapping but incommensurate communities of allegiance and moral obligation' (p 99). How these forms of citizenship are characterised and conferred is critical to the formation and functioning of any sustainable and functioning spatial economy and (sustainable) communities. Such a focus on relational citizenship, Rose (2000) contends, has come to dominate the politics of citizenship in what he terms 'advanced liberal societies', such as the UK.

And it is in the process of conferring citizenship that we need to understand some of the recent changes in spatial policy, and social policy more broadly. In many ways, the process of governing modern societies has become increasingly focused on the creation of the right types of citizens and communities, who are able to act as both the objects and subjects of policy. The construction of citizenship is actively forged and cultivated through policy (see Clarke, J., 2005). This is a complex process involving many different, interrelated dimensions, and changes in one sphere of policy have intended, and unintended, consequences for others. In the field of housing, for example, the Right to Buy legislation of the 1980s enabled social tenants to become property owners, usually for the first time. This had the effect of reducing the quality of the housing stock left in the public sector, through a process of residualisation, and this, in turn, encouraged more tenants and potential tenants to seek out their own homes, rather than relying on the retreating public sector. One of the primary objectives of this move was, therefore, not only to address questions of social housing but also to engender new forms of individualised citizenship and to break one of the institutionalised links between civil society and the direct provision of social, or collective, consumption by the state (see Saunders, 1995).

The process of making better citizens has also dominated debates over the meaning and significance of so-called 'Third Way' politics or what Giddens (2002a, 2005) has recently attempted to rebrand the 'neo-progressivist' movement. For Giddens, new forms of progressive citizenship should be focused on the *co-production* of public goods in which there 'should be collaboration between the state and the citizen in the production of socially desirable outcomes' (2005, p 16). The popular conception of the state as an enabler that was developed in the 1980s and 1990s was an attempt to move away from the top-down managerial, bureaucratic governance that characterised the post-war era. This, it is argued, has been supplanted by the Blair government (and others) by a new understanding of the 'ensuring state' in which 'there exists a public responsibility after enabling and that there are certain guarantees that the state has a moral and political responsibility to provide' (Schuppert, 2005, p 57). According to these neo-progressives the role of an ensuring state is to use politics to establish 'new tools with which to bring together disparate constituencies and persuade them to behave in ways which make collective solutions possible' (Bentley and Halpern, 2005, p 74). In other words, through a process of institutional reform and a re-imagining of social policy, neo-progressives believe that the state can engender new forms of citizenship and new ways of thinking and behaving.

While such debates have been fruitful and have shed much light on new modes of state action, they have little to say about the spatialities and temporalities of these new forms of state–citizen interactions. For example, the emphasis on balanced economies and places that has underpinned spatial policy agendas since the Second World War has been premised on differential relations between different types of citizens and their *spatial relationships to each other*. Spatial policy has been one vehicle for the creation of new (often divisive) relationships between different groups, as selection always involves a set of boundary-drawing processes in which lines of exclusion and inclusion are drawn. Decisions are made over what types of expertise and knowledge are essential to the delivery of policy proposals (and what types are not) and the ordering of spaces and places so that they become more socially cohesive and economically competitive (see Kenny and Meadowcroft, 1999; Gordon and Buck, 2005).

This raises a series of policy questions. If certain groups or citizens are labelled as 'essential', how are they to be defined and identified and what policy measures should be developed to support them? In more practical terms, what types of housing and employment should be promoted, where should it be located, what should it cost, and who should provide it? The ways in which such questions are addressed by development agencies depends on a series of imaginations and political perspectives concerning the formation and implementation of spatial policy agendas and the roles and responsibilities of states, citizens, private sector actors, and communities. The next section will now expand on this discussion to examine the ways in which questions of entitlement have become bound up with citizenship and work.

Labour, citizenship, and the welfare state

> The word work embraces equally those for whom it is exhausting, boring, disagreeable, and those for whom it is a clear pleasure with no sense of the obligatory. There may be a satisfying feeling of personal importance or the acknowledged superiority of having others under one's command. Work describes both what is compelled and what is the source of the prestige and pay that others seek ardently and enjoy ... fraud is evident in having the same word for both circumstances. (Galbraith, 2004, p 18)

Historically, individual entitlements under the British welfare state were dependent on a citizen's position in the labour market. In the Victorian era, for example, distinctions were made between the so-called deserving and undeserving poor in which (albeit limited) welfare support was conditional on the individual's perceived ability to work (see Briggs, 1979). Those who could work had a moral and social responsibility to do so, whatever the conditions under which they were employed. Other writers such as Weber and Marx saw the regulation and control of the labour process as the primary foundation of modernity. Weber (1968), for example, identified the complex relationships between modern bureaucratic systems, capitalism, and the importance of the 'work ethic' in shaping the consciousness of workers and employers. Marx's chapter on 'The working day' in *Capital* (1974) graphically illustrates the relationships between workers (and their bodies), employment, and the capitalist system (see Braverman, 1977). As later chapters will show, during the first half of the 20th century embryonic welfare state systems in countries such as Britain were still based primarily on the relationships between work and citizenship. The evidence documents the close interrelationships between work, citizenship, and state strategies and the policy dilemmas and challenges faced by post-war governments and their *imaginations* of what constitutes a 'healthy' labour market and the role of policy in bringing them to fruition.

The rise of the post-war welfare state was designed to provide a new system for collectivising the risks associated with employment and its loss. The payment of unemployment benefits had both a moral and economic purpose. It was moral in that society had a duty to protect its most vulnerable members from hardship and destitution and economic in that supporting workers would help maintain economic demand and therefore ward off the threat of deep recessions such as that of the early 1930s. However, this emerging welfare state was always underpinned by the principle that in some way 'rights *should* depend on discharging some moral obligations such as labour' (Plant, 1991, p 61; emphasis added). Citizens were still expected to take responsibility for making themselves more employable and take up employment opportunities once they arose. It is sometimes forgotten now that some of the most vehement critics of the welfare state system in the 1960s and 1970s came from the political Left who saw it as a vehicle for entrenching patriarchy, supporting the existing (capitalist) socioeconomic system, and stigmatising welfare recipients (see Miliband, 1968; Gough, 1979).

For Giddens (2002a, p 16), the consequence of these social, political, and economic changes since the mid-1970s has been a series of welfare reforms that reduce 'unsustainable' commitments, tackle the culture of dependency that exists, and 'stress responsibilities as well as rights, in order to encourage active citizenship as well as to reduce welfare dependency'. The new concern is with the 'employability' of workers or the mechanisms through which individual citizens can raise their skills and aspirations to make themselves more attractive to prospective employers (McQuaid and Lindsay, 2005; McQuaid et al, 2005). The unemployed have become both the subjects and objects of welfare reform, to be defined, identified, and mobilised in order to tackle 'a vast array of economic and social problems ... encompassing everything from weak competition and low productivity to unemployment and community breakdown' (Lloyd and Payne, 2003, p 367).

These changing imaginations of labour market processes have increasingly drawn on the foundations of classical political economy in which labour markets are conceptualised in abstract, a-spatial, and a-temporal terms. At their most extreme, such approaches 'assume systematic relationships between prices and quantities, purged of all social and institutional processes' (Picchio, 1992, p 2). Explanations are increasingly derived from *individualist* or *atomistic* conceptions of the labour process in which the distribution and character of labour markets can be explained through the laws governing price signal adaptations, market exchanges, and rational decision-making. The focus turns to individual subjects and their employability, capacities, and aspirations (see De Brunhoff, 1976). As Peck (1996, p 30) forcefully argues, they represent 'a powerful fiction. The competitive model performs a fundamental ideological function, justifying rewards to those thought to have earned them and issuing penalties to those who have not'. Social or institutional factors that shape the everyday functioning of labour markets in different contexts are abstracted out of explanatory models.

These changing conceptions of citizenship and the role of the welfare state draw attention to the broader social and economic functions of labour markets. Labour markets represent the core, mediating interface between the 'realms of production and consumption' (Jonas, 1996, p 324). The problem for capitalists is that they have always had to rely on efficient, functioning local labour markets to accumulate profit and yet they 'lack direct control over the conditions of labour reproduction or workers' consumption' (p 325). For Jonas this dependent relationship necessitates:

> a contextual approach to local labour market governance
> which recognises capital's on-going need for place-based
> labour control practices while at the same time holding on
> to a vision that forces are about which are profoundly
> disruptive of these local ties. (p 326)

Consequently, labour regulation requires the formation of 'institutional fixes in different localities and at different points in time' (Jonas, 1996, p 326). It is an inherently *political* process forged in and through existing, historically embedded social relations and institutional practices. In building balanced communities and labour markets, spatial policy initiatives represent strategic attempts to bring about a spatial fix in which the needs of production and social reproduction are brought together and met in place or in 'institutional sites at which place and space intersect' (Peck, 1996, p 16; see also Harvey, 1994). Understanding how and why spatial labour markets are defined, identified, and turned into objects of government, therefore, becomes a critical part of any analysis of spatial policy.

A focus on spatially differentiated labour markets does not, of course, limit analysis to crude generalisations concerning the links between the availability of employment and the employment of local populations. Labour markets are highly segmented between different groups of workers. They represent 'complex socio-political structures' and an analysis of them has to be 'inseparable from a consideration of the complex institutional forms, patterns of governance and processes of social regulation that together constitute its institutional underpinning' (Haughton and Peck, 1996a, p 319). Thus, different groups of workers coexist in local labour markets and carry out very different types of interrelated employment to the extent that 'there is no such thing as a local labour market if we mean by this a set of jobs in any one place which are open to all the residents of that place' (Duncan and Savage, 1989, p 189). Eliding co-presence with employment is, therefore, a dangerous (policy) assumption that simplifies the relationships between spatial co-presence and labour market access.

A broad range of studies show how such processes operate in practice. Sennett's (1998) research on the differential rhythms of work patterns in cities such as London, for instance, highlights the ways in which a mass of low-paid, low-skilled workers, such as cleaners and cafe waiters, work in shifts, often at unsociable hours, their little-noticed existence barely registering with the highly paid workers who inhabit their offices during the day. Toynbee (2002) and Ehrenreich (2001) provide graphic accounts of life for low-paid workers in the UK and US respectively and others such as Mike Davis (2003) have written about the disconnections and fragmentations in labour markets in California and other parts of the US (see also Peck and Theodore, 2000; Wills, 2001). In such contexts, for 'the majority of underprivileged workers ... labour markets are indeed local' (Cooke, 1989, p 264) at the same time, paradoxically, as they are becoming more inaccessible and polarised. As Peck (1996, p 30) writes, the reality has been that:

> whatever the measure chosen the *same* social groups tend to suffer the brunt of labour market disadvantage ... [and this] tends to be distributed in accordance with the ascribed rather than achieved characteristics of the workers, varying more closely with ethnicity, gender and age, for example, than with education and skill.

The processes involved in labour market-building are, therefore, as much social and political as they are economic. Imaginations over how labour markets are constituted and what employment demands consist of within a spatial economy shape labour market policy objectives and practices. For instance, the Blair government has consistently argued that there is a skills shortage in the UK and that, as discussed earlier, improving the skills base of the workforce, particularly in lagging areas, will promote new types of enhanced economic development. However, there is little recognition that employers have consistently failed to demand new skills, as would be anticipated if there existed a significant 'skills gap' (Lloyd and Payne, 2003). There is a failure to re-imagine the economy and accept that many British firms demand low-skilled labour because their competitiveness depends on exploitation, low wages, and little investment in the workforce (see Hutton, 2003). As the risks and rewards of employment become more polarised, so questions over exactly when and how socioeconomic boundaries are drawn between different types of workers take on a new importance. Given the intrinsic interrelationships between the social construction of 'skills' and processes of group labelling, whole sectors of the labour market are *ascribed* as being 'unskilled' or 'semi-skilled' workers, whereas others are seen as 'key' or 'essential' to the competitiveness and cohesion of places and it is to such debates that the chapter now turns.

Labour market politics: skills, divisions of labour, and the definition of key workers

The concept that groups of *essential* or *key workers* (KWs) exist has been a recurring feature of labour market and spatial development policies since the inception of spatial policy in the 1930s. There is no one definition of a 'key worker'. The category only takes on meaning through the material and ideological contexts in which it is developed and understood. It involves the drawing of boundaries around particular groups of workers and the provision of special support to meet their particular needs and requirements in the name of economic efficiency and the wider public 'good' (see Raco, 2006). In this sense, definitions of worker 'value' can be critical in establishing differential relationships between the state and citizens working in different occupations as the notion of essential workers represents 'a contingent identity [that] only constitutes itself in relation to that which it is not' (Du Gay, 1996, p 2). It often involves a binary, dualistic way of thinking that sets out to include particular groups, communities, and individuals while excluding others.

The effects of this process may be profound as in modern societies paid employment is closely bound up with the structuring of identities and subjectivities. People in paid employment 'will frequently use their work as a resource for the construction of their identity but will rarely do this in a way that actually reflects the formalities of the employment contract' (Bradley et al, 2000, p 175). Work constitutes a mode of social identification as well as an economic transaction so that any classification of the work process is constituted by broader relations of social power (see Sennett, 2003). It is the close relationship between economic 'skills' (or what is often termed 'human capital') and social status that makes definitions of skills and therefore KWs such a politically charged and highly significant process.

The most frequent interpretation of the KW within discourses of modernity and economic governance is that of the *expert* who can perform a key *instrumental* role in the functioning of a labour market. Instrumental definitions of KWs are linked to wider conceptions of expertise, expert systems, and knowledge that have arisen since the Enlightenment (Beck, 1992; Rose, 1999a). As later chapters will show, KWs have often been elided with those in positions of managerial expertise or 'creativity' whose skills and knowledge are characterised as pivotal to the competitiveness of particular firms, industries, and places. Where appropriately skilled workers are perceived to be lacking, spatial policy needs to focus on mechanisms that tackle shortages through, for example, training programmes, the redeployment of workers from other activities, or inducements such as subsidised wages or forms of consumption (for example, housing).

This instrumental approach also requires a series of choices to be made over what constitutes 'demand' for particular types of skills, expertise, and knowledge. As Massey (1994, p 96) argues, definitions of skills are 'always related to the definitions of the functions themselves and to the nature of the people performing them' (see also Pringle, 1989; Bowlby et al, 2004). In Peck's (1996, p 33) succinct terms, 'the process of matching a worker to a job is infinitely more complex than determining that she [*sic*] possesses the technical skills to carry out the required task'. Technical ability, or the 'human capital' that workers possess, is always defined in and through particular social contexts so that the identification of KWs and non-KWs reflects and reproduces broader *social divisions of labour* in which specific types of skills and employment are linked to broader social questions about which groups in society predominate in different forms of employment and which types of skills are advantageous in the broader pursuit of capital accumulation (see Pahl, 1988).

However, alongside these changing instrumental and social definitions, KWs are also identified through *spatial divisions of labour* in that skills and knowledge are embodied in specific actors who are either present or absent in particular spaces at particular times. As later chapters will argue, it is this spatial aspect of KW definitions that, in many ways, has been the driving force of KW policies in countries such as Britain. Local or regional labour markets are perceived not to be functioning efficiently if the needs of different workers and their means of social reproduction are not being met by existing market conditions. KW strategies, therefore, seek to 'fix' idealised, balanced labour markets in particular places on the assumption that they have become ill-balanced and can only be redeemed through the active support of certain defined economic sectors and skilled workers. Place is equated with the existence of the means of social reproduction and collective consumption, particularly housing, healthcare, and educational facilities. It is in places where there is a failure to provide such consumption needs that, it is argued, the sustainability of economic development is threatened and the social fabric of particular places is undermined. Given the importance of these spatial dynamics, the chapter now turns to the central role that labour mobility and movement has in the construction and development of functioning spatial labour markets and places.

Labour market-building, migration, and mobility

Processes of mobility and movement are critical to the construction of balanced places and in labour market-building. As Allen and Pryke (1999, p 54) note, movement 'has an effect on how people experience and give meaning to their surroundings and to others'. Mobility, or ordered movement, plays an important role in the 'production and reproduction of regional [or spatial] consciousness' (Paasi, 1991, p 244) and the associations that individuals and communities have with the places in which they live. In the field of spatial policy, for example, the process of creating balanced places is bound up with broader questions over exactly what types of *fixity* and *mobility* are required and how this can be best achieved. Planners and policy-makers have had to overcome the apparent paradox that in order to create relatively fixed, self-contained communities and labour markets in particular places, specific types of mobility need to be actively promoted in a controlled and regulated way.

This simultaneous embracing and rejection of mobility as a mechanism of change reflects some of the wider tensions within the discourses and practices of planning. Modernist development has long been concerned with spatial ordering and 'a wider suspicion of all things mobile' (Cresswell, 2001, p 15). Order has been elided with fixity whereas disorder and dysfunctionality have been associated with mobility and movement. If socioeconomic systems are organised in an optimal manner then it is perceived that the need for mobility and movement is reduced. However, unregulated mobility, particularly through migration, is characterised by what Cresswell (p 15) terms 'a furtive and transgressive character' so that mobile people and groups tend to be portrayed as rootless and lacking in authenticity. Mobility is, therefore, inherently political and 'any account of mobilities in general has to recognise the diversity of mobilities and the material conditions that produce and are produced by them' (p 24).

As later chapters will show, the polarised debates over issues such as the out-migration of businesses and people from Britain's major cities in the 1960s and 1970s or the in-migration of international workers during the 2000s are not simply about mobility per se but also about *unplanned* mobility. It is the perceived disorder that unregulated mobility and social and economic flows bring that has made them politically controversial (see, for example, *The Economist*, 1977). Regulating mobilities has, therefore, become a priority for modern states, although at different times, different types of problems and policy solutions have taken centre stage. Again, in Cresswell's (2001, p 24) terms:

> mobilities are located in specific geographies, networks and economic contexts and these need to be explored.... It is a question of how mobilities get produced both materially and in terms of ideas, who moves, how do they move, how do particular forms of mobility become meaningful, [and] who benefits from this movement.

In the context of contemporary discourses on globalisation, for example, the mobility of capital is seen by policy-making elites as an acceptable and unchallengeable 'reality', whereas the mobility of workers is always heavily regulated and controlled (see Harvey, 2000; Massey, 2004a). In Sheller and Urry's (2006, p 208) terms, 'issues of movement, of too little movement or too much, or of the wrong sort or at the wrong time, are central to many lives and many organisations'.

The whole question of *labour* mobility and the links between migration, employment, and spatial structures has been a central theme in planning and development discourses. Labour migration can be defined as 'those movements of population that involve changes of residence associated with a change of job' (Johnson et al, 1974, p 1; see also Mueller, 1982). Neo-classical theory assumes that 'individual and household migration decisions are motivated by the expectation that they will lead to the migrant – or their family if they are part of a family unit – becoming better off' (Dixon, 2004, p 194). If better jobs and prospects lie in a particular place, then an individual worker will be incentivised to move to where they will receive the greatest rewards. Within neo-classical economics, labour migration represents a vehicle through which differences between places are levelled out, so that efficiency across the spatial economy is optimised. The role of the state becomes one of facilitating such mobility to allow labour markets and employers within them to function as efficiently and effectively as possible.

And yet this characterisation of labour mobility and its core assumptions are inherently limited. The principles of individual 'choice' on which it is constructed are, in practice, highly constrained, partial, and limited. In the UK, for example, approximately 10-11% of the working-age population change address annually, with 2% moving to a different region (Dixon, 2004). This mobility is strongly correlated with levels of skill, with older and more highly skilled individuals likely to move more often and further. They tend to be employed in sectors of the labour market that are more stretched out across space; they often respond to specific job opportunities, located in different areas; and by having more income they possess the practical means to cover the economic costs of relocation (Frogner, 2002). Choices over mobility are, therefore, highly structured and differ significantly for different groups. Practical, political, and psychological boundaries exist which are often only selectively permeable. In addition, individual workers have a range of needs, expectations, and aspirations beyond that of employment and are embedded within particular places and social networks.

These complexities are exemplified by recent debates over the extent to which urban policy should encourage the residential and labour fixity/mobility of deprived urban communities. During the 1990s and 2000s there has been a significant shift in many western countries towards community-driven, area-based policies initiatives. Their purpose is to draw on local resources, knowledge, and capacities in order to improve the quality of life in deprived places (see Mulgan, 1998; Cochrane, 1999). However, as Spirings and Allen (2005) argue, such policies promote forms of fixity that may paradoxically undermine the life chances of individuals living in such areas as they restrict:

> the residential mobility of poorer households and this exacerbates (rather than combats) their social exclusion because a key indicator of social inclusion is their ability to

take advantage of the social, cultural, and economic opportunities that so often exist 'elsewhere'. (p 389)

Contemporary initiatives, they argue, focus too much on 'improving' places, and too little on developing support mechanisms to encourage the spatial, social, and economic mobility of individuals from deprived backgrounds (see also Forrest and Kearns, 2001). As later chapters will show, there is a long history to such debates and the extent to which citizen (or community) transfers to different areas, primarily to take up labour opportunities, should be encouraged or discouraged by policy. The obvious danger of encouraging mobility is that it becomes selective in form (helping those most able to help themselves) and effectively abandons some of the most marginalised places and communities in society. It should also be noted that contemporary sustainable communities and migration policies do promote selected forms of mobility and fixity in response to identified 'needs' and 'problems', although, as we will see, these policies primarily relate to those defined as skilled or KWs.

Such debates reflect the fact that the politics of migration and labour mobility has been among the most controversial and contested of any policy field in the post-war era (Weiner, 1995; Sassen, 1999a, 1999b). Conceptualisations of labour needs, the location and availability of supply, and the structures of labour demand have been subject to significant change and re-imagination. As such, any definition or understanding of labour mobility 'demands critical reflection on the autonomy of modern subjects and their capacity to use physical movement as a tool for creativity and self-fulfilment' (Kesselring, 2006, p 270). Migration policy presents significant challenges for governments and simple characterisations of who migrants are, how they behave in given circumstances, and/or what their motivations consist of are doomed to failure as migration represents a 'complex system of short-term, long-term, short-distance and long-distance movements' (Skeldon, 1997, p 2; see also Urry, 2000; Gogia, 2006). Understanding and controlling such mobility is, therefore, an extremely complex task, made all the more difficult by its direct engagement with the contested imaginations of identity, social (and economic) justice, and integrated, balanced, and harmonious places. In short, migration policy becomes a lightning rod for concerns over the building blocks of social reproduction – jobs, homes, and citizenship entitlements. Consequently, 'migration policies are rarely implemented to facilitate the free movement of people; they generally seek to control, regulate or limit population mobility' (Skeldon, 1997, p 8).

Any conceptualisation of labour mobility processes requires an acceptance that the capacities of different citizens to migrate *across boundaries* is highly differentiated, selective, and politically structured. As Skeldon (1997) notes, it is a common myth within policy discourses that it is the poor who tend to migrate more. Instead, it is wealthier groups that 'are likely to move further and more often than poorer people' (p 8; see also Megoran, 2005). As with any political right, the (in)ability to cross boundaries is a direct reflection of relations of power and resources (Bauman, 2005). Thus, in the late 20th century it has become commonplace for state authorities at different scales to simultaneously promote strategies of exclusion for certain groups at the same time as measures are taken to attract those with greater resources and investment power. Indeed, the whole concept of territorial competition and place entrepreneurialism is founded on these strategically selective and power-infused processes of mobility and fixity (see Harvey, 1989; Hall and Hubbard, 1998). In other words, there are direct relationships between labour migration policies and spatial development strategies, relationships that will be teased out empirically in later chapters.

The politics of migration, however, is related to more than this debate on economic 'value'. Sassen's (1999a) historical analysis of labour movements across Europe demonstrates that 'labour migration took place within systematic settings and there appear to have been multiple mechanisms contributing to their size, geography and duration' (p 134). Moreover, different eras of migration policy were characterised by different attitudes and perceptions on the part of both migrants and the populations of recipient countries. When migration is seen by host populations and governments as an economic necessity, then the perceived threat posed by an influx of external (often foreign) workers becomes a calculable and controllable policy field. Tackling labour shortages through migration, particularly when it involves the movement of skilled workers whose social status is perceived to be high, has tended to be a politically acceptable policy agenda. It is when migration is perceived as an external threat, as the consequence of a set of social and economic processes outside of the direct control of the hosts, that political and social resistance to immigration tends to become stronger. Movements of poorer, less skilled workers are often characterised in this way. This rather generalised argument does, however, require greater contextualisation in the grounded politics and practices of immigration and place-building. As Chapters Five and Eight will show, the politics of building balanced labour markets and communities through international migration has always been controversial at different scales, whether or not they were underpinned by a clear economic rationality or perceptions of 'internally' or 'externally' generated problems.

Conclusions: spatial policy as an active social policy

This chapter has argued that in capitalist societies conceptions of balanced places or communities have long been associated with 'healthy labour markets' or locations that contain a broad range of employable and active workers. An important element of any spatial policy is, therefore, to ensure that labour markets are constructed in which the right types of citizens/workers are (co-)present in the right places, at the right times. If labour markets are balanced then this enables the twin objectives of social cohesion and economic competitiveness to be met in ways that are mutually constitutive and reinforcing. The chapter has demonstrated that the process of building labour markets and balanced and ordered mobility places is inherently political as it involves the selection and support of particular groups, workers, and citizens.

A number of key issues are raised for subsequent chapters to address. First, it is clear that more historical and contemporary *empirical evidence* is required to make sense of dominant narratives concerning macro-regulation and the rationalities and impacts of policy agendas. If spatial policy is conceptualised as *an active field of social policy*, then greater attention needs to be paid to the processes through which policy is constructed, what imaginations shape policy actions, what the grounded, multi-scalar politics of policy development and implementation consist of, and what the relationships are between different domains of policy. For example, the chapter has examined the broader contention that countries like the UK are entering a new phase in which the boundaries of the Keynesian welfare settlement are being redrawn so that what was previously conceptualised as social policy, such as education and housing, is now seen as a springboard for the promotion of Schumpeterian innovation and entrepreneurialism. However, as later chapters will show, spatial policy since the Second World War has reflected and reproduced a range of competing rationalities and that even during the high water mark of Keynesian regulation in the 1940s, 1950s, and 1960s, the regulatory capacities of the British state were characterised by an *inability* to develop concerted, thought-through programmes of action. The extent to which 'state selection strategies' and other accumulation projects take on coherent forms, which can be associated with particular periods of thinking, must remain an open question when states represent a fractured and often incoherent assemblage of different institutions and actors (see Hogwood and Gunn, 1994; Bourdieu, 1998).

Second, on a related point the chapter has argued that within much of the governance literature there is a tendency to underplay policy *continuities* and overemphasise 'new' ways of thinking and writing about socioeconomic processes. However, rather than adding to our understanding, oversimplifications can create intellectual distractions. It is not always clear at what point, for example, spatial policy agendas in European and North American countries really shifted from being 'Keynesian' to 'post-Keynesian' and the extent and timing of the 'jump'. This is compounded by the fact that in some policy areas it is much easier to define eras of change than in others and that all governments inherit programmes, institutions, and actors when they come into power. In the UK, local government, for example, still plays a key role in local decision-making processes and has been at the forefront of the Blair government's modernisation agendas, even though its bureaucratic structures of operation and its representative modes of accountability are relics of earlier rounds of welfare state formation (see Atkinson and Wilks-Heeg, 2001).

Third, the chapter has highlighted the importance of *imaginations* in shaping policy. Particular diagnoses are made about the 'problems' afflicting identified places and various solutions are called upon to 'cure' them. These 'frames of reference' (cf Rose, 1999a) cover a broad range of interrelated elements, all of which have significant implications for spatial policy. There have been changing imaginations about the capacities and limitations of state action and what the balance and distribution of responsibilities should be between the state, citizens, and other elements of civil society, such as the private sector. Later chapters will highlight the *contested* nature of these imaginations and the multiplicity of interpretations and perspectives that have existed, across different scales, over what the appropriate boundaries, priorities, and objectives of social (and spatial) policy should consist of.

Fourth, the chapter has also suggested that in order to understand spatial policy as an active field of social policy, there needs to be a greater engagement with questions of *social consumption* and the relationships between the provision of infrastructure, social justice, and economic development. Too much of the work on state regulation draws on accumulation-based interpretations of governance and policy. Less is written about the relationships between social consumption and production or the state's role in providing the conditions in and through which social reproduction is met. In many ways spatial policy in the UK and elsewhere has been as much concerned with providing the social infrastructure for development as it has with the productivist regulation of national, regional, and local economies. Indeed, as Chapter Seven will show, the recent rise of the concept of *sustainability* and its incorporation into spatial development policy agendas represents a new concern with the management of 'tensions between local economic development and the collective provision of social and physical infrastructure' (While et al, 2004, p 279).

Finally, the chapter has argued that any understanding of spatial policy and its parameters requires a full engagement with processes of *migration and mobility*. Spatial policy programmes always have to engage with a series of underlying tensions between the promotion of fixity on the one hand and mobility on the other. Decisions have to be taken over the types of mobility that should be actively promoted and how this should be linked to broader social, economic, and demographic policy objectives across different scales and territories. Subsequent chapters will explore the relationships between spatial policies and labour migration in the UK and interrogate the ways in which the imaginations and policy practices of different eras were constructed and implemented. They will show that contemporary concerns over the 'impacts' of immigration on labour markets and the availability of social consumption (particularly housing) have strong continuities with those expressed during earlier periods, both in terms of dominant conceptions of community 'harmony' and competing characterisations of socioeconomic 'needs'.

Part Two
Post-war spatial policy, 1945-79

THREE

Reconstruction, regional policy, and labour market-building: inter-regional labour transfer policies in the post-war period

Introduction

The period from 1945 to the late 1970s is often characterised as the high water mark of direct state intervention in the spatial economy of the UK. The experiences of recession in the 1930s and the obvious achievements of the wartime administrations created a political climate in which strong welfare state programmes and strategies could be established and implemented. The provision of a just and equitable spatial distribution of work and economic activity was seen as a moral requirement for the state and from the end of the Second World War up until the late 1970s both Conservative and Labour governments worked, to a greater or lesser extent, towards this end. This chapter, drawing on archival sources and contemporary accounts, examines the diverse ways in which the object of what would now be termed sustainable labour markets was defined and redefined in this post-war period. It argues that the state's role became one of regulating and controlling spatial development and matching labour supply with labour demand in ways that were seen to 'balance' spatial, social, and technical divisions of labour. The chapter demonstrates how more interventionist British governments in the first decades after the Second World War saw the engineering of regional economies, through selected inter-regional labour migration and resettlement, as a core component of broader regional development agendas.

The focus of policy was on the presence or absence of particular types of skilled private sector workers and their needs and aspirations. This, in turn, required the implementation of positive discrimination programmes by the state towards particular types of worker-citizen or 'key worker' (KW) based on the ascribed skills that they possessed and how these could be mobilised to fulfil the wider agendas of spatial development policy.The chapter begins by exploring inter-war policy towards labour migration as the experiences of the 1930s were instrumental in shaping post-war agendas. It then discusses the role of labour market policy during the Second World War before looking at the period 1945-79. It shows that while such strategies existed, their form, character, and implementation were subject to contestation and challenge. In many ways these worker mobility and labour market strategies reflected wider problems within regional policy, succinctly expressed by *The Economist* (1969, p 75) as being 'beset by confusion in the analysis of the problem, fuzziness about objectives, ignorance of the benefits, rampant anomalies and outrageous political opportunism about results that cannot be achieved'.

The inter-war period: labour mobility and economic crisis

It was during the inter-war period that governments became increasingly aware of the potential of state policy to organise inter-regional labour transfers in the pursuit of enhanced spatial efficiency and competitiveness. During the First World War the Asquith government, in large part, fell because of its perceived inability to reorganise the productive capacity of the British economy to meet the wider needs of the fighting forces (see Holmes, 1999). Lloyd-George's subsequent War Committee 'ruled with almost unlimited authority' (Keegan, 1999, p 342) and took the first steps towards the deployment of state power to ensure that the social and economic needs of skilled, essential workers in industrial areas were met to enable the war effort to be sustained. It banned strikes, took over production, and embarked on an 'unprecedented programme of house building for workers engaged in the production of munitions' (Swenarton, 1981, p 48). In so doing, it began to reorganise the spatial distribution of skilled workers within the economy to fulfil wider productivity objectives.

However, it was during the inter-war period and the emergence of significant uneven development between the regions that governments began to use labour migration as a purposeful strategy to reorder the spatial economy into a more efficient and productive unit.As Linehan (2000) demonstrates, during the 1920s and 1930s uneven regional development began to be categorised as a 'problem', based on imaginations that 'depicted the industrial region as beyond the tide' (p 110). This perception was reinforced in and through a series of government enquiries and strategies 'that led to the proliferation of a whole range of economic geographies, academic, popular, commercial and official' and these 'helped to sustain a coherent set of economic policies which revolved around non-intervention and control' (Linehan, 2003, p 99). A spatial policy emerged based on neo-classical understandings of labour mobility, with workers conceptualised as a commodity that could be moved and shaped to meet the requirements of accumulation much like any other. Consequently, as Scott (2000) demonstrates, the state's 'main geographically-oriented policy' in the 1930s became 'the migration of industrial workers' (p 337) from the so-called depressed areas to the prosperous regions of the UK.

The 1934 Special (Depressed) Areas Act provided some minor assistance to distressed areas. Two Commissioners, one under the Ministry of Labour (MoL), the other under the Secretary of State for Scotland, were given limited powers for 'the initiation, organisation, prosecution and assistance of measures designed to facilitate economic development and social improvement' (Hannington, 1937, p 22). However, the main strategy of inter-war governments was to move workers to the work. Through a network of Labour Exchanges grant payments were made to assist unemployed individuals and their families to move (one-way) to areas where employment was available. These were supplemented by government Training Centres and other local authority support programmes. The concept that became known as 'industrial transference' involved the abandonment of some areas so that 'instead of attempting to re-organise their economic life ... the government has treated them as doomed' (Hannington, 1937, p 115). Whole families were expected to uproot themselves and move so that geographical mobility could play a part in reconfiguring the economic geography of the UK.

The net effect of these transference programmes was significant for the economic geography of Britain. Hannington (1937) estimates that, between 1921 and 1935, 608,000 people migrated from the distressed areas as a consequence of the scheme. In Durham, Glamorgan, and Monmouthshire this represented the selective out-migration of one sixth of the population. At the same time this migration played a critical role in underpinning the economic expansion of prosperous regions by reducing wage pressures and providing a cheap and plentiful source of labour. The moves involved the significant dislocation and disembedding of whole communities and was characterised by unscrupulous 'taking advantage of migrants ... in order to secure cheap labour' (p 119). The negotiating position of trades unions and existing labour in the recipient areas was effectively undermined by the influx of workers and tensions were created between different groups. In Scott's terms:

> Internal migration played an important role in the expansion of the most rapidly growing new industrial centres during the period, by removing the upward pressure on wages that would otherwise have been inevitable as industrial growth outstripped the capacity of their local labour markets. (2000, p 352)

The policy of inter-regional labour migration, therefore, reached its zenith in the inter-war period as governments accepted the principle that citizens living in deprived regions had no right to expect the state to deliver economic growth and employment. Instead, regional policy was underpinned by a responsibilisation strategy that encouraged workers to move to where work was plentiful. Individuals were compelled to be active citizens in the wider interests of economic efficiency and the management of the spatial economy. Labour migration became a mechanism for equalising economic growth thereby tackling the problems facing unemployed communities while at the same time maintaining the economic efficiency and competitiveness of fast-growing regions. As we will see below the experiences of industrial transference had shown that ordered labour mobility could play a vital part in spatial development strategies.

The war, reconstruction, and labour mobility

During the Second World War the spatial distribution of labour and production became core problems for the government to tackle. The 1940 Emergency Powers Act gave the state significant control over the distribution of labour in a context where 'it was necessary for large armies to be assembled almost from scratch without depriving industry of the skilled workers who would be needed for the expansion of the munitions industries and other aspects of war production' (Powell, 1992, p 108). The shortages of skilled manual male workers forced the national government to introduce a 'schedule of reserved labour' in which it ensured that so-called 'essential workers' were maintained in the labour force in defined 'core' sectors of the economy which would assist the war effort, rather than being conscripted into the army (Cullingworth, 1975). A scheme for the establishment of Essential Work Orders was used 'to register skilled workers and direct them to where they were most needed' (Powell, 1992, p 109). The process was overseen by a Programmes Review Committee consisting of representatives of the MoL, the Board of Trade (BoT), and the Ministry of Production (see *The Economist*, 1945a). Scarlet Areas were identified where labour was in short supply and the Committee had the power to initiate emergency measures to plug the gaps. Women were also deployed as a reserve army of labour to take up the roles left by fighting men in a context where a range of employment was reclassified as essential (Calder, 1994).

This wartime experience of a mobilised, active government, shaping the contours of economic policy and labour distribution, influenced subsequent rounds of policy-making, initially by Attlee's Labour administration of 1945-51 and then by the Conservative governments of Churchill, Eden, and Macmillan. The changes in the relationships between citizens and states that the war brought about led to 'far reaching changes in the position and status of the Labour movement, in relations between industry and government and ideas about social and industrial policy' (Powell, 1992, p 108). As one of the foremost advocates of stronger state planning, Douglas Jay (1947, p 558), argued in a speech to the Fabian Society:

> Before the war we didn't trust the state and doubted the sheer practical ability of central authorities to control big sections of the nation's economic life. I believe that the last seven years have proved that, in a highly organised democracy like Great Britain, that job can be done. Those years have shown the remarkable power of large scale organisation at its best.

This new mood of optimism was shared across the Labour movement with political advocates such as Nye Bevan and Clement Attlee and intellectuals such as John Maynard Keynes, William Beveridge, and T.H. Marshall.

Territorial justice, in terms of regional development, became a key element in the philosophy of *reconstruction* and new policy measures were implemented on the 'shared understanding that the national economy was both manageable, and that such management was politically inescapable' (Tiratsoo and Tomlinson, 1998, p 29). In contrast to the inter-war period, post-war governments initiated a series of spatial policy measures with the aim of reducing growing regional inequalities by supporting the economies of 'Development Areas' (DAs). The 1945 Distribution of Industry Act represented perhaps the most significant spatial policy statement in the history of the UK. Rather than focusing on the regional problem as something to be cured by abandoning places, the new policy was underpinned by a donor–recipient model of redistribution as new development initiatives in the prosperous regions of the South and Midlands were restricted by licences, while grants and loans were made available to firms to set themselves up in selected DAs (Wren, 1996; Chick, 1998). The emphasis of policy measures focused on the core principle of taking 'work to the workers' by regulating the economy so that work opportunities were decentralised from 'core' to 'peripheral' regions (Massey, 1995). The Attlee Labour government committed itself to the incentivised relocation of at least 400 major firms and over 200,000 jobs from the South to the North of Britain (see Cullingworth, 1975). In the contemporary words of *The Economist* (1945b, p 270), the change in spatial policy reflected:

> a new attitude, in which the scheduled areas are no longer regarded as plague-spots, to be diagnosed by specialists and treated as something apart from the rest of the community.

During the same period the MoL commissioned a major report to examine the mobility of labour based on the premise that 'the distribution of the industrial population through Great Britain is a big factor in determining the prosperity of certain areas'.[1] Labour mobility was defined in both human capital terms (in relation to workers' skills) and in spatial terms (concerning who was located where at a particular time). The MoL's philosophy was that 'the importance or desirability to the nation of changes of occupation, industry and town are determined mainly by the prevailing economic situation and the possible changes that might take place in it'.[2] A development strategy was, therefore, required to ensure that worker mobility was limited so that it did not have 'disadvantages for the country as a whole'. Individual decisions over the taking up of an employment opportunity or the movement to another area became 'events of industrial importance. It is necessary for us to know, therefore, what kinds of change are included in the changes of occupation and industry already listed, what are the consequences of those changes to the individual and to the distribution of the industrial population and whether those changes are orderly and stable'.[3]

However, it was apparent to policy-makers from the outset that the redistribution of industry was dependent upon 'the relationship between the demand for labour and housing accommodation' (Jay, 1947, p 558). The reorganisation of the spatial economy required the relocation of particular *types of workers*, possessing the necessary skills and entrepreneurial drive to enhance economic growth in DAs. The emphasis quickly became one of 'distributing it in the way best calculated to meet industrial requirements in a situation where the demand for labour has continuously outstripped the supply' (Jefferys, 1954, p 2). Encouraging firms to develop or relocate to DAs would require the attraction or creation of a diverse, mixed, and multi-skilled labour force that would meet the requirements of accumulation. As *The Economist* (1945b, p 272) noted, for many firms location decisions were based on more than simple economic calculations and DAs were being criticised by many firms for their perceived:

> remoteness and bleakness of life; absence of amenities; traditions of labour unrest; and [their inability to compete with] the superior social attractions of the Home Counties for the directional and managerial grades.

Tackling these problems of place became a critical element in facilitating the transference of limited numbers of so-called KWs across the country and it is to such programmes and their effects that the chapter now turns.

Spatial policy and labour market-building: inter-regional KW migration strategies in the post-war period

The identification, mobilisation, and support of KWs represents a significant, yet under-researched, element of regional development programmes in the post-war period. The KW support programme launched in 1945 survived in one form or another up to the cuts of the Thatcher government in 1979 (see Table 3.1). Its objectives and very existence was indicative of the imagined relationships that existed between the characteristics of places, economic growth, and the development of the regions. Archival sources show that as early as January 1946 civil servants were highlighting the 'difficulty in attracting firms to move from the more prosperous areas ... owing from an early stage to the provision of an adequate supply of suitable housing accommodation'.[4] It was argued that unless KWs were encouraged to move, then firms would be unable or unwilling to relocate thereby undermining the effectiveness of regional policy programmes. KWs, therefore, became critical subjects and objects of regional policy. On the one hand, they were to be the recipients or objects of policy

Table 3.1: KW mobility support legislation, 1945-79

Legislation	Date	Administration	Labour mobility support measures
Distribution of Industry Act	1945	Labour (Attlee)	KW support scheme for firms moving to DAs
Housing and Town Development Act	1957	Conservative (Macmillan)	KW support scheme continued with definitions of KWs attempted for the first time
Local Employment Act	1960	Conservative (Macmillan)	KW support scheme continued with clearer definitions of key workers
Housing Act	1961	Conservative (Macmillan)	KW support scheme continued; additional support where moves were 'in the national interest'
Housing Subsidies Act	1967	Labour (Wilson)	KW support scheme continued; additional clause that conditional on 'no increases in the rate burden or rents of other local authority dwellers'
Industry Act	1972	Conservative (Heath)	KW support scheme extended to Intermediate Areas

support, to be encouraged to move to particular places. On the other, through their physical presence they would act as subjects in helping to bring to fruition wider state objectives and enhanced regional economic performance. Their presence would also, it was argued, play a part in 'stimulating industry already in the DAs by bringing new skills and entrepreneurial dynamism' (Jay, 1947, p 558), with the clear implication that existing workers did not possess such entrepreneurial traits.

It was the BoT that was given the responsibility to encourage firms and KWs to move. The BoT had a wider remit to encourage economic development, enterprise, and trading policy. It played a dual role as both a government department with spending powers and priorities and a representative of business communities (particularly the manufacturing sector) within government. From 1942 the BoT acquired 'many new functions such as location of industry, control of monopolies, consumer protection and a major share in the work of sponsoring contacts between industry and government' (DTI, 2004, p 1). Archival evidence shows that civil servants at the BoT in the 1940s were reporting that firms had been making it clear that 'if houses cannot be provided it will be impossible for them to move their "key-men" [*sic*] to DAs and that without them factories and other forms of assistance will be of no use to them'.[5] The then President of the BoT, Sir Stafford Cripps, pointed out in a letter to Cabinet colleague Nye Bevan that 'difficulties with KW housing will stop firms from locating in DAs where unemployment is rising' and that 'factory building should be given equal priority with housing'.[6]

Given the widespread political support that existed for labour mobility initiatives, attention shifted to the selection process of particular types of workers and their needs. Policy had to encourage firm and worker mobility and it did this through a combination of direct subsidies to aid production and to make mobility and resettlement (fixity) an attractive option for certain workers. And yet, despite this clearly identified strategy, the definition of KWs remained one of the most contested and divisive issues within post-war regional policy. Right from the outset ministers and civil servants argued that owing to the practical complexities of such a programme it was 'impractical to define the term "key worker" in detail … each case is [to be] considered carefully on its merits'.[7] There was to be no blanket, working definition that was to be adopted by all for the purposes of the wider strategy.

Indeed, within government the vexed question of who did and who did not constitute a KW became the subject of vigorous disagreement. The archives show that it acted as a lightning rod for wider discontents and differences over what the role and function of the post-war state should be. The BoT, for example, set out to identify and define KWs in primarily *managerial* terms as those who 'would not ordinarily be satisfied to live in the working class type of housing provided by local authorities'.[8] Managers' careers were understood to be dependent upon their ability to move up management hierarchies through frequent promotions and relocations (for a wider discussion see Pahl and Pahl, 1971). Such mobility, it was argued, would be hindered by the view that the quality of life in DAs was of a 'lower standard', with the condition of housing and housing neighbourhoods playing a critical part in such perceptions. Managers were identified as 'essential citizens' with whom the state should develop selective, cohesive, and supportive relationships over and above those of other citizens. Given that their investment decisions 'were vital to the community', it was considered 'only reasonable to … give them preferential treatment in regard to housing'.[9] The BoT was concerned that a failure to provide housing of a high standard would impact on management decisions and its capacities to attract inward investors from the South.

To support its arguments attempts were made to categorise the types of houses that should be provided for three different 'classes' of KWs to reflect their differential needs, expectations, incomes, and requirements (see Table 3.2). The BoT calculated that those earning £400 or more per year fitted into the Class 1 category and that 'demand for superior houses is likely to come from a small class of employers, directors and managers, not more than 2% of the workforce'.[10] Moreover, such statements and policy initiatives are revealing of a wider concern with creating environments and a quality of life that would be appealing to KWs. This involved a series of subjective, class-based understandings and judgements over what types of housing and neighbourhoods would 'appeal' to KWs – particularly executives and managers whose relocation decisions, it was argued, would be particularly dependent on the availability of high-quality housing.

This attempt to abstract from individual cases and identify different 'types' of workers is indicative of the processes and practices of state selection in the aftermath of the Second World War. Imaginations of regional economies as dependent on a balance of different classes and types of people possessing different skills were evident. The location decisions of such individuals were conceptualised as a function not only of their employment but also of the quality of the environments in which they lived and resided – the same factors that dominate contemporary debates over sustainable communities, attractive neighbourhoods, the needs of key workers, and what Richard Florida would define as the Creative Class (see Chapters Two, Seven, and Eight; Schoon, 2002).

These definitions were also indicative of broader imaginations over the gendering of family life, the roles of men and women in managerial households, and the importance of creating housing and neighbourhoods that provided quality homes for managers' families. In order to encourage mobility, it was argued, spatial policy had to focus on the broader (consumption-based) needs of male KWs and

Table 3.2: Definitions of KW housing, 1945

Class 1	Key manual workers, with houses not exceeding 1,000 square feet in size. Cost £1,200.
Class 2	Houses for foremen or superintendent grades. Up to 1,300 square feet in size. Cost £1,600-£1,800
Class 3	Managers' housing, 2,000 square feet in size. Cost £3,000-£4,000

Source: Adapted from BoT Circular, BT 177/481, 16 July 1945

their wives and children. It was recognised from an early stage that community-building would, therefore, play a vital role in what was an ostensibly *economic* development strategy. The debate over KW housing reflected and reproduced the wider, contested politics of spatial policy. For example, as the archival evidence shows, there was resistance within government to expanding the scheme to cover female-dominated jobs in the DAs. Limited resources were, instead, to be targeted on those (ie male workers) whose presence would have the greatest impact on competitive performance (see also *The Economist*, 1946a).

It was in response to this scalar politics and the perceived fragmentation of responsibilities that the decision was made in early 1946 to establish BoT and Ministry of Health (MoH) Regional Controllers (RCs) part of whose remit would be to coordinate and deliver KW housing policy. RCs were given these responsibilities because it was felt that they could simultaneously obtain a sufficient grasp of local circumstances and strategies surrounding individual requests and take a more strategic overview. In the post-war period the regional scale has often been associated (by governments and other interest groups) with this binary role of bringing together strategic direction and an awareness and sensitivity to spatially diverse needs and social relations (see Jones and MacLeod, 2004). However, in practical terms this regionalism has not been supported by the decentralisation of power to the regional level and KW programmes were no exception. RCs acted as representatives for Whitehall ministries and did not operate with the backing of any regional tier of government. As a BoT Circular[11] made clear:

> Where provision of the houses required cannot be secured by regional action, the RC will refer the case with all the essential details to their [London] HQ for consideration as a special case of difficulty.

In other policy areas the Labour government similarly developed a highly centralist and technocratic approach to policy with RCs acting as the main points of contact but whose existence, simultaneously, undermined the case for enhanced regional devolution (see Parsons, 1988).

However, the archival evidence indicates that RCs did operate with a significant degree of discretion and autonomy. Significantly it was left to them to define who constituted a KW as, even by 1948, the BoT in Whitehall still had no clear, working definition. Indeed, it argued that 'no clear definition [of KWs] could be attempted. It was the clear responsibility of the RC to decide whether an applicant was essential to a firm and should therefore be sponsored for a house'.[12] While their roles and responsibilities were determined by central government (and these included the management and monitoring of the programme), their capacities for autonomous action enabled them to develop diverse strategies and relationships with local authorities in different DAs. In Scotland, for example, so many subsidies for housing were established after the Second World War that the KW subsidy was rarely needed or used by local authorities who were constructing KW homes anyway and there was little pressure on the Scottish Office to extend the scheme beyond the development districts.

These regional variations were also indicative of the different political contexts within which the programme was being implemented. The spatially defined, institutional set-up of programme delivery ensured that central government's capacities were directly dependent on the practices of actors working on different scales. At the regional scale, as the evidence suggests, different interpretations of what KWs should be and what types of support they should receive became paramount. These decisions, in turn, were dependent on politically mediated understandings and interpretations constructed at different spatial scales and from an early stage central government actors were concerned about the influence this would have on the programme. RCs were ordered to keep an 'urgent check' on the situation in their regions and act as monitors of the programme. They were required to act reflexively and proactively as project implementation became a core element of the strategy-formation process. For example, the loss of shipbuilding employment in Northern Ireland after the Second World War became an urgent issue for the national government and efforts were made to encourage KW transfers from that area to the West of Scotland and North East of England.

The politics of KW support

The economic logic of the BoT's approach to KWs and labour market-building was not shared by others at national, regional, and local level. In the immediate post-war period it was not the BoT but the MoH and local authorities that had a primary responsibility for the construction and allocation of housing.[13] The direct linking of housing and health reflected a broader 'social' shift in state philosophies following the destruction wrought by the war and the need to house a growing and demobilising population. The division of responsibilities between the BoT and MoH typified development planning and reflected the broader confusion over the role and purpose of regional policy agendas. As Parsons (1988) notes, all policies relating to DAs were 'a matter of interdepartmental concern that should be facilitated through the formal machinery [of government]' (p 62).

Yet, the differences in the objectives and philosophies represented by different departments within the government generated significant tensions in the policy and its outcomes. Throughout the 1940s BoT officers were frequently frustrated by what they saw as anti-business attitudes within other departments. As one BoT civil servant complained, 'little or nothing is being done by other government departments to discover or meet the need of houses for KWs'.[14] Such evidence supports the findings of other commentators who argue that the Whitehall civil service was unwilling to adapt and change in the immediate post-war period to take account of new, more interventionist ways of operating (see Hennessy, 1993; Shaw, 1996). To complicate matters further it was local authorities, as local planning agencies, whose duty it was to make final decisions over local allocations of KWs and other types of housing. Despite the 'national' emphasis of the proposals, local authorities could not be compelled to accept the dictums of central government departments. As Houlihan (1988, pp 38-9) notes, the MoH 'was content to provide local authorities with financial incentives and powers, delegated discretion and more efficient procedures relying primarily on the salience of housing with the electorate to provide its own momentum'. This focus on persuasion, rather than compulsion, was to become critical to the programme's wider (in)effectiveness. For in establishing a *dependent* relationship on local authorities, central government lacked the power to oversee the programme's implementation and opened up new opportunities for *local* actors, working in and through local socio-political circumstances, to reshape agendas from the bottom up. Despite the wider focus on nationally oriented state strategies, 'it was at the local scale that the contradictions and difficulties of project delivery began to force change within national agendas' (Houlihan, 1988, p 40).

For example, the archival evidence reveals that the BoT was frequently frustrated by its impotence in regard to local authorities and it launched a concerted campaign to put pressure on them to accept KW housing as a priority. In one meeting with MoH officials it called on the MoH to do all it could to '*persuade*' local authorities of the need to provide KW housing and sought to establish a '*fast-track scheme*' in which significant investors were to receive fast-tracked housing in DAs to encourage them to move. The response of the MoH was to reassert its priorities and principles:

> Responsibility for ensuring an adequate provision of houses in any place for any purpose lies with the Health Departments and local authorities…. There are physical limits to what can be done to secure [KW] housing requests … and the BoT may need to help out overwhelmed local authorities trying to cope.[15]

It was a division of responsibilities that reflected the broader politicisation of the issue of KWs beyond technical and economic concerns. As one MoH official wrote to the BoT:

> It is one of the most cherished rights of local authorities that they select the individual tenants … the MoH would certainly not be prepared to take any active steps to encourage argument which would amount to a derogation of the rights of local authorities.[16]

Such proclamations reflect Jones and Keating's (1985, p 87) observation that the post-war Labour government 'was reluctant to assume the greater powers of state control … rely[ing] on the power of persuasion'. Compulsion and strong, coherent government action were not apparent in regard to such strategies.

Establishing the 'strategic rationality' (see Jessop, 2002; Brenner, 2003) of regional policy and KW support policies in this period more generally is, therefore, relatively difficult. In many ways the lack of coherence was a reflection of disagreements over the social and economic priorities of housing and regional policy and how the 'success' of the programme should be measured. Should priority, as the BoT argued, be given to the 'economic' needs of the business community, whose growth and presence in DAs would tackle problems of unemployment and social deprivation or should resources be used to directly provide housing and welfare support to deprived local communities? For the MoH, KWs represented an already privileged minority who possessed their own homes in affluent parts of the country. Offering them subsidised housing and a fast track up the housing waiting list in DAs – in which social deprivation and housing problems were at their most acute – was seen as politically and morally unacceptable. As one MoH civil servant noted in response to a BoT memorandum, 'It is unlikely that many local authorities will be willing to build housing for KWs in view of their present embarrassments with their rate payers who are queuing for housing'.[17] In response, BoT ministers and civil servants highlighted the economic consequences of inaction. One, in response to MoH warnings of political difficulties ahead, replied that 'there would still be greater opposition to continued unemployment in the DAs if we could not induce suitable manufacturers to go there by provision of suitable houses for their transferred KWs'.[18]

The period 1945-50 represented the high point of the KW scheme, although, as Table 3.3 shows, the quantitative scale of KW support remained relatively modest and regionally diverse. Concern was expressed by BoT ministers and officials that the physical construction of Class 2 and Class 3 houses in Wales and the North East was lagging behind and subject to severe delays and restrictions.

This diversity reflected both practical and political circumstances. In practical terms both regions possessed significant shortfalls of construction workers and this was hampering general house-building beyond that of KWs (see Hayes, 2005). In political terms KW support proved particularly controversial in both areas. For instance, the archives reveal that in South Wales, the selection of KWs proved to be extremely contentious, where existing local firms began to complain that KW support was having a detrimental effect on local labour markets because of its insistence on support for non-local in-migrant skilled labour. Local employers' organisations, such as the Industrial Association of Wales and Monmouthshire, argued that it was 'a serious anomaly' that support could not be given to existing skilled workers and that this was leading to an 'exodus of those whose loss could be least afforded'. Similarly local Trades Union Congress (TUC) representatives complained of a 'feeling of frustration in the local industrial workers who resent the favouritism given to a section of the community [KWs],

Table 3.3: The scale of the KW housing scheme in DAs, 1945-50

Region	Class 1 houses			Class 2 and Class 3 houses		
	Application by firm	Not yet granted	Occupied	Application by firm	Not yet granted	Occupied
North East	930	111	730	261	241	41
Wales	1603	607	984	247	214	83
Scotland	801	78	635	165	163	110
West Cumberland	308	63	183	29	25	22
South Lancashire	150	36	63	18	15	13
Merseyside	65	15	10	0	0	0

Source: Adapted from R. Chapman, BT 171/181, 1 April 1950

who in their opinion are no more vital to the national effort than themselves'.[19] Their complaints were supported by the national TUC whose Secretary General complained that 'if housing is not provided for … local inhabitants there will not be work in the neighbourhoods and our export trade will suffer'.[20]

These tensions were reflected in local arguments over the specific assistance given to firms. In 1947, for example, the BoT had encouraged a major firm, named Standard Telephone and Cables, to relocate its highly skilled production facilities from West London to a former Royal Ordnance factory owned by the Ministry of Supply in Newport, South Wales. A core element underpinning the move was the provision by Newport County Council of subsidised rented houses for 71 KWs. However, following growing local housing and political pressures, and an increasingly hostile campaign by existing residents, the council decided to end the subsidy two years after the initial agreement and the KWs faced a fourfold increase in rents in line with local rates. This move prompted a strong response from the firm, which identified the 'sacrifices' made by KWs in moving to the town as a critical element in its decision to move.[21] The firm's chief executive indicated that the rent hike was only one manifestation of local hostility towards the KWs who 'are considered as strangers in the town and treated as a race apart even though they were brought to Newport [at] some sacrifice to themselves'.[22] In addition, it was argued by the firm that the council had assumed that all KWs were of high-income groups, when, in practice, they reflected all classes of workers.

The outcome of such disputes was that the BoT and the Ministry of Supply were unable to compel the local authority to sustain its existing agreements. They tried to reassure the firm that 'all possible pressure will be applied to avoid this act of discrimination against KWs'.[23] However, the KWs' cause was not popular with local electorates or with some sections of government. The local authority argued that it was simply treating all local residents equally and that it had the right to do this. It was not compelled to treat KWs any differently to others, a fact that was acknowledged by the BoT, which admitted to the firm that it was powerless to act. Eventually, as a concession, the council agreed to look at specific 'hardship' cases but refused to back down.

Similarly in the North East region a number of cases highlight the difficulties faced in delivering the programme. In one instance houses built for KWs in Aycliffe, near Darlington, were seen as a hindrance to BoT efforts to attract significant industrial developments to the area as they were 'not popular with the type of person for whom they were intended owing to the lack of general services and educational provision'.[24] In consultation with the local authority new housing units for KWs would, therefore, be constructed to the north of town where it was felt that the quality of the environment would be more appropriate to the needs of KWs and their families. However, this move prompted significant local resistance from existing residents given the desperate shortages of homes for local people who were increasingly reliant on the availability of prefabricated units.[25] Similarly, on Teesside BoT officials launched an investigation into the slackness of the local authority to bring KW projects to fruition after complaints from local employers' organisations that 'there does not appear to be a readiness to allot the houses for this purpose as there does elsewhere … with many firms in Teesside area finding difficulties in having their requirements met and delays'.[26]

Defining KWs proved to be an extremely complex task that varied from region to region and firm to firm. In essence, KWs were defined as those in manufacturing firms 'who are essential for the establishment and successful operation of new factories … which will materially assist in meeting the employment needs of the area'.[27] They should 'possess the appropriate skill and knowledge to make it essential for them to be brought to the area to enable an industry to be built up there who by imparting their knowledge to local workers, will provide a nucleus on which good local employment can be based'.[28] A BoT memorandum in 1946 pinpointed the immobility of KWs as a core problem in firm migration and the 'natural disinclination of the British public individually and *en masse* to uproot themselves and re-establish interest and new relationships in a strange environment'.[29] The MoL's 1949 survey of labour mobility[30] also found that those in more skilled positions were more adaptable to economic change and most likely to maintain their skills and entrepreneurial capacities. It also found that 'entry to the Professional and Technical class from other classes [of workers] is comparatively infrequent, and it would appear to be the most stable of all occupational groups' (p 17). Its spatial distribution across the national economy was, therefore, a vital element in shaping the (un)competitiveness of particular regions.

The drive to establish KW programmes within regional policy frameworks was initially strongly supported by business and TUC representatives at national, regional, and local scales. In an unpublished 'Joint Statement on the Balanced Distribution of Industry and Labour', the Federation of British Industries, the British Employers' Confederation, and the TUC called for new post-war programmes in which labour mobility had a limited and selected role in the context of the development of DAs and the national economy. The transfer of workers was 'not a satisfactory solution to DAs' but there was a recognition that 'there may be cases in which the transfer of work people to another district would be the only sensible and economic solution' (paragraph 33). Housing policy would be vital to a sensible and sustained process of labour market change through migration and regional policy should be designed to even out the costs of housing 'within the reach of the average wage earner ... between different areas of the country as part of any long term project to increase the mobility of labour' (paragraph 35). Similar sentiments were expressed by the corporatist-style regional development councils. For example, as early as 1945 the Cumberland Development Council was calling on central government to establish a programme of labour market-building alongside firm migration strategies in that 'a proportion of the housing programme in several districts should be earmarked for executives and key personnel of new industries until such time as the present difficulties disappear'.[31] The focus of policy was on the selection of individuals to be supported through housing subsidies so that their location within the spatial economy could be ordered and optimised.

However, this wider enthusiasm for the KW programme generated tensions within the wider trades union movement as it would when KW schemes were officially reinvented in the 2000s (see Chapter 7). The principle that work was stratified between different groups was something that unions had long fought for. In 1948 the Secretary of the TUC, E.P. Harries, wrote to the Attlee government to argue that the scheme was failing to deliver quality support to its members and that local authorities with their non-industrial housing policies were standing in the way: 'I have been receiving complaints from various quarters that houses which have been allocated by the government to KWs through local authorities are not ... getting to KWs at all'.[32] He went on to argue:

> The General Council's view on KWs is that if housing is not provided for them, irrespective of the demands of local inhabitants there will not be work in the neighbourhoods, our export trade will suffer and so will our food supplies ... the arrangements that the local authorities shall have the disposal of housing allocated for KWs needs looking into and I ask that it be [re]considered.[33]

The TUC was therefore highly supportive of the productivist nature of KW support schemes and the trickle-down effects of KW presence for 'laggard' places and communities.

And yet, in some places TUC representatives were among the most vociferous critics of the KW programme and the perceived injustices that it created for local members. As discussed in Chapter Two, the politics of worker mobility is often contentious as it directly engages with the everyday lives of individuals, the character of their communities, and the availability and quality of employment opportunities. The arrival of external workers to take up local employment and housing can be seen as a threat at the local level, even if at the national level the policy appears to be rational and fulfils wider objectives. Later chapters will show how this contested politics of labour market-building is repeated in a range of policy contexts.

The inception of the KW housing programme in the immediate post-war period therefore exemplified some of the difficulties in developing coherent and effective state selection strategies and programmes. The general policy principles were clear. The presence of KWs could help to reconcile the 'ill-balanced' technical, social, and spatial divisions of labour within the economy and play a significant role in the post-war reconstruction effort. However, the mechanisms of implementation were anything but clear. Rather than compelling movements of labour, as in the inter-war period, the government sought to use a strategy of persuasion and support. Arguments over broader questions of social justice and economic efficiency hampered attempts to establish a clear programme of action. Selection strategies were inherently politicised and therefore subject to contestation and amendment in specific contexts and this was reinforced by a fragmented and diverse set of institutional systems to implement them. Despite the best efforts of some within government, a coherent, business-friendly, KW agenda was not established. It was an example of how 'despite all the rhetoric little by the way of planning or strategic intervention took place' (Shaw, 1996, p 47). Even though this period is often characterised as the high point of Keynesian-style state intervention, in practice the relationships created between state agencies and specific groups of KWs were piecemeal, fragmented, and limited. As *The Economist* (1947, p 514) noted at the time, 'the assumption ... that government officials can accurately assess the national interest becomes more doubtful with each passing day'. As the next section shows, during the 1950s and 1960s these tensions became more acute and the scheme began to falter.

The modernisation of regional policy and the KW programme, 1951-79

During the 1950s the KW support programme underwent significant changes as a consequence of the scheme's obvious limitations and changing political and economic circumstances. The BoT, still intent on providing some state assistance to KWs and their firms, decided to reorient its strategy towards a more targeted approach, in the knowledge that its scheme was unlikely to be saved from the cutbacks. A secret internal memorandum in 1955 outlined the emerging problems:

> The Ministry of Housing[34] has taken the line that ... industry should build houses for its own workers ... they have told their principal Regional Officers to cease pressing local authorities to provide for KWs....We cannot expect an immigrant firm to face the extra financial and administrative burden of building houses for their own migrating KW.[35]

The response was, therefore, to 'concentrate on plugging the special and unique features of certain cases' such as firms oriented to strategic exporting sectors or others that could be justified by the 'national interest'. The principle that states should select certain workers was downplayed and different types of market-based citizenship were encouraged.

In seeking to resolve this problem the scheme became more bureaucratised and formalised with a greater centrally directed focus on who KWs actually were and what could best be done to assist them, although this was only achieved to a limited extent. This modernisation of the scheme was carried out through a series of Acts including the 1957 Housing and Town Development Act, the 1960 Local Employment Act, and Section 3 of the 1961 Housing Act, which stated that a housing subsidy would be available to local authorities where (a) there was a housing need as a result of a major new development vital to the national economy, and (b) where houses for incoming KWs were required and KWs could not be recruited locally. The process was operated through a 'Certificate of Need' scheme in which firms applied to the BoT's regional offices and were given a certificate if they matched the relevant criteria, which would then be handed to the local authority whose duty it was to consider the proposal and act on it if it wished.

The criteria were much clearer than they had been in earlier rounds of the KW programme. A BoT Circular was issued to all of its RCs in March 1961, which sought to clarify exactly what constituted a KW and demanded that RCs monitor the extent to which there were shortages of 'essential' and 'non-local' KWs in their districts.[36] It identified two types of KW: those working in (i) 'bottleneck' jobs on whom a number of semi-skilled workers depend, and (ii) supervisory or coordinating jobs such that an operation would break down without such supervision or coordination (20 persons upwards was a reasonable level of dependence). In addition, KWs were defined by other criteria, which stipulated that no one was locally available, they must be married men who were recruited from outside the local Travel to Work Area, and must already be in the employment of the firm.

These definitions were again reflective of the broader socio-political relations in which the scheme was operating. They enshrined particular notions of technical divisions of labour, with managerial KWs' needs prioritised, particularly in industries that were 'vital to the national economic interest' and on whom lower-class, less skilled workers depended. At the same time they highlighted the significance of spatial divisions in that KWs were to be helped only if they encouraged workers to move with the work. Existing workers in DAs were not eligible for assistance. In this sense, the strategy was an attempt to alter the spatial divisions of labour within the economy. It represented a clear example of the differential state selection of some interests over others in order to develop programmes through the subjectivities and capacities of others. Other selection processes were also evident. The provisions aimed at married men institutionalised a set of gender norms by which KWs could be defined and identified, with women expected to defer to their husbands' career needs. This de facto privileged those in more established positions and increased the demand for 'family-sized', large executive housing.

Between 1956 and 1964, a further 8,000 houses were provided under the scheme – a not insignificant number. However, there were signs that the scheme was not working effectively. Of the 603 project certificates authorised by the BoT only 193 had been taken up by local authorities in 15 of the 32 areas covered. In only nine areas had there been a clear correspondence between the numbers of subsidised dwellings specifically provided and the number of KWs included in the BoT certificates. Although this partly reflected a lack of take-up by firms, it was primarily due to the reticence of local authorities who were still unwilling to expand the number of subsidised KW houses, particularly for senior staff. The lack of take-up also reflected ongoing disputes over KW eligibility. The burden of proof in proposing assistance lay with the BoT RCs who had to convince local authorities and Ministry of Housing and Ministry of Labour RCs that the workers in question 'contributed to the nucleus of skill without which the new industrial plant could not operate'.[37] Once again the politicised and contested nature of the programmes had a significant impact on their implementation and breadth.

Even within the BoT, concerns over the morality of providing homes for KWs resurfaced. Archives show that a number of RCs expressed disquiet that the legislation was unjust and unfair. Given the relative power of discretion that such actors possessed in the definition and implementation of the programme this lack of legitimacy undoubtedly had some impact on the ground. As the RC for the Manchester BoT complained after assisting KWs for a printing firm moving to Merseyside:

> What bothers me is that in granting a certificate we are providing these people with subsidised housing which will thus be let to them at lower rents than would seem to be justified, particularly at a time when apart from this type of KW house the subsidy has been largely discontinued.[38]

Such sentiments were also expressed by other RCs, particularly in Wales and the North East of England, who had had difficulties in dealing with local authorities and argued that KWs warranted special treatment and support. In addition, studies such as Pahl and Pahl's (1971) during the 1960s showed that managers and their families who had moved to DAs regarded their job 'as a stepping stone to another in a pleasanter neighbourhood elsewhere' (p 65). Tensions were often generated with local communities as executives kept themselves detached from local social life and saw their location in DAs primarily as a means to an end.

By the late 1960s support for the scheme within the civil service and the business community was waning. The Labour government of 1964 sought to reform and eventually abolish specific KW housing support. Section 5 of the 1967 Housing Subsidies Act added the stipulation that KW subsidies would only be provided if they did not cause 'increases in the rate burden or rents of other local authority dwellers' in order to try to limit the potential impacts of the scheme on local authority housing projects. In addition, the issue of 'tying' properties to firms had become increasingly difficult to manage. From the outset there existed confusion over the extent to which KW housing was tied either to the individual or the company or to the local authority. One BoT RC's view on the matter was that tying 'does provide a new firm with some stability by influencing the availability of its KWs during the early, difficult years.... However, it should not continue once the firm has become established as this has the effect of impeding the free movement of labour'.[39] This issue of the stability as opposed to the mobility of labour raised a number of difficulties concerning not only the practicalities of the scheme but also its wider ethos.

Defining workers as 'essential' also imposed a fixity both on the workers' employment status and definitions of what constituted an 'essential' worker – categories that were subject to change over time. Fixing skills in places in this way underplayed the fluidity and socially constituted nature of local labour markets. Government agents were expected to 'explain to tenants moving in the philosophies of KW housing so that any subsequent decision to leave the job must be considered in the light of the knowledge that the tenancy might have to be surrendered'.[40] The net effect of this was to tie workers to particular firms in dependent relations so that their KW status became a limiting factor on their mobility and, in a collective sense, on their bargaining power. The institutionalisation of KW definitions became a part of the process by which firms increased their control over workers and divisions of labour. Ironically, this 'fixing' of KW also posed problems for expanding firms. For example, it reinforced rigidities within, often specialised, labour markets.

Efforts were made to broaden the appeal of the scheme. Leaflets were produced (see Figure 3.1) that sought to encourage individuals and firms to take up assistance. In addition, a new closely related scheme, *The Nucleus Labour Force Scheme*, was initiated in which individuals could qualify for temporary relocation expenses in order to improve their skills with an expanding firm. Changing housing markets and expectations were also undermining the attraction of the programme to KWs. In a prelude to the problems faced by contemporary KW schemes, those involved sought to become owner–occupiers themselves, at all social levels, and rented council houses were no longer a strong inducement to moving. By 1968 internal briefing papers were highlighting the rapid decreases in take-up as firms found the inducements to attract KWs less and less significant. From May 1968 onwards BoT Certificates of Need were no longer required to assist local authorities in DAs to obtain a special rate of subsidy. Instead local authorities were left to work out their own strategies and relations with incoming firms, a part of which may have included assistance for KWs. Gradually the assistance for KWs in DAs was wound down.

Figure 3.1: Promotional leaflets for the KW housing programme, 1976 (Employment Service Agency, 1976, Crown copyright)

Table 3.4: Number of KWs assisted, 1966-74

Year	Total number of KWs assisted	Number of applications for lodging allowance	Number of applications for removals
1966-67	368	133	415
1967-68	408	223	367
1968-69	369	121	353
1969-70	512	196	382
1970-71	801	281	649
1971-72	739	312	438
1972-73	792	354	667
1973-74	691	284	596
1974-75	753	184	580

Sources: 1972 Industry Act; Ministry of Labour Annual Report (1974-75) (HMSO, London)

Between 1960 and 1968 it was only assisting 400–500 workers per annum, often to support flagship projects, such as Ford's move to Halewood in Merseyside, that would have gone ahead regardless (see Table 3.4).[41] It remained a part of the regional policy support programme in the 1972 Industry Bill and remained on the statute books until it was abolished by the Thatcher government in its downsizing of regional support grants from 1979 to 1982 (see *The Economist*, 1972, 1979).

Conclusions

The experiences of the KW relocation programmes of the post-war decades were indicative of the broader rationalities and practices of regional policy. They involved the formation and mobilisation of particular ways of thinking about how economies functioned, the social practices and formations that underpinned economic development, and the ways in which the spatial co-presence of different types of workers could and should be organised through policy. These imaginations directly related to what we would today call regional competitiveness in that the focus was on improving the economic efficiency of the UK's DAs and the ability of firms within them to compete in national and international markets. In so doing, the wider social 'sustainability' of the DAs would be improved and living standards and levels of entrepreneurialism and self-sufficiency raised. Such policies also reflected Brenner's (2003) contention that in the immediate decades after the Second World War it was the national economy and society that represented the primary scale of state action. The movement of skilled workers within the national economy could contribute to the overall well-being of society. The chapter has shown in empirical detail how this process operated in relation to a particular strand of spatial policy and what the limitations and possibilities of state action were during this period.

Labour transfer strategies also relied on particular forms of mobility and fixity. They assumed that defined groups of workers could and should be moved in an ordered, rational, and directed manner. Directed mobility was to be the vehicle through which control could be taken over 'disorganised' flows of social and economic forces and new types of more desirable places could be created. However, in order to achieve this, new types of fixity had to be established in which the defined consumption needs of different groups were to be identified and catered for. The chapter has demonstrated that it was this process of selecting groups of workers/citizens and resourcing their mobility and fixity that created political controversy, particularly at the local level where local authorities were already struggling to cope with massive demands on increasingly stretched resources. Defining 'key' workers was always a complex, contradictory, and contested process and the politics surrounding their mobility was, therefore, far from straightforward. It involved a redeployment of resources to meet the needs of certain types of migrating workers over existing residents in the name of economic efficiency. The spatial economy of the UK could be 'rebalanced' if the right types of citizens could be encouraged to migrate in order to create thriving, entrepreneurial, and sustainable labour markets and communities.

And yet, at the same time the chapter has shown that this process was far from uniform, uncontested, or successful. Central state capacities, even at this 'high water mark' of post-war Keynesianism, were never sufficient to impose national agendas on local or regional actors. The primary role given to local authorities and RCs, for example, created nodes of resistance in the institutional structures of implementation. At the same time, the unwillingness of firms and KWs to move to DAs was indicative of a failure of the programme to mobilise enough agents to make the policy effective. Indeed, there is evidence that the political controversies that were generated locally had a significant impact on national state programmes and that policy rationalities were, in part, *generated through these interactions between different scales*. Spatial policy provides a clear example of the limitations that states have on their capacities for action and how their power is relationally generated through the capacities of others. Much has been written about how government works in this way during periods of neo-liberalism (see Rose, 1999a; Peck and Tickell, 2002), the assumption is often implicit that during eras of 'strong' state action there is less reliance on non-state actors. The evidence presented here is, conversely, of a relatively weak central state seeking, but often failing, to direct and mobilise others in the pursuit of its policy agendas.

Notes

[1] Ministry of Labour, *Industrial Mobility: Social Survey*, LAB 8/1531, August 1949.

[2] G. Blacker, *Key Worker Housing*, BT 177/616, 1 November 1946, p 1.

[3] G. Blacker, *Key Worker Housing*, BT 177/616, 1 November 1946, p 10.

[4] Minutes of Meeting of Board of Trade and Ministry of Health at Ministry of Health, BT 177/616, 22 January 1946.

[5] G. Blacker, *Key Worker Housing*, BT 177/616, 1 November 1946.

[6] S. Cripps, Letter to A. Bevan, BT 177/616, 19 March 1946.

[7] S. Cripps, Letter to A. Bevan, BT 177/616, 19 March 1946.

[8] BoT, Minutes of Interdepartmental Group on the Physical Development of the Development Areas, BT 177/481, 3 May 1945.

[9] R. Daniel, BoT, Letter to F. Blaine-Gillie, BT 177/482, no date.

[10] BoT Circular 2297/45, BT 177/481, 16 July 1945.

[11] *Development Areas – Provision of Houses for Key Workers*, BoT Circular 3/13, BT 173/616, 15 April 1946.

[12] H. Crook, BoT, Letter to Regional Controllers, 31 July 1948.

[13] Other departments such as the Ministry of Supply and Ministry of Food also had some residual wartime powers to provide housing for military personnel and agriculture workers, and the newly established Ministry of Town and Country Planning brought a range of different, less economically focused perspectives.

[14] R. Hammond, Letter to Ministry of Health, BT 177/616, 31 May 1946.

[15] Notes of meeting held in the Ministry of Health to discuss provision of houses for workers and factory managers of new industries, BT 177/481, 20 March 1946.

[16] L. Chasanovitich, untitled letter to BoT, BT 177/482, 12 October 1950.

[17] G. Blacker, *Key Worker Housing*, BT 177/481, 11 November 1946.

[18] G. Blacker, *Key Worker Housing*, BT 177/481, 11 November 1946.

[19] Barry and District TUC, Letter to the President of the BoT, BT 171/181, 19 August 1950.

[20] E. Harries, Letter to Office of Economic Affairs, BT 171/181, 14 May 1948.

[21] E. Byng, Standard Telephones and Cables Limited, Letter to Board of Trade, BT 177/273, 9 May 1950.

[22] H. Shrimpton, Standard Telephones and Cables Limited, Letter to Ministry of Supply, BT 177/273, 14 February 1950.

[23] W. Gray, Controller, Ministry of Supply (Wales), Letter to Standard Telephones and Cables Limited, BT 177/273, 28 February 1950.

[24] M. Stephen, Ministry of Labour, Correspondence Regarding the Provision of Homes for KWs and Executives, LAB 8/1475, 21 June 1946.

[25] S. Sharp, Letter to G. Calder, Board of Trade, BT 177/616, 29 May 1946.

[26] J. Ridley, Northern Regional Board for Industry, Letter to Board of Trade, BT 171/181, 11 February 1948.

[27] V. Chapman, Letter to Hamilton and District Trades Council, BT 171/181, 7 October 1949.

[28] V. Chapman, Letter to Barry and Districts TUC, BT 171/181, 5 September 1950.

[29] BoT memorandum, *Location of Industry*, MSS 292/540.1/8 Distribution of Industry 1944–1960, 13 March 1946.

[30] Ministry of Labour, *Industrial Mobility: Social Survey*, LAB 8/1531, August 1949.

[31] *Memorandum on Cumberland – With Special Reference to the Development Area, Cumberland Development Council*, 1945, MSS 292/540/2 Industrial Development of Certain Regions 1945-1947.

[32] E.P. Harries, Letter to Office of Economic Affairs, BT 171/181, 14 May 1948.

[33] E.P. Harries, Letter to Office of Economic Affairs, BT 171/181, 14 May 1948.

[34] The Ministry of Housing and Local Government was established in 1951 to take control of housing policy and reforms to local government. It acted as a precursor to the Department of the Environment and its subsequent forms and disappeared as a separate ministry in 1970 (National Archives, 2004).

[35] B. Payman, *Policy on the Sponsorship of Key Workers for local authority houses*, BT 177/479, 3 February 1955.

[36] *Key Worker Housing Briefing*, BT 177/2188, July 1966.

[37] J. Elliott, *What is a Key Worker?*, BT Briefing, BT 177/2188, March 1961.

[38] R. Forbes, Letter to Board of Trade London, 24 October 1961.

[39] M. Brennan, BoT, Northern Office, Letter to C. Taylor, Ministry of Housing and Local Government, BT 177/2188, 6 December 1968.

[40] M. Brennan, BoT, Northern Office, *Letter to C. Taylor, Ministry of Housing and Local Government,* BT 177/2188, 6 December 1968.

[41] C. Broadbent, Letter from Ford's, LAB 8/2897, 28 August 1963.

FOUR

Building balanced labour markets in the post-war New Towns

Introduction

At the same time as post-war governments were seeking to encourage employers to move to DAs, they were also embarking on a longer-term strategy to redistribute populations and employment away from the large conurbations. The Second World War had exacerbated the housing problems of Britain's cities and demonstrated the potential effectiveness of decentralisation strategies. The resulting development of New and Expanding Towns (NETs) in the post-war period was to become one of the most significant spatial development programmes ever undertaken in any European country. This chapter assesses the rationalities and practices involved in the building of the NETs and focuses on the key relationships that were established between *employment* and community-building. It shows how development agendas were underpinned by particular imaginations of place and specific understandings of how labour markets operated and could be constructed through policy programmes. Migration was seen as a mechanism for sustainable labour market-building and the optimisation of economic growth and social activity.

The chapter argues that NET policy was indicative of a wider politics of mobility and fixity that involved contested understandings of what constituted a balanced place and how this was to be defined. In debates that mirrored those in DAs, decisions were made concerning the types of worker mobility that should be promoted and how this should be done. Policy-makers had to decide on how processes of selection should function and how different socioeconomic groups should be spatially distributed in order to fulfil wider policy objectives. Questions were raised over the form and character of state regulation and what role the state should be playing in the creation of new places. The chapter begins by examining the rationalities underpinning the NET policy and how selective interpretations of the concept of balance were interpreted and deployed in policy discourses. It then assesses the relationships between employment and community change and how the priorities and objectives of policy changed as processes of mobility became increasingly complex and difficult to steer. The example of the Industrial Selection Scheme is used to highlight some of the rationalities and practices of labour mobility policies in the NETs and the regulatory challenges that such schemes raised for policy-makers and development agencies.

Building New and Expanding Towns: balancing space and place

The principles that underpinned the building of NETs were set out before the Second World War when planners and governments began to turn their attention to the problems facing Britain's urban areas and the potential of organised spatial planning to bring into existence a more efficient and just social order. The rationale for such towns had been premised on the ideas of the Garden City movement and thinkers such as Ebenezer Howard (1902) who advocated the construction of new, mixed urban spaces and the establishment of self-contained and harmonious communities (see Ward, 2004, for a thorough discussion). The chronic social and economic problems of the inter-war period, combined with the existence of densely populated and polluted industrial cities, focused attention on the chaotic and unplanned nature of British urbanism. In 1921, for example, the Unhealthy Areas Committee, chaired by Neville Chamberlain, recommended a Garden City type decentralisation from the congested cities through the creation of new satellite towns and the expansion of existing small towns. It was argued, even at this early stage, that whichever method of *controlled expansion* was adopted it was essential that both industry and population should be persuaded or forced to move in accordance with wider planning objectives.

Other writers such Patrick Abercrombie and Alker Tripp were arguing for new types of urban planning in which spatial efficiency could be married with new types of community-focused programmes. The latter, for example, argued that 'the idea of community life is the big human factor which the planners have detected and which underlies all their planning' (Tripp, 1942, p 31). In developing his conception of what he termed '*precinct planning*' he argued that redevelopment should be about giving power 'as a creative agency to build up new associations and to define new patterns as lively as the old and to remove and destroy whatever is bad' (p 32; see also Matless, 1993). However, in the period leading up to the Second World War little was actually done to prevent the continued drift of population to the large urban centres.

As discussed in Chapter Three, the war fundamentally changed the political and regulatory climate in which decisions over spatial development policy were made. Bomb damage to cities was significant and, with the return to domestic matters, attention turned to questions of urban planning and quality of life. There was a new optimism about the capacities of the state to deliver social improvements and to redistribute the benefits of economic growth to the wider population. Urban planning and the spatial distribution of jobs and populations were seen as key battlegrounds in the construction of a fairer and more inclusive social order. The Barlow Commission of 1937 and the Abercrombie plan for Greater London of 1943, for example, called on the construction of New Towns to act as an 'overspill' for the city's growing population and new rounds of development to facilitate a controlled and coordinated outflow of population and industry. The Barlow Commission, in particular, outlined the social, economic, and strategic dangers of large urban aggregations and recommended decentralisation by the creation of new satellites and the expansion of existing small towns. Such arguments were echoed in the Labour Party (1943), which argued in its policy statement *Housing and Planning After the War* that:

> If we are to solve the problem of large agglomerations of population which existed in London, Lancashire and other parts of the country, there must be a considerable measure of decentralisation ... satellite towns will have to be created for those industries which need not necessarily be located in the neighbourhood of large towns. It might be found useful to expand existing (small) towns. (p 71)

During the Second World War the national government accepted the main recommendations of the Barlow Commission and the 1944 Town and Country Planning Act established powers for the acquisition of land for the relocation of population and industry away from the large conurbations. NETs would be built and these would be supplemented by satellite towns 'established within the orbit of, but not immediately contiguous to, the built-up area of a large town or conurbation planned so as to provide for all purposes, including industry' (Carter and Goldfinger, 1945, p 26). Abercrombie's Greater London 1943 plan proposed that one million people should be relocated to eight satellite towns around the city and rejected 'the idea that life in the Metropolis must be bad in itself; it recognises the vitality of the old central units and aims only at thinning them out to the maximum extent necessary for ample spacing of buildings and to give enough open space' (Carter and Goldfinger, 1945, p 26). As Abercrombie stated in his report, selective out-migration would 'give London order and efficiency and beauty and spaciousness' (p 28). The alternative would be a return to 'the old unplanned city blocks, to the same old wild activity of private speculation, to recreate the same old jumble of courtyards and streets and competing facades' (p 28). Similar plans were drawn up for other conurbations drawing on similar rationalities.

However, while it was acknowledged that NET-building would require forms of state selection to be developed and initiated, it was not clear exactly whose mobility (and fixity) should be encouraged. Moreover, the mechanisms through which state-led mobility could fulfil broader objectives and rebalance spatial economies and communities were untested and controversial. The Reith Committee, for example, established some of the principles that, it argued, should underpin the NETs. It outlined a vision of the social structure of decentralised development in which:

> all social classes should be represented; that to attract and retain all classes it was essential to establish the diverse character of the NET at the beginning and to take the earliest opportunity to provide groups of larger houses built for sale and leasing and building sites for owner-occupiers; and that segregation of classes within the town should be avoided as far as possible. (Reith Committee, 1947, paragraphs 22-5)

In a similar vein the Barlow Commission report (1940) had examined the ways in which a 'better' distribution of population and industry throughout the country could be created and one of its key recommendations was similarly that the government should be pressed to 'recognise the importance of small towns and to urge that as part of the dispersal policy, a number of such towns should be given an opportunity for suitable expansion with the necessary industrial development' (p 23).

The debate went much wider than this. Other organisations such as the Town and Country Planning Association (TCPA) called for an expansion policy for existing small towns, with less of a focus on NETs. In a statement to government ministers in 1944[1] the organisation argued that 'for the social life of the average family, the town of moderate size in rural surroundings presents great advantages' (p 1). These included short commuting distances, access to the 'open' countryside, the ability for families to live in houses with gardens, and new opportunities for industries to expand and create jobs. The TCPA recommended that 'small towns, suitably placed, should be given the necessary administrative and financial assistance to enable them to expand' (p 1).

The post-war New and Expanding Towns programme

This wider debate culminated in the publication of the 1946 New Towns Act. From the outset the stated ambition of the Act was twofold. On the one hand, it was concerned with relieving the perceived problems of overcrowding in Britain's large conurbations. These were seen as suboptimal places whose populations and industries should be decentralised in a planned and coordinated way (for a list of principal NETs see Table 4.1). On the other hand, the strategy was to create balanced communities through the principle of *self-contained* places. NETs would be at least 25 miles from London, and industry and population 'would be systematically decamped ... to ensure that they became self-contained, yet near enough to induce industrialists and workers to move' (Orlans, 1953, p 23). As the Attlee government succinctly put it, the stated aim of the NETs was 'to decentralise both living and working accommodation so that living conditions in the central areas may be improved and real communities, properly planned, may be established in the outer country ring'.[2]

The 1946 New Towns Act embodies most of the principles outlined by the Reith Committee. Towns were to be socially mixed and not dominated by one single 'type' of citizen. They were to be designed to cater for a variety of housing needs and requirements in an effort to ensure that migration away from the conurbations became as diverse as possible. Their form was based on 'neighbourhood principles, with grouped communal facilities ... placed centrally in neighbourhoods' (Ward, 2004, p 95) and the concept of balance was deployed as the mechanism through which what might now be termed 'sustainable communities' could be created and could reproduce themselves. This sustainability through self-containment would be achieved through an adequate level of local employment, development that was not dominated by a single employer; and programmes that encouraged a range of classes and social groups to in-migrate to promote community diversity and prevent domination by a single class or group. The

Table 4.1: Principal NETs in Britain

NET	Date of establishment
1st generation	
Stevenage, Hertfordshire	1947
Crawley, Sussex	1947
Hemel Hempstead, Sussex	1947
Harlow, Essex	1947
Newton Aycliffe, Durham	1947
East Kilbride, South Lanarkshire	1947
Glenrothes, Fife	1948
Cwmbran, South Wales	1949
Peterlee, Durham	1948
Hatfield, Hertfordshire	1948
Welwyn Garden City, Hertfordshire	1948
Basildon, Essex	1949
Bracknell, Berkshire	1949
Cumbernauld, North Lanarkshire	1955
2nd generation	
Skelmersdale, Lancashire	1961
Redditch, West Midlands	1964
Runcorn, Cheshire	1964
Washington, Tyne & Wear	1964
3rd generation	
Milton Keynes, Buckinghamshire	1967
Peterborough, Cambridgeshire	1967
Telford, Shropshire	1968
Northampton, Northamptonshire	1968
Warrington, Cheshire	1968

presence of different types of work and workers was, therefore, an essential component of any successful NET-building strategy, although as we will see the mechanisms through which this 'balanced' development was to be achieved were patchy and only partially successful.

NETs were to be built by powerful New Town Development Corporations (NTDCs) that had the power to purchase land and raise revenues through land sales and the charging of rents for the construction of public infrastructure. They were given local planning authority powers and were designed to be strategic bodies that could oversee the development of new communities in a coordinated and planned manner. However, government records show that there was much interdepartmental debate over the most appropriate strategy for the building of the NETs. A memorandum from the Ministry of Housing and Local Government (MHLG) to the Ministry of Health (MoH) in 1947, for example, argued that even though the plans were for the creation of NETs of 50,000-60,000 people in size, the NTDCs would 'need to submit a full statement of our NET proposals showing the claims on labour and materials, in consultation with the Ministry of Works as well as the MoL [Ministry of Labour] and the BoT [Board of Trade]'.[3] It was clear that the resources for NET construction would not be adequate to meet these early plans. Estimates for the number of 'man years' per unit were made so that, for example, the construction of a cinema was estimated to involve 38.34 man years of time, a 900-square-foot house 1.31 man years, and a 500-bed hospital 721 man years.[4] These levels of inputs could not be adequately initiated or sustained in the pursuit of policy owing to severe constraints in the construction industry (see Hayes, 2005).

In addition, the NET programme also represented a threat to the programmes for the DAs outlined in Chapter Three. Many of the NETs were based in and around London and the West Midlands, areas that were supposed to be donor regions in the context of national development policy. Providing new spaces for the expansion and development of industry in such areas was seen by some civil servants and government officials as a step in the wrong direction. It would encourage profitable firms to become more competitive in the 'wrong' places. Labour market differentials would be increasingly skewed across the country and areas that were already competitive would become even more so, thereby attracting more skilled key workers (KWs) and entrepreneurs from both the major conurbations and, ironically, the DAs. In this sense the significant resources given to the NET programme represented, for some, a reverse regional policy and indicated a lack of coherence to the state's economic development 'strategies'.

Overall, then, the introduction of the NET programme was designed, in the words of the New Towns Committee, to 'conduct an essay in civilisation by seizing an opportunity to design, evolve and carry into execution for the benefit of coming generations the means for a happy and gracious way of life' (Reith Committee, 1946, p 4). Socioeconomic balance, in terms of class, skills, gender, and age was therefore seen as both a core part of the process and a desirable outcome – the simultaneous means and end of the overspill strategy. For the Attlee government this was vital for 'as in old towns all sections of the community should be represented ... the last thing we want would be to see the NETs developing into one-class communities'.[5] Through this process of balancing, the NETs were to act as both the objects of policy, to be created, and the subjects of policy that would possess the appropriate balance and functionality to sustain themselves in the longer term.

Labour market-building in the New and Expanding Towns

From the outset the object of the balanced place was bound up with the provision, availability, and location of *employment*. The in-migration of jobs into the NETs was seen as the basis for the creation of a balanced social order. As the minister responsible for the 1946 New Towns Act, Lewis Silkin, argued at the time, 'it is essential that a sufficient amount of industry shall be available to enable every worker living in the [New] towns to find his [*sic*] work there'.[6] In parallel with debates that had dominated policy for the DAs, the emphasis was on how to encourage employers and employees (and their families) to be mobile in ways that fulfilled wider spatial development agendas. The form and character of mobility had to be defined and identified and mechanisms established through which this mobility could be channelled and directed.

The early expectation was that the NETs would be characterised by a spatial juxtaposition of housing, skilled labour, and employment so that new self-contained and functioning labour markets could be created. For example, advocates of the NETs argued that:

> Industry and all types of employment have nothing to lose and everything to gain if their workers do not exhaust themselves by long journeys to and from work on crowded transport everyday. In the NT they can be given good houses and decent living conditions generally.[7]

This selective mobility was a contentious policy that depended upon particular judgements over how spatial economies functioned and what the requirements of a balanced community consisted of. There were significant debates over, for example, the provision of infrastructure and housing in the NETs and who should cover the costs of labour and population movements. Local authorities in Expanding Towns complained that they were expected to meet the costs of housing subsidies that were an essential element of expansion policy and that 'those places from which people were decanted should cover the costs'.[8] If major cities were to benefit from an emigration of their populations then, it was argued, their ratepayers should contribute towards the significant infrastructure costs that movement would bring. Again there were clear parallels with contemporary debates on planning for sustainable communities in which it is unclear where the relative costs and benefits should be drawn between different interests and groups (see Raco et al, 2006).

There were also disagreements over what exactly a balanced community required in terms of social infrastructure. Blueprints were laid out for planned communities in which 'you will get both working class and middle class types of housing and you must have an industrial area and a shopping area'.[9] The changing character of industry also needed to be reflected as, in the words of one London-based civil servant:

> Industry now requires much more land than it did 25 years ago ... most industrialists want one storey factories, an increasing proportion of workers are not merely going to [go to] work on their bicycles but will come to work in their cars ... you need to make provision for schools and churches and we have got to recognise that the public house is an integral part of our social life.[10]

There was a clear recognition that industries and their workers were key subjects, whose presence or absence would make or break the NET programme. Through their mobility and presence they directly contributed to the 'financial and social success of the towns' and represented the building blocks of new communities.

Two principal reasons were put forward for why new houses should be matched with local jobs. First, as an MHLG memorandum made clear, 'this tends towards producing communities with local roots rather than a repetition of the inter-war L.C.C. [London County Council] out-county estates'.[11] Second, poorer people tended to be in the greatest housing need and could not afford commuter fares. Their lack of mobility meant that local jobs needed to be provided to enable them to work and the town to function as a unit. A particular sense of community and labour market balance was also envisaged in which the presence of a range of different groups would enable firms to be more competitive by allowing them to select the most appropriate workers.

However, from the outset these plans were hampered by the ambivalent attitudes of ministers and government officials, and differences between government departments. As we saw in Chapter Three the BoT saw the promotion of development in the regions, not the NETs, as its primary concern. There were discussions over what types of assistance should be made available to migrating firms and their workers and who should have the power to make the final decisions. For example, in 1948 some NTDCs asked the government if they were allowed to develop KW housing for managerial staff and given the response by the MHLG that 'the NTs have the same case as the DAs, with the weakness that the BoT is not as much interested in getting industries to move to the NTs as they are in getting them to move to the DAs'.[12] Others experienced similar difficulties with the BoT. The District Councils (New Towns) Association, for example, complained in 1951 that 'the general policy of the BoT is damaging to one of the main concepts of the creation of a New Town, namely that the importation of population should be balanced by the provision of suitable industry and other means of employment'.[13] The Association was angry at what it saw as an attempt to block the industrial development of NETs for political reasons and the damage that this would have on the social composition and balance of the places being created. It was particularly fearful that the NETs would become '*dormitory towns*', attracting commuters who would not be part of a living and working community.

As one BoT official noted in relation to NET policy it seemed unwise 'to seek to solve the problems of the South East by promoting the movement of the right sort of labour from the North'.[14] The fear of the BoT was that NET policy was undermining its efforts to attract high-quality industry and KWs to DAs. Two different spatial policy programmes were, in its eyes, in conflict. Some archival evidence shows that South Eastern planners were aware of such tensions and sought to find ways of playing them down. As one civil servant noted in a Secret Letter:

> The South East in particular and the nation in general are being sacrificed to the complaining North. It is thus politic not to risk raising their combative instincts but to exude an odour of sweet reasonableness and seek to divert their attention to more fundamental matters.[15]

This was compounded by BoT decisions such as the refusal to allow expansion of the British Oxygen Company in Harlow NT in the late 1950s on the grounds that 'in considering applications … we shall have particular regard to the need to provide employment in the DAs. If we are satisfied that a project could go to a DA, we refuse the application even if it is for a NT'.[17] The decision was justified by the claim that in practice this type of selection and restriction had not meant any shortages in employment opportunities in the NETs as many businesses would not be able to migrate.

However, there were wider concerns over the essentially conservative nature of the NET plans. As Orlans (1953, p 24) argued, the 'notion of balanced communities posited the existence of social classes and set forth a basis on which they should live together'. In the same way that labour market-building initiatives in DAs had presupposed and reinforced class divisions, needs, and aspirations, so NET discourses also drew upon selective imaginations of ideal and balanced communities. The needs of different groups would have to be catered for if some sense of 'balance' was to be achieved. This principle effectively institutionalised unequal forms of state support as enhanced levels of assistance would need to be given to those in already advantageous socioeconomic positions in order to encourage their mobility and relocation.

For example, as the Reith Committee (1947, paragraph 25) argued, it was seen as important 'to take the earliest opportunity to provide groups of larger houses built for sale and leasing and building sites for owner-occupiers' in an effort to attract middle-class groups and KWs. In ways that echoed policy in DAs the NET strategy sought to make places more attractive to individuals whose managerial and technical skills were seen as essential ingredients in the process of economic development. Efforts were made to encourage the development of large, private houses in order to ensure that middle-class groups would be attracted and their 'needs' catered for. Debates were held within government over how such groups could be attracted and what types of development should be encouraged and how. As Evelyn Sharp, Permanent Secretary to the MHLG made clear:

> It is important to build houses of all types as soon as they start to build any ... the NTDCs ought to have a free hand to build whatever type of house is necessary with the small amount of labour and materials they will get.[17]

More specifically, NET planners from an early stage were concerned that not enough 'middle-class' employment would migrate, or that the quality of life associated within NETs was not of a sufficiently high standard to attract KWs and managers. Their absence from the NETs, it was argued, would be a severe blow to their economic and social sustainability.

In summary, we can see that the rationalities that underpinned the development of NETs in the aftermath of the Second World War were characterised by the principles of social and economic balance, harmony, and diversity. Programmes were developed to encourage particular forms of migration, mobility, and fixity in order that spatial economies could become more balanced and work more efficiently. In the words of a government minister of the time, the stated aim of the NETs was 'to decentralise both living and working accommodation so that living conditions in the central areas may be improved and real communities, properly planned, may be established in the outer county ring'.[18] In so doing, the problems of overcrowding and the difficulties faced by firms in dilapidated inner-city premises could be tackled in a planned and coordinated manner.

The state's role was to use planning to (re)create ideal, functioning communities and urban and regional labour markets with selective mobility programmes presented as the way to achieve this. Private enterprise had a relatively limited role for, as Aneurin Bevan succinctly argued in 1946, in words that have a strong resonance for contemporary planning debates:

> Housing [on a] vast scale has to be planned ... private enterprise is not a plannable instrument ... you do not know what they are doing, where they are doing it, or how they are doing it ... the only plannable instruments ready to hand are the big public authorities.[19]

However, in reproducing models of socioeconomic diversity, planning policy in the NETs was in effect institutionalising conservative visions of an ordered society and the needs of capital accumulation. As the next section shows, the implementation of the programme was a difficult and challenging task and it became increasingly dependent on the locational decisions of employers and their employees over which the state had a guiding and persuasive, rather than compulsive, role.

Place-building and the experiences of the New and Expanding Towns

Encouraging selective forms of mobility to the NETs proved to be an extremely difficult problem of government. The key to the decentralisation of populations lay in the readiness of employers to move and this, in turn, depended on the availability and quality of new housing provision. By the early 1950s, the Conservative government admitted that the programme had experienced severe difficulties in its opening years but argued that the BoT was seeking to 'bridge the gap between houses and industry in the NETs to encourage industrialists to take a stake in the NETs and to introduce new and varied industries as soon as possible'.[20] And yet, the mechanisms through which balance and harmony were to be achieved were subject to ongoing change and alteration. The attraction of core employers was seen as the key to the success of the NETs as 'self-containment' meant that 'the people who lived and worked in the NTs would have jobs there and all other necessary facilities' (Schaffer, 1970, p 120). By the early 1950s, the difficulty in attracting KWs was proving to be a major stumbling block in the expansion programme. In tones that echo contemporary urban redevelopment agendas, government ministers were arguing that:

> In the narrow sense of the term, mixed development is the problem of the extent to which better-class housing should be mixed with standard housing ... the solution ranges from scattering fairly small groups of better-class houses throughout the neighbourhood to setting aside only one area for such houses in each neighbourhood or the town as a whole.[21]

This 'better class of workers', it was argued, had higher aspirations and needs and the NETs were unable to attract them as they were 'soulless' places that offered a relatively poor quality of life. In many NETs early development had focused on the construction of industrial and housing units but little had been spent on social infrastructure such as churches, shops, pubs, and cinemas. In this respect the NETs were little different from other places where the costs of reconstruction were severely limiting the extent and scale of rebuilding.

Evidence from the early years of the NETs demonstrates some of the effects of these resource limitations. In Letchworth NT, for example, one contemporary source claimed that:

> New industrial development continues to be frustrated by the housing shortage. It is not easy to induce firms to migrate when one is unable to help them to accommodate the nucleus of operatives they wish to bring with them. (MacFadyen, 1951, p 17)

Similarly, during the late 1940s and early '50s the NT of Hemel Hempstead had struggled to attract industries owing to a 'lack' of executive and managerial housing. This had restricted the growth of hi-tech and high-quality investors moving in and had reduced the sustainability of the town as a functioning community (see Brooke-Taylor, 1951). In the first NT, Stevenage, the early emphasis was on 'creating job opportunities where the housing and households would be and would be likely to remain' (Mullen, 1980, p 181). The Stevenage Development Corporation (SDC, 1949, p 17) outlined its rationale for expanding KW housing:

> The first step is to get a balance between different occupations to reduce unemployment. The town should have its share of better-off people, whose presence is beneficial because it means that the community as a whole can afford a wider and more interesting range of services and amusements.

Consequently, 'when houses and flats are available in considerable numbers it will be necessary to allot them so as best to assist the industrial, commercial, and social development of the town' (p 35). For people wishing to move from London 'the best qualification for a house is to have a job there ... subsidised housing will only be let to applicants who have got themselves a job in the NT' (pp 35-6).

This dovetailing of jobs and houses meant that preference would be given 'to the man or woman whose profession or business is functionally related to the town' (p 36). By the 1950s, the provision of widespread infrastructure to support firms and the certificates and grants on offer had been so successful that the lack of high-quality, KW housing became the biggest impediment to continued expansion (Mullan, 1980). The problems were exacerbated by the type of development in the early NETs in which less than 5% of house-building was carried out by the private sector. The result was that 'the professional and other staff needed for developing the town could not be recruited' (p 151). Consequently, 'managerial staffs coming into Stevenage with the new industries were electing to live outside of the NT ... there being no alternative to rented housing' (p 152). The need for a specific KW focus to relocation policy was, therefore, increasingly being made.

The strategy of social selection was made explicit in a secret government memorandum to NTDCs that told local executives that they should 'keep available a margin of spare housing in order to attract industry ... [and] would not wish to import unemployment into their area making houses available on attractive terms to people for whom no work was available'.[22] In some NETs illicit prioritisations were made in which particular types of housing were to be prioritised for particular essential groups. In Washington in the North East of

England, for example, the local Development Corporation identified three types of local housing – new housing, substandard older properties, and other properties in reasonable condition. It gave 'careful consideration to the various categories of applicants' and decided that new housing with rebates and subsidies should be offered to KWs in new industry and commerce who were moving into designated areas, whereas commuters into the town and non-essential workers were designated properties without a rebate.[23] Such discrimination was common yet was kept secret for fear of antagonising local opinion.

This focus on who should live in an NET not only related to those whose presence was seen as necessary to its functioning but also to those whose absence was desirable. For example, the NETs did not attract populations of Commonwealth Immigrants (CIs) who came to the UK after the Second World War. Owing to discrimination, and the desire of many in-migrants to establish identifiable, supportive communities, many CIs quickly came to occupy the lowest-quality and most overcrowded housing in England's industrial cities. Consequently, CIs were exactly the types of citizens who were, in theory, to be the most significant beneficiaries of the NET programme (see Chapter Five for a full discussion). As a contemporary commentator noted:

> The NTs are peculiarly suited to accept larger numbers of coloured [sic] people … largely free of depressed Victorian housing which invites overcrowding and the creation of ghettos … and largely populated with white immigrants, mobile and disproportionately young, they are without the deep roots and tradition-consciousness which can resist change. (Barr, 1965, p 2)

However, by 1965 it became apparent that these groups represented only a tiny proportion (0.003%) of the total population of the NETs. Despite being 'suited' for the NETs, the selection procedures of the NTDCs and the lack of attention given to the needs of minority ethnic families limited the extent of mobility. While it would be too extreme to say that there was a deliberate strategy of exclusion for such groups (although as Chapter Five demonstrates there were local tensions, particularly in the Expanded Towns), the dominant imaginations of what a balanced and harmonious community should consist of focused on questions of class and gender rather than ethnic diversity. There was little attempt to encourage such groups to migrate as their presence was not necessary to, or desirable for, the successful operationalisation of the programme and they were, therefore, not prioritised. Indeed, attempts to move minority ethnic immigrants from London to smaller towns, such as Mildenhall (Suffolk) in the mid-1960s, raised fierce local opposition on the grounds that it would undermine community 'harmony' and aggravate local shortages of housing. For 'donor' areas such as London, the unwillingness of such authorities to take immigrant populations was seen as an explicit example of racism.[24]

Government departments, Regional Controllers (RCs), and NTDCs applied significant pressure to migrating firms to set out their employment plans in terms of how many people they would employ, how skilled such workers needed to be, and where they would live. Priority would be given to those firms migrating from the major conurbations who could demonstrate that they would bring their workers (and their families) with them. By the mid-1960s civil servants were even drawing up criteria for 'ideal' migrating firms (see Box 4.1). The focus, as always with the NETs, was to ensure that a diverse and skilled labour supply could be provided to in-migrating employers. For example, the guidance stated that 'by the end of the expansion period the age and occupational structure of the population should be reasonably well spread so as to avoid any serious shortages or surpluses of labour in any particular age group or occupation'.[25] In-migration of firms should be encouraged so that 'demand for labour from existing and newly arrived firms should be just a little ahead of the labour supply … it creates a situation where the attractiveness of the area will get recruits in'.[26] The guidance warns that a failure to attract a steady flow of workers would leave houses standing empty, whereas the attraction of too many employers, too quickly, could also 'lead to a situation which damages the progress of the scheme'.[27] At the same time, housing provision must, it was argued, keep up with new employment opportunities as 'serious problems would develop if housing and industry are not introduced in reasonable balance'.[28] Any significant delay would encourage in-migrating firms to 'recruit local labour rather than attracting migrants to the area … [and] cause the acceptance of poorly trained and unsuitable labour and the bidding up of wage rates'.[29]

Box 4.1: Department of Employment and Productivity's 'ideal' migrating firm, 1968[30]

To secure a 'balanced' industrial structure in-migrant firms should:

*   not be in the same industries as the larger employers already established in the NET;
*   represent a balance of fast-growing industries and slower growth industries whose employment demand is more stable;
*   operate in ways that facilitate easy transfer of labour from the donor conurbation;
*   be predominantly male 'breadwinner' employing and be able to bring their workers with them; but
*   look to employ local less-skilled workers where appropriate.

The BoT and MHLG archives are full of examples of correspondence between civil servants and migrating firms. One engineering firm, for example, that was being offered assistance to move from London to Corby, asked for preferential treatment to be given to 50 of its core workers. However, the government and NTDC's response was limited by the 'difficulty in obtaining reliable forecasts from the firm about their long term labour requirements'.[31] Such plans were essential as, in the words of senior MHLG civil servant, 'the Corporations have tied themselves to taking London's overspill and we would like them to maximise their contribution to London's overspill needs'.[32]

As with KW policies in DAs outlined in Chapter Three, the emergence of such programmes also generated political tensions. Regional and national Trades Union Congress (TUC) lobbyists, for example, were arguing that labour mobility provided a key mechanism through which balanced places could be created as 'the unrestricted mobility of labour might at one and the same time improve rates in one place and conditions in another'.[33] However, within the TUC archive there is evidence of a very different approach among local activists. In 1951 the Stevenage branch of the TUC wrote to the General Secretary to:

> protest strongly at the restrictions on the employment of local labour on the NT site and we ask the TUC to take up this matter with the Ministry of Housing and Local Government ... the position at Stevenage is that local building labour is not being employed on Stevenage's development with the result that unemployed local labour

has to travel very considerable distances to obtain employment which is actually available on the doorstep.[34]

In Hatfield the local branch complained about the allocation of houses in the town to KWs in major local employers, such as the De Havilland aircraft manufacturer.[35] The factory was a major employer of 7,000 skilled workers, 1,500 of whom lived in Central London and commuted to the factory daily. Local houses were being given over to these workers in order to increase the attractiveness of the town. Similarly in Berkshire local TUC representatives called for a broadening of the definition of KWs and community balance to go beyond skilled workers and managers to include 'many other workers to be considered including hospital workers and those engaged in public services'.[36]

And yet, through the post-war period the leadership of the TUC gave its full backing to the activities of the NTDCs and their sponsoring government departments. They were among the strongest advocates of balanced community-building. The 1959 TUC Congress, for instance, passed a motion calling for guarantees of adequate opportunities for employment with special regard to young persons leaving school; new hospitals and maternity homes; and community centres and social amenities for in-migrants given the absence of other facilities usually provided by voluntary organisations, such as church halls, working men's clubs, and other meeting venues.[37] Once again, therefore, the issue of labour mobility and impacts over different scales created cleavages among workers' representatives across different scales – a trend that would have strong echoes with later rounds of KW and labour mobility policies.

To summarise, the NET focus on balanced communities and diverse employment, in the context of an 'overspill' policy, necessitated the definition and promotion of particular types of KW and, therefore, raised tensions between the programme's economic and social objectives. While the principles applied to NETs' KWs were similar to those in DAs, the institutional mechanisms of implementation were very different. Rather than the 'persuasive' DA policy in which firms and the BoT had to negotiate with local authorities to try to get KW housing established, the NET programme built KW needs and requirements into the fabric of policy-making and implementation. NTDCs saw KW attraction as a core element of their strategies to attract industry. They had the power to provide infrastructure for relocating firms *and* to create neighbourhoods for incoming workers, with few of the local political controversies endemic to DAs. Moreover, they were working in an institutional context that saw the migration of KWs as a central policy objective, rather than something that was an add-on to wider regional policy measures. Despite this prioritisation of KW policies the next section exemplifies the difficulties they had in linking social and economic mobility and reflects on the limitations faced by state actors in the pursuit of wider planning agendas.

The rationality and effectiveness of mobility policies: Key Worker house-building and the Industrial Selection Scheme

The Industrial Selection Scheme (ISS) was the most significant of a number of bureaucratic programmes that were established to assist the process of labour market- and community-building in the NETs. The ISS began in 1953 to ensure that 'the offer of a house in an NT was linked to the possession of an offer or a job there' (Hall et al, 1973, p 331). It was designed to be a key component of the policy of self-containment, in that it tried to ensure that a full range of jobs would be relocated to the NETs and that their development would, therefore, be mixed, balanced, and sustainable in the longer term. The rationalities and experiences of the ISS were indicative of the wider dilemmas inherent in the planning of self-contained communities, with clear lessons for contemporary planning priorities and developments. In essence, it was a programme of 'planned migration' that sought to use selected forms of mobility as a vehicle for the spatial balancing of populations and employment. Rather than relying on haphazard market mechanisms and individual choices, it was believed that schemes such as the ISS opened up new opportunities for the more equitable and efficient operation of spatial economies and social processes. As with DA policy, state agencies were initially perceived to be powerful instruments of social and economic control who could oversee the relationships between mobility, fixity, and functionality in ways invisible to other actors such as business, communities, and individuals.

Through the ISS, workers in London registered themselves for selection at local Employment Exchanges where they were asked a range of questions about their 'skills' and capacities (see Box 4.2). This information was conveyed to local authorities and to the Greater London Council, who then nominated particular workers to move to the NETs on the basis not only of the skills they possessed but also their wider housing needs, thereby adding a social dimension to the process of worker selection.[38] At the same time migrating firms to the NETs listed their employment 'needs' with the NTDCs who, through central government, passed these on to the London Exchanges who then matched workers to suitable positions. For each vacancy 20 'appropriate' KWs were informed of the position (see Gee, 1972). Once a KW was offered a job through the ISS, they were also entitled to an offer of a house, usually one of much superior quality to their existing urban residence.

Box 4.2: Worker classifications under the ISS

Workers joining the ISS were asked to classify themselves as one of the following:

- professional
- clerical
- skilled engineering
- other skilled job
- building
- semi-skilled engineering
- other semi-skilled job
- unskilled.

And yet, despite its relatively simple, bureaucratic logic, the implementation of the ISS was to become indicative of the inherent tensions, contradictions, and difficulties of implementing a programme of planned mobility and fixity. From the early 1960s, records show that it came in for a barrage of criticisms from firms, NTDCs, and government officials. There was confusion over the relationships between agencies in the donor cities and the NETs. One Department of Employment regional officer complained that 'The ISS will never work satisfactorily while two regions control the different ends of the scheme ... performance is uneven and offices with only a small ISS time allowance do not have the necessary expertise'.[39] Other officers reported that firms were getting extremely anxious about the slow progress of the ISS with delays of up to 39 weeks in some London Labour Exchanges. Table 4.2 lists some of the delays in providing a house to an ISS applicant *after* they had been offered an employment position in an NET. This failure had led to a situation where 'there is an unsatisfied demand for skilled workers in all of the NETs'.[40]

There was also much local opposition in NETs. In the Expanded Town of Luton in the early 1970s, for example, support given to in-migrating residents and firms from London was criticised for diverting resources away from existing residents at a time when the town was facing job losses and there was a national and international recession.

Table 4.2: Average length of delays between an ISS applicant being offered a job and a house in selected New and Expanding Towns

Length of delay (months)	NET
1-3	Andover, Ashford, Aylesbury, Banbury, Basildon, Basingstoke, Burnley, Bury St. Edmunds, Corby, Crewe, Farnborough, Grantham, Harlow, Haverhill, Huntingdon, King's Lynn, Sudbury, Thetford, Wellingborough, Witham
4-6	Ashford, Edenbridge, Gainsborough, Hemel Hempstead, Luton, Mildenhall, Stevenage, Swindon
7-9	Braintree, Crawley, Scunthorpe, St. Neot's
10+	Biggleswade, Bletchley, Hatfield, Letchworth, Peterborough, Welwyn Garden City

Source: Adapted from 'Note to all Housing Officers in GLC area', LAB 8/3439 New and Expanding Towns – Industrial Selection Scheme – Miscellaneous, 2 October 1968

The local press highlighted the 'scandal of vanishing jobs' in the town where 'an administrative loophole is allowing jobs which should be available in Luton – hit by the biggest unemployment problem in living memory – to be filtered off to Londoners' (*Luton Evening Post*, 1 February 1972, p 1). Similarly, in Basildon in 1968 a 'special housing allocation' scheme that had been established to provide houses for semi-skilled and unskilled workers in London was abandoned after local campaigns to encourage employment among existing workers in a context where local unemployment was rising. In some NETs employers' organisations, such as the New Towns Industrial Group Association (representing over 200 firms that employed over 40,000 people), were also arguing that there:

> should be more flexibility in allocating houses and the rule of allocating them to London people should be relaxed ... some should also be given to local people working in the NTs where the local council cannot provide them with houses.[41]

Questions over mobility and entitlement, therefore, dogged the wider legitimacy of the programme.

In addition, it was increasingly argued that NET communities were, in effect, being selected in and through the requirements of employers. The policy of moving people to rented houses in NETs only after they had obtained a job there meant that 'the nature of the industry in the town has a major influence on the sort of people who may come to live in it'.[42] The profile of jobs that existed in any one place shaped the character of the population so that in almost all NETs there was a clear bias towards skilled people in their population structures (see Hall et al, 1973; Mullan, 1980). This was institutionalised through the ISS, which required the exporting local authorities in London to visit the homes of KWs and check on their 'suitability' for a move through a series of subjective judgements over the 'cleanliness' of their homes and the 'manners' of the residents (Gee, 1972). In addition, the 'social' element of the process gradually became less and less important as development agencies became focused on the needs of firms in NETs, rather than those of workers in poor housing in London. Evidence from contemporary accounts indicates that 'administrators were not really interested in the housing applicants they selected to put forward to employers' (Turok, 1989, p 99).

Such findings were not surprising given that, through the ISS and NTDC, housing allocations would be prioritised 'as far as is consistent with the demands of industry' (Thompson, 1973, p 7). Even by the early 1970s the result was that 'people in the worst kind of housing conditions in places like London are finding great difficulty in getting into the NTs'.[43] One additional problem was that the types of jobs attracted to many of the NETs were not easily filled by non-specialist labour. The London Dispersal Liaison Group (LDLG) reported that efforts to migrate unskilled workers from London and train them up to take on new, more skilled positions in the surrounding NETs failed as it was found that:

> the skills required at this level by the engineering firms were of such variety and the requirements in particular skills so intermittent or limited in numbers, that in practical terms training could only be given by the individual firms and not collectively.[44]

The result was that dedicated training courses were extremely difficult to operationalise and there was an increasing mismatch between the employment needs of the NETs and their social balance.

As a consequence the ISS contributed to a broader problem – that NETs attracted relatively high concentrations of skilled manufacturing employment through the post-war period. As Thompson (1973) noted, 80% of new job vacancies in NETs were for skilled men from the 20-29 age group. The focus on KWs meant that social and spatial divisions of labour in the South East of England were directly altered through government policy. Approximately 20,000 people per year through the 1960s were assisted by schemes such as the ISS to move away from

London, 55% of whom were in manual skilled labour sectors, such as engineering. The impacts on London of this selective out-migration were profound as it compounded many of the socioeconomic problems already faced by the city and its manufacturing decline. The Greater London Council, for example, complained that the NETs 'should accept a broader cross-section of London's population, including the unemployed and families unable to work' (Field and Crofts, 1977, p 24). There is evidence that London boroughs did not want to cooperate with the ISS as they feared losing their best people and, as a Ministry of Labour briefing made clear, being 'saddled with more and more problem families unable to move out'.[45] By the late 1960s even NET managers were complaining that the ISS was skewing their housing priorities and that firms were using the scheme to bend resources towards skilled and relatively well-paid employees. The Manager of Welwyn Garden City NT, for example, pleaded with the government to allow the town 'to achieve normality in regard to housing demand and in relation to migration and the ISS. It would seem an opportune moment to cut off the ISS completely in 1968'.[46]

Aside from this erosion of legitimacy, the other factor that reduced the effectiveness of the ISS over time was the declining importance of manufacturing industry and the emergence of a new generation of NETs focused to a much greater degree on the attraction of white collar, service sector jobs in both public and private sectors. In the later generation of NETs, built in the 1960s and 1970s, the emphasis became one of providing housing for knowledge workers, office employees, and other producer services without whom the 'success' of the new developments would be significantly hampered. As one of the planning frameworks for Hook NT in Hampshire, for instance, stated:

> If as we hope office, research and other organisations are to ... [relocate], it will be necessary to ensure that the character of the town as expressed in such things as technological and other educational provision, cultural and recreational facilities, and arrangements for housing for all income groups, is attractive to the existing staffs of such establishments. (London County Council, 1961, p 26)

The focus was increasingly on a different class of skilled worker, with firms being encouraged to move to NET greenfield sites where new offices would be constructed rather than factories.

In addition, the failure to attract balanced and mixed communities in the NETs led to another socioeconomic strategy being introduced – that of promoting commuter settlement. In 1968, Telford in the West Midlands, for example, became the first NET to actively promote itself as a location for commuters, something that found favour within the MHLG and the BoT. An internal memorandum between policy advisors stated that:

> The experience of Telford in mounting a campaign to attract commuters is significant and should be applied elsewhere too. I am as much a believer in the balanced community approach – i.e. social mix, age mix, work provision etc – as ever I was but I do not think that the encouragement of building houses must always be restrained to immediate prospects of employment in order to achieve the balance by the time the NETs are completed.[47]

The NET Housing Minister at the time, George Chipperfield, noted in response that 'Clearly commuters are not ideal but it would be wrong to neglect homes for several thousand people and a valuable contribution to our overall stock just because industry is slow to move'.[48]

This view was echoed by the LDLG, who wrote a report to ministers arguing for the extension of commuter-resident communities in the NETs around London, even though this went against the founding principles of balanced communities outlined in the early days of the programme. A scheme with the NTDCs allocated a percentage of their housing to nominated, semi-skilled or unskilled workers in housing need in large cities and would 'have the advantage of seeing that the allocation was fully used to give the intended relief and would put those who moved in a better position to seek both jobs and training at their level in the NT'.[49] In 1969 the Wilson government decided to allow the NETs to pursue active commuter-attraction policies if they so wished. The move was justified by reference to the ways in which local employment had got out of sync with house production and the:

> policy and practice of [NTD] Corporations ... are flexible enough to ensure that undue insistence on something which is desirable but not essential does not hold up the development of new towns or get in the way of maximum house production.[50]

It was in this context then that the ISS became increasingly irrelevant and was wound up. Its objectives and failings were indicative of the wider strategies of place- and labour market-building enshrined in the NET policies. It was an attempt to bureaucratise and control mobility in ordered ways so that the right types of labour markets and communities could be established in the NETs. However, the difficulties involved in enlisting other actors in the implementation of such policies and the wider confusion over the purpose of and role of labour mobility within spatial policy more broadly undermined its effectiveness. Economic changes and the shift away from manufacturing industry in the 1960s and 1970s also encouraged NETs to develop post-industrial strategies within which the category of the 'industrial worker' became less and less significant.

Conclusions

This chapter has shown that the discourse of the balanced and harmonious community was an essential element in the planning and construction of the NET programme in the post-war period. Drawing on original archival sources it has demonstrated that the construction of new places required the mobilisation of particular, selective imaginations of what a 'model' community consisted of as both an object and subject of development policy. This process was simultaneously enlightened, in seeking to plan for the needs of a broad range of social groups, at the same time as it was reactionary in using planning to fossilise an imagined social (and economic) structure through new forms of community-building. Despite the emphasis on state-driven development, through the powerful NTDCs, the success or otherwise of the NETs was ultimately dependent upon the actions of individuals and companies operating in rapidly changing social, economic, and political environments. Imaginations of what constituted functioning and harmonious places was, therefore, subject to repeated change and reinterpretation.

The chapter has also shown that one of the most challenging features of NET planning was the process through which particular types of employment would be attracted to sustain and reproduce a 'balanced' community. In order to facilitate this, a particular politics of mobility had to be developed that would encourage close relationships to be established between the movement of employers and appropriate workers. This process was also designed to tackle existing spatial development problems in the conurbations and to ensure that a 'balanced' migration of workers and communities would take place.

And yet, the ineffectiveness of initiatives such as the ISS was indicative of the intrinsically selective nature of the migration process and the difficulties that states face in the ordering and spatial distribution of industry and labour. In establishing the NET programme, the state was creating places that would, by definition, have to be attractive to entrepreneurs and entrepreneurial businesses and individuals, whose *presence* was deemed to be necessary to the delivery of the wider policy programme. While such agendas did not explicitly call for the *absence* of particular socioeconomic groups, those whose presence was less significant to the implementation of the wider strategy, such as CIs, were clearly given less priority. In this sense, we see a coming together of the key issues outlined in the opening chapters, namely the selective character of place imaginations, the contested and controversial politics of mobility, and the circumscribed character of state powers and resources to shape and control the actions of policy subjects.

As Chapter Seven will show, there are interesting parallels with today's sustainable communities agendas in which the process of ordering spaces and building new places has re-emerged. Identifying and directing the mobility of non-state actors represents a significant challenge. Even in a context of relatively 'strong' Keynesian state regulation, there were significant bureaucratic hurdles to the creation of balanced NETs. Leaving decisions over mobility to the vagaries of markets and individual choices disorganises the very processes that spatial policies are ostensibly seeking to control. In addition, the emphasis on building self-contained places underplayed the impacts of mobility on places *from* which movements occur. While the NET policy was explicitly concerned with spreading development and growth across boundaries, the inability to control the movements that took place meant that donor communities suffered from selective forms of migration that undermined their own socioeconomic balance and stability.

Notes

[1] TCPA statement to Ministry of Reconstruction, Ministry of Town and Country Planning, Ministry of Health and the Board of Trade, HLG 90/66 Survey of England and Wales: Expansion of the Existing New Towns 1946-1948.

[2] L. Silkin, New Towns Bill Debate, *Hansard*, 3 April 1946, vol 422, col 1234.

[3] Dame Evelyn Sharp, MHLG, Letter to Sir John Wrigley, MoH, *New Towns – Labour*, HLG 90/108 Labour Requirements Estimates for New Towns Industries 1946-1950, 7 January 1947.

[4] Ministry of Works Planning and General Division, HLG 90/108 Labour Requirements Estimates for New Towns Industries 1946-1950, 15 November 1946.

[5] L. Silkin, New Towns Bill Debate, *Hansard*, 3 April 1946, vol 422, cols 1231-8.

[6] L. Silkin, New Towns Bill Debate, *Hansard*, 3 April 1946, vol 422, cols 1089-90.

[7] Lord Mancroft, *Statement to the House of Lords*, HLG 90/64 House of Lords Motion on New Towns, 24 June 1953.

[8] Deputy General of Region 5 (London), Report, HLG 90/66 Survey of England and Wales, Expansion of the Existing Towns 1946-1948, October 1947.

[9] Deputy General of Region 5 (London), Report, HLG 90/66 Survey of England and Wales, Expansion of the Existing Towns 1946-1948, October 1947, p 1.

[10] Deputy General of Region 5 (London), Report, HLG 90/66 Survey of England and Wales, Expansion of the Existing Towns 1946-1948, October 1947, p 1.

[11] *English New Towns: House Building by Development Corporations*, HLG 116/558.

[12] E. Sharp, Internal memorandum, *New Towns – Housing for Different Population Groups*, HLG 90/92, 5 March 1948.

[13] The District Councils (New Towns) Association, Letter to G. Lindgren, Ministry of Local Government and Planning, HLC 90/84, Introduction of Industry into New Towns, 20 February 1951.

[14] E. Warne, Letter to F. Lacey, Board of Trade, BT 177/2189, 15 August 1969.

[15] D. O'Connell, Letter to E. Warne, Board of Trade, BT 177/2189, 22 May 1969.

[16] H. Erroll, BoT, Letter to TUC Congress, MSS 292B 540/1/Regional Policy 1960-1962, 23 March 1962.

[17] E. Sharp, Letter to Sir John Wrigley, MoH, *New Towns – Labour*, HLG 90/108, Labour Requirements Estimates for New Towns Industries 1946-1950, p 1.

[18] Lord Mancroft, *Statement to the House of Lords*, HLG 90/64 House of Lords Motion on New Towns, 24 June 1953.

[19] *London's Housing – The Minister Rt Hon Aneurin Bevan Reports*, Farleigh Press, Herts, 1946, p 7.

[20] Lord Mancroft, *Statement to the House of Lords*, HLG 90/64 House of Lords Motion on New Towns, 24 June 1953.

[21] Lord Mancroft, *Statement to the House of Lords*, HLG 90/64 House of Lords Motion on New Towns, 24 June 1953.

[22] Ministerial Note on the Sale of Empty Homes in New Towns, Discussion Paper 3, HLG 116/561 English New Towns Quarterly Return to Secretary of State of Unemployed Labour and Unoccupied Houses, 3 July 1972.

[23] Washington Development Corporation, Letter to Department of the Environment, HLG 116/561 English New Towns Quarterly Return to Secretary of State of Unemployed Labour and Unoccupied Houses, 23 February 1972.

[24] E. Hambly, 'Mildenhall, Suffolk', in Minutes of London County Council Meeting on Immigration Housing Policy, HLG 118/545, 2 March 1965.

[25] Department of Employment and Productivity – Expansion of Peterborough, LAB 8/3439 New and Expanding Towns – Industrial Selection Scheme – Miscellaneous 1974.

[26] Department of Employment and Productivity – Expansion of Peterborough, LAB 8/3439 New and Expanding Towns – Industrial Selection Scheme – Miscellaneous 1974.

[27] Department of Employment and Productivity – Expansion of Peterborough, LAB 8/3439 New and Expanding Towns – Industrial Selection Scheme – Miscellaneous 1974.

[28] Department of Employment and Productivity – Expansion of Peterborough, LAB 8/3439 New and Expanding Towns – Industrial Selection Scheme – Miscellaneous 1974.

[29] Department of Employment and Productivity – Expansion of Peterborough, LAB 8/3439 New and Expanding Towns – Industrial Selection Scheme – Miscellaneous 1974.

[30] Department of Employment and Productivity – Expansion of Peterborough, LAB 8/3439 New and Expanding Towns – Industrial Selection Scheme – Miscellaneous 1974.

[31] F. Garwood, MHLG, Letter to Mr Roberts, 'Industrial Selection and the Housing of Londoners at Corby', HLG 116/312 Industrial Selection Scheme 1967-1970.

[32] F. Garwood, MHLG, Letter to Mr Roberts 'Industrial Selection and the Housing of Londoners at Corby', HLG 116/312 Industrial Selection Scheme, 1967-1970.

[33] Home Counties Federation of Trades Councils, Letter to TUC General Secretary, MSS 292/830.1/3/New Towns 1945-59, 15 April 1952.

[34] Home Counties Federation of Trades Councils, Letter to TUC General Secretary, MSS 292/830.1/3/New Towns 1945-59, 5 December 1951.

[35] TUC General Secretary's Office, Letter to Hatfield Trades Council, MSS 292/830.1/3/New Towns 1945-59, 16 January 1953.

[36] Windsor Trades Council, Meeting to discuss Bracknell New Town, MSS 292/830.1/3/New Towns 1945-59, 26 January 1952.

[37] TUC Education Committee, Amenities in New Towns, MSS 292/830.1/4/New Towns 1959-1960, 28 June 1960.

[38] Alternatively, in some cases, London boroughs had made specific agreements with specific NETs (there was such a relationship between Stevenage NT and North East London Borough, for instance), or individuals could simply move to the area.

[39] J. Towehill, East & Southern Regional Controller, Department of Employment and Productivity, Letter to HQ, LAB 8/3439 New and Expanding Towns – Industrial Selection Scheme – Miscellaneous, 10 February 1969.

[40] J. Wood, Letter to MHLG, LAB 8/3439 New and Expanding Towns – Industrial Selection Scheme – Miscellaneous, 9 September 1970.

[41] New Town Industrial Group Association Press Release, MSS 292/830.1/3 New Towns 1945-1959, 8 January 1957.

[42] London Dispersal Liaison Group, Memorandum by the Ministry of Housing and Local Government, Internal memo, HLG 116/558, 1969, p 2.

[43] J. Fraser, Prime Minister's Question Time, *Hansard*, 1 April 1971, p 1031.

[44] LDLG, *Commuters for London Towns*, Internal memo, HLG 116/558, 1969, p 3.

[45] LAB 8/3439 New and Expanding Towns – Industrial Selection Scheme – Miscellaneous, 1974.

[46] Notes of meeting between F. Garwood, MHLG, and M. Restall, Housing Manager, Welwyn and Hatfield Commission for the New Town, HLG 116/312 Industrial Selection Scheme, 1967–1970.

[47] R. Brain, Internal memorandum to R. Coates, *Commuters for the New Town Housing 1968-1972*, HLG 116/558, 23 October 1969.

[48] G. Chipperfield, Memorandum to M. Brain, *Commuters for the New Town Housing 1968-1972*, HLG 116/558, 12 November 1969.

[49] LDLG, Internal memo, *Commuters for London Towns*, HLG 116/558, 1969, p 2.

[50] LDLG, Internal memo, *Commuters for London Towns*, HLG 116/558, 1969, p 4.

FIVE

Economic modernisation and post-war emigration and immigration

Introduction

Labour mobility programmes in the post-war decades were not only concerned with the movement of workers within the UK. Debates over whose presence or absence was necessary in the pursuit of economic growth and community well-being also related to broader questions concerning international migration and the types of policy that the UK should pursue. On the one hand, the supported *emigration* of workers to expanding parts of the Commonwealth had represented a key foreign and economic policy objective since the late 19th century. The mission to 'people the Commonwealth' with UK subjects was seen to have both political and economic dividends in creating pro-UK countries across the world that would provide guaranteed export markets for UK products. On the other hand, from the 1950s policy also became focused on the (often reluctant) promotion of international immigration as a vehicle to 'rebalance' labour markets in expanding regions and thereby underpin the modernisation of the British economy. During the 1950s and 1960s it became clear that notions of 'essential' work would have to be expanded to include those areas of the economy in which labour shortages were having the greatest impact, partly as a consequence of emigration policy.

Drawing on archival sources this chapter focuses on *intra-Commonwealth migration* during the post-war decades and examines how and why international migration policies emerged, what their core principles and rationalities were, and what impact they had on spatial labour markets and economic development trajectories. The emergence of such programmes was extremely controversial and this was reflected in (and in part produced by) government policies that were muddled and at times contradictory. Despite being commonly associated with globalisation and modern forms of governance, the chapter shows that concerns over how labour mobility should be structured and in whose interests underpinned the politics of migration throughout the period of post-war Keynesianism. The rationalities and practices of policy were underpinned by relational understandings of citizenship (see Rose, 1999a) in that immigrants were seen as *relationally different types of citizens and workers* to those in existing communities who should be treated differently to 'native' citizens. The former's presence had to be directly related to the well-being of the latter and the chapter shows how such decisions were taken and what the rationalities and practices of government policy were. The discussion begins by examining how emigration policy came into existence before moving on to immigration policy, with a particular focus on the experiences of Caribbean migration to exemplify the wider processes in action.

Economic modernisation and emigration policy in the post-war period

> It has been said that the British people are the most migratory-minded in the world. Certainly through the years they have always been to the fore in the movements of people around the world. Today that urge still exists. (*The Scotsman*, 1953, p 13)

Throughout the post-war period governments were concerned with the quantity and quality of emigration from the UK and its implications for economic development and regional growth. During the first half of the 20th century emigration had been closely related to the wider politics of Empire-building and the 'peopling' primarily of the so-called Dominion territories.[1] The 1922 Empire Settlement Act included a range of measures to support UK emigrants such as an Assisted Passage Scheme to Australia and New Zealand that gave financial help and practical assistance. Emigration was designed to underpin the settlement of the Empire. In so doing, it would provide labour to enable the exploitation of the enormous natural resources of the new countries and ensure that their governments would adopt a pro-UK outlook in matters of trade and foreign affairs. In the reflective words of the UK's Interdepartmental Committee on Emigration, 'It was believed to be in Britain's best interests to have a country of British-minded Australians'.[2] The same was true for other parts of the world where it was felt that there would be significant strategic and moral advantages in promoting the emigration of UK subjects.

This general policy was followed by the Attlee government of 1945 and subsequent Conservative administrations of the 1950s. As Paul (1997, p 25) notes, from 1946 to 1960 UK emigration averaged 125,000 per annum, out of a population of approximately 47 million. Eighty per cent of these, a total of 1.5 million, went to the Dominions. The focus was on encouraging a broad range of people to migrate, with a particular emphasis on women, without whom, as one Foreign Office planner wrote in a secret minute, 'you will not succeed in peopling the Commonwealth with British stock and ... as time goes by we will be compelled to take in an increasing number of Europeans of doubtful breed [sic]'.[3] This peopling strategy also had an economic rationale. Expanded trade was always a core element in the growth and maintenance of the Empire, and migration was seen as a vehicle for enhancing economic relations and assisting the UK to boost its export industries (see Sharma, 2002). With high levels of UK immigration, the economies of the new countries would expand and provide readily available markets for UK firms to exploit.

The burden of post-war reconstruction and the growing spatial inequalities across the UK put pressure on governments to manage and shape the spatial economy and available labour markets in new and more efficient ways. The loss of people from the UK was not perceived to be a significant problem in and of itself. Indeed, government records show that some within the government saw emigration in the context of a more comprehensive 'population management' strategy. They argued that the lack of productivity in UK industry meant that there would be an inevitable lowering of living standards if the national population continued to increase at post-war levels. One government advisor even went as far as to call for a 'considerable reduction in our population' drawing on geographical imaginations to argue that a lack of physical space meant that the UK was 'over-populated' in relation to its Empire and that it was becoming increasingly difficult to sustain an adequate quality of life.[4] In a similar vein, others argued that emigration represented a mechanism of 'rebalancing' the UK's spatial economy with some, for example, calling for 'the Empire to be treated as a single entity as far as financial solvency is concerned' (Carson, 1952, p 23). In order to achieve this, a review was required of 'our present distribution of manpower' not only in the UK but in relation to the Empire's population and employment balance.

However, by the early 1950s the dominant view within government was that policy was creating more problems for the UK than it was solving. There was particular concern over the *selective nature* of emigration and its impact on the skills base of the UK economy. It became clear that emigrants were not representing a 'fair cross-section of the population by occupation, age and sex'[5] and a government report noted that 'the Empire countries now want not farmers as prewar but skilled and semi-skilled workers – bricklayers, carpenters and mechanics, fitters – with young people preferred. These are the very people Britain wants to keep at home' (Carrier and Jeffrey, 1953, p 17). As early as August 1947 the Conservative leader Winston Churchill was calling on would-be emigrants to cancel or postpone their moves from the UK in order to help in the reconstruction of their home country (*The Times*, 1947, p 1). Archives reveal that within government many were arguing that the Dominions needed to 'take their fair proportion of non-workers – dependants of one sort or another – as well as active workers ... any planned emigration scheme would alter the age distribution of the population further'.[6] By 1951 the Attlee administration had amended its procedures so that it had the right to withhold financial assistance to those with 'certain qualifications whose services may be urgently needed in the UK in the national interest'.[7] It was not clear what the 'national interest' constituted and decisions were taken by the Ministry of Labour (MoL) on a case-by-case basis. The measure was designed to put pressure on the Dominion country governments to take, what one minister called, a 'fair cross section of society'.[8]

The problem was that migrants tended to be those with more secure and well-paid employment prospects and also those below the age of 45 for whom the prospect of 'making a new life' took on greater appeal. As one civil servant reported to ministers in November 1953:

> It is quite clear that there is a very substantial drain to various parts of the Commonwealth of technically qualified engineers of all grades of skilled craftsmen, technicians and professionally qualified men.... I am not suggesting that anything can or should be done to stop the drain but I think it very important that those concerned with scientific and technical manpower should be aware of the position.[9]

The post-Attlee Conservative government became so concerned with this exodus that it collected statistics on the net flows of key workers (KWs) such as skilled engineers (see Table 5.1) and established an Overseas Migration Board in 1953 to 'consider and advise the Secretary of State upon specific proposals for schemes of emigration from the UK to other Commonwealth countries'.[10]

There was also growing concern over the impacts that emigration was having on the regions and the damage that was being done to the

Table 5.1: Migration of skilled engineers to and from the UK, 1952-55

Year	Numbers coming into the UK	Numbers going out of the UK	Net change
1952	608	1,354	–746
1953	848	1,762	–934
1954	900	1,310	–410
1955	718	1,096	–378

Source: LAB 8/1871 Emigration of Professionals and Skilled Engineers to Commonwealth and USA, 1953-1956

skills base of Development Areas (DAs). In Scotland, for example, population levels and the presence (and absence) of particular skills was long regarded as a politically sensitive and important issue. In 1953 *The Scotsman* reported that the emigration of skilled workers from the country was particularly high with a net loss of 236,000 between 1946 and 1951. As with the rest of the UK, it was argued that the root problem was not only the numbers involved but also the quality of those leaving. In the inter-war period these had mainly been agriculturalists and low-skilled workers. However, from the end of the Second World War, the trend had become an out-migration of the skilled workers whose presence was seen as a necessary ingredient in the rebuilding of the Scottish economy. As later chapters will show, the politics of population loss has continued to be a critical feature of debates over Scotland's economic development, many of which date from the emigrations of the post-war decades.

As the 1950s proceeded the nature of labour demands in the UK changed significantly. The Dominion countries required more people for their own post-war rebuilding programmes and developed more targeted strategies to find and support the movement of the 'right' kind of emigrant. In 1957 the *Sunday Express* reported that the Dominions wanted at least 200,000 UK workers to supply their growing industries, figures that helped fuel a wider discourse of fear within the UK media (see *Financial Times*, 1955; *The Guardian*, 1955). Attention was increasingly drawn to programmes such as the *Bring Out a Briton* scheme in which Australian communities were being encouraged by their government to nominate people they knew in the UK to emigrate. The Canadian government similarly developed a number of schemes in an effort to attract UK workers and their families and over 300,000 emigrated between 1946 and 1954 (Paul, 1997, p 34). Despite its obvious dislike of the emigration process the Conservative Party's wider commitment to the Empire and its unwillingness to impede on the free mobility of individual citizens prevented it from taking significant restrictive measures during the 1950s.

State (in)capacities and emigration policy in the 1960s

By the early 1960s secret files indicate that the UK government was contemplating measures to try and halt the movement of workers. A confidential interdepartmental report of 1961 argued that there was:

> a growing competition for skilled workers between the sending and receiving countries ... [and] Britain should shape emigration policy in her own interests. These are to maintain a buoyant economy and to maintain and develop her links with the Commonwealth.[11]

Such statements reflected real concern within the government. It was not only the numbers of workers that were being lost but also their quality and their geographical location. The loss of skilled workers was 'seriously hampering the efficient working of the economy out of all proportion to the numbers involved'.[12] Once again state agencies were directly concerned with broader questions over the economic damage that an absence of KWs would have on the economic competitiveness of the UK. It was particularly damaging because it ran counter to the KW programmes and NET strategies outlined in Chapters Three and Four as the majority of emigrants originated in the regions where they were desperately needed. Ministry of Labour officials argued that skilled workers were essential for the economic competitiveness of healthy labour markets at local, regional, and national levels so that 'even slight increases in shortages could have big effects'.[13] One minister wrote to the government's Overseas Migration Board to ask: 'Can we be happy about the UK's role as an exporter of skilled manpower to the Old Commonwealth and an importer of mainly unskilled manpower from the new?'.[14] A new set of more restrictive government policies was required to tackle this or, at the very least, less direct support for those who wished to move.

The government's own working party on the economic effects of increased emigration reported that the failure to link emigration policy to the needs of 'key industries' had encouraged the governments of the receiving countries to adopt a more selective approach with the problem that 'precisely the same sorts of skills [are required in these countries] as are required for economic growth in Britain'.[15] The problem had been compounded by the slowing of the post–war boom in the Dominions and the growing unwillingness to accept 'unskilled' UK migrants. Identified sectors included scientists and technologists, mathematicians, and mechanical and electrical engineers. The working party warned that small losses in these areas were:

> particularly significant because they must be measured against a total qualified population of about 300,000 and there is also an important qualitative element in that migration may have particular attraction for the most highly qualified individuals within each profession.[16]

Similar sentiments were also expressed by trades unions and business representatives.

Despite this growing political pressure, however, governments throughout the 1960s failed to adopt significant measures to limit emigration. Secret files (a categorisation that indicates the sensitivity and seriousness with which governments treated the issue) reveal that the Wilson administration of 1964 did not want to officially discourage further emigration as it was fearful of the national and international political difficulties that any change in tone would engender.[17] In 1965 it crossed a Rubicon when Wilson told a meeting of Commonwealth Prime Ministers that although the UK had been a willing exporter of workers, the time had come for it to adopt a more cautious approach as:

> economic indicators suggest that general labour shortages are developing in many sectors of our economy and particularly for carpenters, bricklayers, skilled general engineering and aircraft workers.[18]

And yet, despite this rhetoric little was practically done to try to halt emigration as to do so would be seen as an admission that the UK's relationship within its Commonwealth had changed and that the state had no right to limit the mobility of its citizens if they made the choice to move.

One response was a greater emphasis on the collection of statistics, particularly of skilled workers to ensure that their loss 'didn't cause serious embarrassment to industry in this country'.[19] A Technical Personnel Committee had been established in the MoL in 1956 to oversee this process but it was during the 1960s that procedures became more formalised and of greater significance. As Rose (1999a) argues, the collection and deployment of statistics is one of the defining features of modern systems of government as they allow disordered realities to be dissected and ordered into calculable problems of government. Accurate knowledge of exactly which citizens were leaving the country was seen as essential to government policy. Indeed, statistical data collection proved to be one of the biggest areas of contention between the UK and the Dominions. The latter were reluctant to publish or collect accurate figures on the different types of citizens that were migrating from the UK, fearing that if the true extent of KW emigration from the UK was known then this might act as an incentive for stronger limits on worker mobility.[20]

Governments also tried to use statistics to develop more 'rational' responses. In 1964, for example, the Department of Education and Science drew up a list of A and B type citizens whose emigration needed to be monitored and regulated. Table 5.2 lists the variety of occupations that were included in each group.

Records show that there were a series of long and often heated debates over how shortages should be defined and what effects they had had on the prospects for regional and national economic development. It was noted that in some sectors the lack of workers resulted from factors that were not primarily related to emigration. For example, in most of the category A and B sectors, there were shortages of female workers, something that reflected the social structuring of labour markets. Attempts were made to collect statistics on trades and their employment needs but, as was frequently noted, it was extremely difficult to get an accurate picture of exactly how priorities should be worked out and how such agendas should be implemented, a recurring problem as we will see in later chapters.

Policy also began to develop a more explicitly spatial dimension.

Table 5.2: Department of Education and Science categorisations of different types of KWs

List	Persons with first degree or equivalent or professionally qualified in the following
A	*Science* – agricultural science, biology, chemistry/pharmacy, geology, mathematics, physics, general science *Technology* – metallurgy, chemical engineering, civil and structural engineering, electrical engineering, mechanical engineering, other engineering, plastics technology, rubber technology, textile technology *Other qualifications* – technicians, draughtsmen [sic], research assistants
B	Workers with experience and skills in short supply in science and technology

Source: LAB 8/2988 Economic Effect of Increased Emigration to the Old Dominions 1964-1967.

For example, in the early 1960s, regular letters were sent from the MoL to Australia House in London in order to give the Australian government lists of UK sectors that were suffering from skills shortages. If the Australian government asked for skilled workers in a particular sector, the UK government passed on the request to local authorities and Labour Exchanges in areas of high unemployment where it was felt that emigration would be most 'beneficial' for the UK.[21] The existence of spatial selection policy reveals that labour transference from areas of unemployment was still a policy option that could contribute to the rebalancing of spatial labour markets and communities. If unemployed workers could be encouraged to leave the UK altogether, then one of the 'problems' that the state faced, namely that of providing for economically marginalised communities, could be addressed.

There was also some evidence that workers' representatives in Australia were increasingly unhappy at the influx of UK workers. As economic growth slowed so workers' representatives became increasingly concerned about the continuing influx of UK émigrés. Table 5.3 shows that, by 1960, 331,139 people had migrated from the UK to Australia. Some tried to change this perception. Australian trades unions, for example, began to question migration policy, fearful that in-migrants would take the dwindling supply of jobs. One Queensland trade union, for example, used UK newspapers to put across the message that even skilled workers were not wanted as wages were relatively low and the quality of life poor (*The Australian*, 1964). As with labour mobility programmes in the UK, the fears of those in recipient communities that in-migrants would disturb the socioeconomic balance and harmony of place were of growing importance, particularly in the context of periodic economic recessions.

To summarise, the politics of post-war emigration was indicative of the contested and controversial character of the politics of (labour) mobility. Government agendas were driven by multiple and contrasting rationalities that drew on specific imaginations of places, communities, and economies and how they functioned. Questions emerged over

Table 5.3: Total number of emigrants from the UK to the Dominion territories, 1946-60

Country	Total number of emigrants from the UK
Australia	331,139
New Zealand	151,730
Canada	582,787
South Africa	82,178

Source: LAB 8/2736, British Emigration Policy 1961-1967

whose presence was necessary for their functioning and how policy should adapt to their absence if processes of movement became 'excessive' and began to undermine the balance, harmony, and sustainability of places and labour markets. At the same time, UK governments were concerned with a wider international political agenda and wanted to be seen to be acting in particular ways. The state assisted its citizens to voluntarily migrate overseas if they so wished, even if this principle appeared at odds with spatial and social policy objectives in the UK. A very different politics of mobility began to characterise *immigration* policy, however, particularly from the Commonwealth, and it is to this that the chapter now turns.

Immigration, labour market-building, and the politics of mobility

As discussed in Chapters Three and Four, the experience of war had shown that state power could be used to optimise the efficiency and effectiveness of the economy and the spatial distribution of labour. However, the effects of emigration, mass military mobilisation, and socioeconomic dislocation were profound and the problem of labour shortages began to affect the capacity of the economy to grow and develop. Shortages were particularly acute in 'essential' sectors such as 'agriculture, coal mining, textiles, construction, foundry work, health services and international domestic service' (Paul, 1997, p 67). The Attlee government's Foreign Labour Committee in 1946 reported that there was a shortage of between one and one and a half million key workers across the UK (Spencer, 1997, p 38). The government's response was to look to international labour mobility, particularly from its Commonwealth, to solve its labour force problems and rebalance its spatial economies. After the Second World War various groups of Europeans, including Irish, Polish, and Italian workers, were encouraged to migrate to the UK to fill specific KW positions in core industries, particularly coal mining, transport, and agriculture. And yet, under pressure from Commonwealth governments, such as those in the Caribbean, and drawing on a sense of colonial responsibility, the UK government began to look to its former colonies for a natural supply of workers (see Spencer, 1997).

The 1948 British Nationality Act essentially established an open borders policy between the UK and Commonwealth countries. As Phillips (2004, p 1) notes, 'British passports designated their bearers as citizens of the "United Kingdom and the Colonies", with the implication that every Commonwealth citizen was also a British subject'. In 1948 the first Caribbean immigrants began to arrive and establish communities in the entry ports of Liverpool and London. However, from the outset the Attlee administration saw the geographical concentration of these migrants as a social and economic 'problem'. It developed a strategy of *organised dispersal* aimed at creating a more 'even' distribution of migrant workers across the economy so that the impacts of immigration could be managed, coordinated, and controlled in the pursuit of wider objectives. For instance, Regional Controllers (RCs) were told by central government that 'the best we can do is to place skilled men in jobs for which English labour is not readily available'.[22] Active efforts were made to match up the immigrants with specific job placements across the UK, and the MoL implored RCs to find opportunities for dispersal as 'there is already a problem in London with unemployed coloured men [*sic*], and it will be necessary to make special efforts to find employment for as many as possible'.[23] RCs were warned that 'unless something can be done there will remain a nasty residual problem of a comparatively large group of men unemployed and all together ... very few of whom are likely to be skilled in the sense that we would understand the term'.[24] RCs were ordered to develop programmes in which small groups of 10 to 12 immigrants at a time would be moved to different places 'where they might be expected to be absorbed into employment'.[25]

This organised dispersal was not only a mechanism for matching labour supply with demand. It was also part of a wider strategy to ensure that some sense of community balance and socioeconomic harmony could be promoted within DAs and the UK's cities. An MoL minister, for example, argued in 1948 that 'there is a colour prejudice and that is at its most fierce, naturally enough, in places where there is already unemployment amongst white people'.[26] It was considered that policy should therefore seek to move the immigrants away from such areas to reduce the 'potential' for community conflict and disharmony. Liverpool and London became identified as particular trouble spots and were contrasted with healthy, balanced, and buoyant labour markets, such as Birmingham or the North Midlands. In such localities 'the problems were very much less; agitators do not get hold of their men and because there is practically no unemployment amongst white men, the prejudice is far less'.[27] Consequently, all government departments were agreed in 1948 that government policy should be to 'spread these men out throughout the country and solve the problem this way'.[28] Assisted mobility was to be used as a mechanism for ensuring that the balance and harmony of communities was maintained.

At its most extreme, government policy secretly encouraged local

Labour Exchanges to organise the dispersal of migrant workers in 'ones and twos' because the movement of greater numbers was perceived to create accommodation problems as landlords were unwilling to accept the new migrants. Indeed, numerous government reports showed that 'the problem of finding living accommodation is a very serious handicap to the placing of coloured [*sic*] workers in most areas of the country'.[29] The government set up a network of hostels to enable a 'constant stream of coloured [*sic*] colonials to be transferred to areas of good employment and dispersed among the working population'.[30] This would be achieved through a programme of 'regional arrangements to ensure that where any region found employment opportunities for Colonials special steps were taken to get them away from Liverpool or London'.[31] Interestingly, it was argued that migrants would only fit into the 'right type' of place. Their presence in market towns and NTs, for example, was frowned upon as their ways of working and living were perceived to be 'ill-suited' to such communities. A government minister at the time, for example, told RCs that the problem of satisfactory location was likely to grow worse as despite the government's best efforts to move workers to areas where their skills were required 'the greatest difficulty in placing was the behaviour of the men [*sic*], the ease with which they were influenced by agitators and the question of accommodation'.[32] In more explicitly racist terms the minister also felt that 'it was doubtful whether we could understand properly the mentality of the coloured [*sic*] person',[33] making their dispersal an urgent priority of government.

The 1950s and new waves of immigration

During the 1950s the numbers of immigrants from the Caribbean increased significantly (see Table 5.4).[34] In ways that mirror contemporary debates, efforts were made to control what one Home Office official described as 'the problem of immigrants coming to the UK in search of employment'.[35] From the outset this 'problem' was couched in a broad range of terms relating not only to the immigrants' economic characteristics but also to the perceived 'inability' of recipient places to absorb increases in minority ethnic populations in a sustainable way. Echoing Sassen's (1999a) concept of internal versus external threat (see Chapter Two), the problem with Commonwealth immigration was increasingly perceived as something that was externally generated, that could only be controlled and regulated through the imposition of strong government action.

Underlying the immigration 'problem', of course, were questions

Table 5.4: Approximate numbers of Caribbean, Indian, and Pakistani immigrants to the UK, 1951-61

	Caribbean	India	Pakistan	Others	Total
1951	1,300	–	–	–	1,300
1952	2,165	–	–	–	2,165
1953	2,000	–	–	–	2,000
1954	11,000	–	–	–	11,000
1955	27,500	5,800	1,850	7,500	42,650
1956	29,800	5,600	2,050	9,350	46,800
1957	23,000	6,600	5,200	7,600	42,400
1958	15,000	6,200	4,700	3,950	29,850
1959	16,400	2,950	850	1,400	21,600
1960	49,650	5,900	2,500	350	57,700
1961	66,300	23,750	25,100	21,250	136,400

Sources: Adapted from W. Cornish, Home Office, Letter to A. Morley, Commonwealth Relations Office, CO 1032/120, 12 May 1955; Hansen (2000, p 265)

over race and the perceived 'balance' of urban and regional communities. In 1955 it was decided to establish a 'Working Party on the Social and Economic Problems Arising from the Growing Influx into the UK of Colonial Workers from Other Commonwealth Countries'. As a secret memorandum at the time made clear, 'controversy would be reduced if it were possible to base the legislation on the recommendations of an impartial committee'.[36] It reported back that, due to buoyant economic conditions, immigrants were finding little problem in accessing employment. The wider 'problem' concerned 'housing difficulties caused by unrestricted immigration … in areas the migrants have congregated'[37] and what would happen in the event of economic recession. The concern was to ensure that some type of sustainable balance was established between employment opportunities and housing so that efficient and working communities could be created in order to underpin economic development. However, the state's limited ability to sustain such a balance and the implications of disharmony were also apparent. A Home Office memorandum in 1954 highlighted the early successes of the immigration programme in filling employment vacancies. However, it also warned that, 'difficulties in relation to fellow workers and TUs [trades unions] will undoubtedly come when the coloured [sic] workers become entitled to promotion in factories and workshops as many will be in the near future'.[38]

The same 'problems' were identified in relation to housing and community-building. There was an inherent tension between a desire for the creation of mixed communities in which people of different backgrounds and races would live together at the same time as immigrant groups were expected to play a subservient role in labour markets. For example, many immigrants were moving to urban areas, particularly around London and Birmingham. Government records indicate that this was perceived to be a problem by ministers, officials, local authorities in those areas, and trades unions, all of whom objected to the 'imbalances' being created. An internal Home Office memorandum, for example, noted how immigrant workers were 'finding their own solutions' in relation to housing problems and building their own communities. Many were 'buying up slum property and creating coloured [*sic*] quarters … finding their own solutions but not always of a kind satisfactory to local residents and local authorities'.[39]

This spatial concentration, and what the government's committee on immigration in 1955 referred to as a '*lack of assimilation*' on the part of ethnic groups, helped to create a perception that immigration was not 'working' in the way that it ought to be. Even the relatively successful addition of workers to the expanding labour markets of the 1950s was presented as a temporary fix as 'it is questionable whether race relations would be so harmonious if there was a significant increase in the coloured [*sic*] population' (Home Office, 1955, p 2). Rather than seeing the newcomers as part of an inclusive community, their presence was seen as a 'necessary evil' required for the functioning and balance of the economy but also represented a threat to the dominant imaginations of what communities in UK cities ought to consist of. In this sense, post-war immigration exemplifies the difficulties in marrying perceptions of what ideal places and communities should consist of with the need to secure economic production and the needs of economic competitiveness.

In response to the perceived threat posed to community harmony governments from the mid-1950s established new forms of selection that would distinguish between different types of citizens and ensure that only those who could play a functional role would be admitted to the UK. A reading of *Hansard* demonstrates the tone of much of the debate with Members of Parliament (MPs) calling for the repealing of the legislation and the establishment of new restrictive measures that 'should exclude the criminal, the idle, and the unfit of all races'.[40] The government considered introducing an industry-specific quota system in which the labour needs of industries would be identified, with limited quotas of workers allowed into the UK to fill specific labour positions. However, with the exception of a small number of easily identifiable sectors, such as transport, this idea was dropped on the grounds of being impractical. The government's own advisors called for a system of Board of Trade (BoT) and MoL regulated employment permits as 'whatever needs exist for immigrants to fill certain types of jobs can be adequately met by a system of individual labour permits which, compared to a quota system, is an instrument of precision'.[41]

However, other sources show that a wider debate was taking place over the functional needs of the economy and the role that different types of immigrants could and should play in maintaining the UK's economic competitiveness. In 1956, for example, *The Times* reported that within the industrial regions of the UK, there were 'still plenty of vacancies for unskilled workers ... and coloured [*sic*] workers do not mind where they are sent or what work they take on' (p 2). An internal government memorandum of 1956 noted that despite policy initiatives there were still 397,000 vacancies in the British economy.[42] As discussed above, large-scale emigration was beginning to reach economically and demographically significant levels with regional economies in particular facing an exodus of skilled workers. The mixture of economic priorities, with broader (often racist) concerns over community harmony made this a particularly complex and sensitive issue for the Conservative administrations of the late 1950s. Conceptions of balanced places included some degree of social diversity but did not extend to people from minority ethnic groups.

So even in economic terms, the employment prospects of the new immigrants were limited by the socially structured nature of labour markets. As other studies have indicated, the skills and knowledge of immigrant workers were systematically downgraded and given a significantly reduced economic and social value. The government's own committee reported in 1955 that:

> The job which an immigrant has obtained may not always have been the type of work which he [*sic*] hoped to find or for which he regarded himself as qualified when he left home. It would appear that a worker classified as 'skilled' in the West Indies would probably not be regarded as equally skilled by the standards of this country and he may have been unacceptable in his former occupation for that reason. (Home Office, 1955)

From an early stage there were reports of skilled workers returning to the Caribbean, disillusioned with the roles they were expected to play in the pursuit of balance, harmony, and efficient UK labour markets.

The influx of Commonwealth workers posed significant dilemmas for workers' representatives. The fear was that in the event of a recession the balance of employment opportunities vis-à-vis immigration would shift and that existing workers needed to be protected. Other concerns were raised over issues such as the 'health' of the British population with a Congress Resolution in 1956, for instance, calling for all 'entrants, regardless of their race or creed [to] be subject to a medical examination prior to being admitted into this country ... to safeguard the health of our members and the whole of the nation'.[43] In an attempt to deflect attention away from the Trades Union Congress' (TUC's) problems broader geographical imaginations were called upon that challenged the legitimacy of an (im)migration strategy. TUC Congress Resolution 51 in 1955, for example, called for new rounds of development in Caribbean countries. After 'welcoming' workers from overseas it pointed out:

> These coloured workers [*sic*] are driven out from their homeland by poverty and social insecurity which are due mainly to unbalanced economies created by years of colonial exploitation ... immediate steps should be taken to develop the resources of the Commonwealth territories so as to establish balanced economies which would make it unnecessary for the native populations to seek employment and security elsewhere.[44]

TUC archives indicate that even though the TUC leadership was staunchly opposed to racial discrimination within the British labour market, it still expressed concerns over various aspects of immigration.

The existence of such sentiments in the TUC leadership reflected a much deeper unease across the movement. Motion number 68 at the Transport and General Workers Union Congress in 1957, for example, called for restrictions on immigration as:

> Owing to changed circumstances during the last five years and to safeguard the people of this country with reference to their employment and standard of living, this conference urges the TUC to demand from the government strict and orderly control over imported labour.[45]

The archives contain a letter written in 1956 by the General Secretary of the TUC to Iain MacLeod MP, then Minister of Labour, that highlights some of the tensions in the TUC's views on immigration:

> Our concern was not, of course, to do with the colour of immigrants [*sic*]. We raised the matter because of the difficulties which would arise from the views bound to be

> expressed that where employment opportunities are scarce,
> priority should be given to British born workers ... in the
> event of full employment not being maintained.[46]

Letters from local TUC branches to the General Secretariat during
this period indicate that 'colour' was an essential concern of many
activists. In St Pancras, London, for example, the General and Municipal
Workers Union reached an informal agreement with major local
employers that in the case of redundancies 'coloured' workers would
be sacked before any white workers regardless of length of service or
other considerations.[47] In 1956 the National Union of Railwaymen
stopped Commonwealth migrants from working as skilled footplate
drivers or firefighters. In Bromwich in the West Midlands, a strike of
local bus workers was organised to 'protest' against the arrival of West
Indian immigrants into the local industry. This local dispute reached
the national media and created significant embarrassment for a TUC
leadership that was trying to convey a broader message of worker
unity and solidarity.

These disputes over immigration within the TUC were indicative
of the central role that labour markets play in mediating economic
and social practices (see Gordon and Turok, 2005). As with industrial
transference during the inter-war period, the perceived 'influx' of new
workers in receiving areas was seen as a threat to collective bargaining
power. These views were expressed to government in a memorandum
in 1955 in which it was argued that 'recent examples of colour prejudice
have not been motivated by colour but by low wages ... the workers'
view was that if coloured labour were not available our wages would
need to be higher to obtain manpower for the industry [*sic*]'.[48] Such
proclamations were indicative of the divisive nature of worker mobility
and labour market change. What governments and firms perceived as
'problematic' skills shortages were seen by others as an opportunity to
increase their incomes and their quality of life. Expanding the supply
of labour was perceived to have an effect on these relationships and
for some workers the new immigrants became visible, threatening
agents. Some on the left, such as the British Communist Party, did,
however, see the arrival of new groups of workers as 'an opportunity
for the British working people. We are being offered a partnership.
Acceptance will immensely increase our strength. Rejection can only
cause disastrous divisions' (Bolsover, 1955, p 3). It tried to highlight
this with poster and publicity campaigns (see Figure 5.1). Despite such
efforts, the arrival of migrants had a significant impact on the Trade
Union movement.

Figure 5.1: British Communist Party poster, 1955

The 1960s and the shifting contours of policy

During the 1960s, the obvious discrimination faced by minority ethnic groups and the continued physical segregation of communities were creating new political and economic tensions at a variety of scales. The government was increasingly concerned that inequalities had the potential to produce significant unrest in British cities and damage the economic potential of the British economy. In 1958 there had been racially motivated public disorder in Nottingham and in the Notting Hill area of London (see *New Statesman*, 1958). As one Home Office official succinctly argued in an internal memorandum, 'The attitude of employers and the TUs [trades unions] to the employment of coloured [*sic*] workers is emerging as one of the most important factors in the whole complex of race relations in the country'.[49] He warned that:

> Unless we ensure that people with coloured skins [*sic*], especially those born and educated here, are able to get the work and their promotion to supervisory positions to which their qualifications entitle them, we may well find ourselves facing all the implications of an American–style situation in which an indigenous minority group is discriminated against solely on the grounds of colour [*sic*].[50]

The problem, it was argued, was to be found at the local level where trades unions and employers would often come to informal agreements over the roles and responsibilities of different types of workers in surreptitious ways.

The solution was to be found in 'strong' immigration policies in which mobilities would be controlled and ordered and linked much more explicitly to employment vacancies as a way, the TUC argued, of ensuring that community balance could be sustained and reinforced by policy. Employment discrimination and a general lack of integration on the part of the new groups, was creating an ill-balanced 'series of communities', rather than the relatively homogeneous communities of the pre-immigration era. In the TUC's blunt terms, 'In the longer term the size of the immigrant population ... [will force] the government to think about what type of society it wants'.[51] For the trades union movement there was, therefore, no contradiction in advocating on the one hand a policy of an end to discrimination in the workplace and on the other a call for strict new limits and quotas on the numbers of immigrants allowed in to the UK (see *Yorkshire Post*, 1965).

During the 1960s successive governments sought to develop new ways of limiting immigration. There were two primary mechanisms. First, there were new, tougher immigration controls and bureaucratic systems that would regulate and control mobility. The 1962 Commonwealth Immigrants Act represented a landmark piece of legislation that effectively ended the free movement of citizens around the Commonwealth. In Spencer's (1997, p 187) terms, 'by far the biggest element contributing to its intensity was undoubtedly the increasing numbers of Asian and black people entering Britain, related to fears about the effectiveness of more traditional administrative measures to counter the increased inward movement'. The Act established a voucher system in which immigrants were divided into three categories (see Table 5.5). Category A vouchers were given to highly skilled workers coming to take up specific employment positions. Such KWs could fill vacancies within the UK economy and their presence could be legitimated and justified in these instrumental terms. Category B vouchers were given to defined 'skilled workers' or those who possessed particular types of skills that the UK economy was lacking, but who were not seeking to move to the UK to take up a specific job vacancy. Category C vouchers, on the other hand, were to be given to 'unskilled' workers who could not claim to be coming for a specific job. Government records in Table 5.5 show that 11% of category C voucher applicants were successful in obtaining a voucher in the first years of the scheme, indicating a high rate of 'filtering' of migrants based on divisions of skills.

This legislation was justified in instrumental terms with the claim that 'immigrants have been highly beneficial to the British community and accepted as such in both the cultural and economic fields by expanding and stimulating the commonwealth of skills and talent'. However, a limit was required on this 'influx of immigrants from

Table 5.5: Immigration vouchers issued under the 1962 Commonwealth Immigrants Act, 1962-64

Category	Definition	Vouchers issued, 1962-64
A	Coming for specific, advertised job vacancies	34,000
B	Skilled workers – such as doctors, teachers, nurses, postgraduates, builders, craftsmen [sic], members of the armed forces	22,000
C	Unskilled persons – those entering without specific employment position or dedicated skills	42,000*

Note: *380,000 applications

Source: Adapted from figures taken from the 1962 Commonwealth Immigrants Act

Commonwealth countries [as it] would provide a breathing space in which some social problems might be tackled'.[52] In other words, the building of selectively permeable barriers to mobility and migration would not only have significant economic dividends but also help to resolve the political and social tensions that were building up in many urban areas. The Act represented a significant step in the state's attempts to control mobility in order, it was argued, to build more harmonious communities and to create more efficient and functioning labour markets at a variety of scales. It treated immigrants as the objects of policy whose mobility should be controlled and restricted at the same time as it saw them as subjects, whose presence in particular places could help meet the wider needs of communities and state policy.

For example, in 1965 official government policy was that: 'On the economic side we must have regard to the fact that most of these immigrants are an asset and indeed life would be harder for all of us if we were deprived of their labour'.[53] To support this claim the government pointed out that 40% of all hospital doctors at consultant level, 20% of student nurses, and the majority of semi-skilled jobs were now reliant on 'coloured [sic]' immigrants. The effects of their absence would be that:

> Some hospitals would have to close. Public transport would be disrupted and bus services in our major cities would be severely curtailed. In many towns dustbins would go uncollected and the streets would become dirtier. The brick shortage would worsen and we would not get so many of the houses we badly need ... [and] many industries would be drastically affected.[54]

A second element of government policy during the 1960s was the attempt to increase the residential mobility of Caribbean immigrants. The Wilson government, in particular, was primarily concerned with mixing urban communities and ensuring that American-style 'ghettoes' did not develop in the UK. The government's thinking on the matter was expressed in the Home Office's working paper entitled *Voluntary Dispersal of Commonwealth Immigrants* (Home Office, 1968). This report was jointly authored with the Department of Employment and Productivity and aimed to highlight the problems caused by the spatial concentration of immigrants and the potential policy solutions. It noted that 86% of all Commonwealth immigrants lived in the regions of London, the South East, the Midlands, the North West, and Yorkshire & Humberside where jobs were plentiful and 'not especially attractive to other workers in the areas' (p 9). These 'reception areas' possessed employment conditions in which jobs could be found quickly, little training was required, and the lack of competence in the English language for immigrants was not a major handicap. Comparisons were made with earlier rounds of Commonwealth and European immigration that 'were dispersed into smaller groups while efforts were made to find them suitable employment ... and the special problems of colour [*sic*] were absent' (pp 7-8). In areas such as Cardiff and Merseyside there had been long-standing minority ethnic communities and the absence of racial tensions in these areas was explained through the incremental nature of the immigration (see Little, 1972).

While fearful of being seen to be positively 'discriminatory' towards immigrants, it was considered that action still needed to be taken to overcome 'a threat to social peace or ... a better chance of integration' (Home Office, 1968, p 9). Area-based initiatives, such as the newly established Urban Programme, were to be used to target groups in ostensibly non-divisive ways. The report explicitly stated that surreptitious discrimination could be applied to 'coloured [*sic*] people as members of some other class e.g. to all inhabitants of districts of special social need within the meaning of the Urban Programme' (p 9). In this sense the fledgling urban policy of the time could be used as an instrument of social control. By creating balanced and mixed communities, the perceived threat of urban unrest in the future' was reduced. A mixing of groups and individuals was seen as the most appropriate mechanism for breaking down barriers of social (dis)advantage for as the Committee argued:

The concentration perpetuated an image of the immigrant as a separate kind of person, and one moreover associated with poverty and overcrowded conditions – a kind of coloured slum dweller [*sic*] – or worse, someone coloured whose nature it is to live in a slum? [*sic*] (p 10)

The solution was, therefore, to promote individual and community mobility for 'unless steps are taken to make it easy for the immigrant to move about freely, the fact that he has less mobility than other citizens may equally go to perpetuate the wrong image' (p 10). A strategy 'to advance greater mobility' was called for based on the understanding that:

(a) dispersal would increase the opportunity for contact between immigrants and the host community;
(b) dispersal on any large scale would help to solve some of the difficulties present in areas of special social need;
(c) it seems likely that individuals or small numbers of people are more likely to be seen and appreciated as people.

Programmes were devised in which spatial policy measures were surreptitiously used to encourage social mixing and to enhance the efficacy or sustainability of existing communities. Table 5.6 highlights some of the strategies that were used for encouraging Caribbean people to move.

Other efforts were made to stimulate advisory groups within the minority ethnic communities themselves that would encourage and support voluntary movements. Box 5.1 provides an example of a proposal for a West Indian Housing Association in the UK in the 1960s and how the government sought to tackle multiple problems simultaneously through such measures.

Box 5.1: The case of the proposed West Indian Housing Association[55]

The confused and, at times, contradictory nature of policy towards Caribbean immigrants was reflected in proposals that were put forward in 1960 to create a dedicated West Indian Housing Association to provide 'hostel type accommodation on a non-profit making basis for migrants'. While such a move would ostensibly be promoted as an attempt to improve the lives and working conditions of, often destitute, migrants, secret archives reveal that the 'improved social welfare of West Indian migrants' was emphatically 'not the prime objective for the proposed Association'. Instead, 'the basic objective would be the improvement of race relations in this country and the promotion of good relations with the Commonwealth'. The government was keen to ensure that through a policy of welfare assistance, racial tensions between the new migrants and existing populations were reduced. Inner urban areas were seen as being 'unbalanced' communities and this was underpinning social and racial tensions. Again, as the memorandum explained, 'the mixture of races in overcrowded housing conditions inevitably leads to racial friction with a constant threat of serious and possibly violent outbreaks of the kind already experienced'. Moreover, the government was concerned with the UK's image abroad as a society that 'not only preaches but practices a belief in inter-racial harmony'. Through concerted state action, it was argued, 'multi-racial societies can be harmoniously maintained and are worth striving to establish'.

Table 5.6: Key components of the government's mobility strategies for Caribbean migrants

Strategy	Key components
Surveys	A survey of job opportunities for immigrants where they were few in number. The survey was to be coupled with one for housing and if the surveys revealed that jobs and housing were both available in the same place then opportunities could be drawn to the attention of immigrants.
NT policy	Special attention might be paid to immigrants who are suitable for employment in an NT. Most employers wanted skilled workers, so employment would need to be combined with training.
Extra training	Training immigrants at Government Training Centres should be carried out to enable them to undertake skilled work and on leaving training they should be assisted in finding work in their new trade areas. Encouragement might also be given to school-leavers to follow careers away from areas of concentration.
Extending priority	Immigrants tend to occupy private rented accommodation and are therefore not subject to assistance available to local authority tenants. New ways should be devised to extend the rules.
Identifying firms	Firms in DAs who would be prepared to take some immigrant workers should be identified.
New inducements	Inducements could be offered to immigrants wishing to get away from their twilight areas or to the children of immigrants who might wish to move further afield.
Discouragement	Measures should be introduced to discourage immigrants from taking up jobs in the areas of immigrant concentration.

What we see, therefore, in these policy discussions is an ongoing tension between the promotion of fixity and mobility. On the one hand, a programme of community-building is advocated in which balanced, mixed, and diverse groups are present and relatively fixed in particular places. On the other hand, the mechanisms through which this fixity will be established are paradoxically those of mobility and the removal of 'barriers' to movement. A mixing of different social groups would overcome the problems of labour market exclusion that the new communities were facing by reducing prejudice and increasing the visibility of the 'positive' contribution that the new citizens were making to community-building. The post-war policy discourses and practices of inter- *and* intra-national migration of Commonwealth immigrants in the UK reflect the tensions inherent in the creation of balanced places between fixity, mobility, presence, and absence.

These tensions became apparent in the political battles between communities and agencies in 'donating' and 'receiving' areas. Many local authorities imposed residential qualifications that effectively selected groups for assistance and marginalised Commonwealth migrants. Others tried to find alternative ways of preventing immigration. One of the highest profile examples in the 1960s was in the Birmingham suburb of Smethwick in which the local authority sought to obtain a loan from central government to purchase houses that had been earmarked as a dispersal site for Commonwealth communities. The local authority argued that it was in the best interests of immigrants themselves to be more evenly distributed across the UK in different areas, rather than establishing themselves in an area that already possessed a relatively high number of immigrants (see *The Guardian*, 1965). The relative merits of dispersal versus concentration and mobility versus fixity became central to the debates that followed.

The Labour government's response was equivocal. On the one hand, it did not want to be seen to be supporting an overtly racist local campaign motivated by a policy of social exclusion. On the other hand, the government's own lack of clear direction and its inability to implement a dispersal strategy meant that it was unable to establish a coherent response. Internal memoranda show that there was considerable uncertainty within government over how to respond to the Smethwick case. There was some sympathy with the argument of the local authority with one senior civil servant advising the minister, Richard Crossman, that 'By preventing heavy concentrations they would, it could be argued, be removing an obstacle to integration and preventing living conditions from deteriorating'.[56] Moreover, it was also noted that: 'If the acquisition to prevent a ghetto developing were seen as part of an integrated policy, which included positive provision for helping immigrants with their housing problems, it may be easier to justify'.[57]

The national effects of this local dispute were significant. Local, anti-immigrant activist Peter Griffiths had defeated the local Labour Party candidate in 1964. As Spencer (1997, p 136) notes, from this example 'it was apparent that voter opposition to further Asian and Black immigration could be exploited'. The Wilson government had originally opposed the 1962 Commonwealth Immigrants Act but owing to political pressure it began to change its own approach and brought in significant new measures. From September 1964 the voucher system became tighter, with only category A and B priority vouchers being given out (Spencer, 1997, p 135; see Table 5.7). The result was a waiting list of 300,000 unskilled and semi-skilled workers for whom there was no policy of admittance. In 1965 the *Immigration from the Commonwealth* White Paper (Prime Minister's Office, 1965) further tightened up the scheme and reduced the total number of vouchers issued to those with a job offer or special skills to a maximum of 8,500 per year and stricter interpretations of who qualified as a skilled worker. From 1969 even category A vouchers would not be

Table 5.7: The scale of the immigration voucher scheme established under the 1962 Commonwealth Immigrants Act (number of vouchers issued)

	Category A		Category B		Category C		
	Canada, Australia, New Zealand	New Commonwealth	Canada, Australia, New Zealand	New Commonwealth	Canada, Australia, New Zealand	New Commonwealth	Dependants of workers from all categories
1962	307	3,063	1,163	3,363	667	16,827	8,832
1963	460	7,002	1,369	9,618	470	22,182	26,234
1964	383	10,219	814	7,187	72	2149	37,460
1965	283	8,361	842	6,560	6,427		41,214
1966	23	2,852	461	4,694	No longer issued		42,026
1967	26	3,013	384	4,986	No longer issued		52,813
1968	24	2,865	429	4,802	No longer issued		48,650
1969	89	2,731	905	3,044	No longer issued		33,820
1970	130	2,736	1,295	2,654	No longer issued		27,407
1971	169	1,788	728	1,077	No longer issued		28,014

Source: Adapted from Hansen (2000, pp 265-6)

issued if labour was available locally. For some the voucher scheme was not, therefore, about economic efficiency but represented 'a convenient device for limiting the number of Asian and black immigrants who would be allowed to enter Britain for the purposes of settlement ... not anything to do with changes in the conditions of labour supply and demand' (Spencer, 1997, p 139).

Despite this toughening of immigration policy during the mid-1960s the Labour government was increasingly anxious not to restrict immigration too much. It sought to draw legitimacy for a controlled immigration policy by arguing that foreign workers were vital to the operation of British public services and that workers from abroad were KWs, whose presence was a necessary element in the operation and functioning of sectors of the labour market and the health of urban and regional communities:

> Had it not been for the availability of doctors and nurses and other workers from overseas, the health service, public transport and other social services would have been severely damaged. Our standard of living could not have increased as it has without the contribution of immigrants. (Labour Party, 1968, p 9)

Others tried to develop similar, instrumental arguments to justify their stance. For example, the Fabian Society published a series of short, glossy publications with titles such as *Immigration Facts versus Myths* (1968) and *Immigration and Race Relations* (1970) in which economic arguments were used to highlight the essential status of foreign workers and generate fearful scenarios in which such labour was absent. Thus the former argued that:

> Sending immigrants home would dislocate many important public sector services without bringing any relief to Scotland, Wales or Northern Ireland ... the availability of jobs depends overwhelmingly on the state of the economy and government policy. (p 15)

In a similar vein the latter argued that 'we could of course halt immigration and watch certain industries run down or even switch elsewhere' (p 4). The railway industry was used as an easily identifiable reference point for such arguments as it demonstrated the highly functional and essential role that such immigrants were playing in daily life (see Box 5.2).

Box 5.2: Immigration, labour, and the London Transport system

The railway industry in post-war Britain was hampered by chronic labour shortages. As Wolmar's (2004) study of London Transport indicates, 'demand for the largely semi-skilled employment on the Underground and buses is highly dependent on the availability of jobs elsewhere' (p 295). The expanding London economy of the 1950s was drawing its labour elsewhere and London Transport was forced to look for alternative sources of labour. In 1956 it opened an office in Barbados and between 1956 and 1965 4,000 Barbadians were recruited. Their experiences were typical of those of many immigrants. Their skills were undervalued in their new positions as they tended to come from the better-educated and higher social classes within their host countries. Many had to live in poor-quality accommodation and districts and suffered from discrimination inside and outside the labour market.

Conclusions

This chapter has argued that the migration of Commonwealth citizens and workers to and from the UK has been closely related to broader agendas of balanced community-building and economic competitiveness. The mobility associated with international movements is, perhaps, more politically charged and explicit than those of inter-regional movements discussed in Chapters Three and Four. In this sense there are some clear differences in the politics and programmes associated with them. However, the chapter has argued that some of the core principles surrounding mobility, imaginations of place, state capacities, and relational citizenship were, in reality, very similar. The discourses and practices of spatial policy in the UK were, by definition, linked to immigration and emigration policies and the extent to which these processes could be rationally controlled and ordered.

The discussion has also centred on the ways in which crossing boundaries *re-ascribes* the 'value' of particular individuals to the social balance of defined places. Caribbean immigrants, whatever their economic or social backgrounds, were reclassified as lower-skilled workers once they moved to the UK. Given the added dimension of racial and cultural differences questions over what types of 'community' policy-makers were seeking to create and what priority should be given to the labour market value of individuals took on greater urgency. International migration was a highly contentious and politicised issue with definitions of citizenship increasingly defined in terms of economic capacity rather than political rights or entitlements. It was used as a mechanism for the creation of more efficient and effective urban and regional labour markets. The arrival of these migrants was also the beginning of a longer-term process of finding workers for the public sector during periods of strong economic growth in which lower paid public and private sector jobs became increasingly unattractive to native workers.

The experience of many (primarily white) UK emigrants was, as discussed above, very different. Many were seen as key or essential workers, whose presence would help to bring about the economic development of the Dominion territories. Their movement was wrapped up in a wider politics in which tensions existed between economic, social, and political objectives. The effects of their out-migration on economic development became a growing concern for spatial planners but little was done to prevent their movement. They were native citizens who had the right to international mobility. They could act as important subjects in the building of a new Commonwealth and their movement was to be tolerated, even if it damaged the economic competitiveness of key sectors of the UK's economy and the economies of its regions. Efforts were made to try to ensure that surplus workers in areas of high unemployment were prioritised for emigration in order to rebalance laggard labour markets and avoid a further tightening of labour markets in faster-growing areas.

The spatial distribution of Commonwealth immigrant communities also became a 'problem' of government during this period. The visible concentrations of minority ethnic communities in relatively poor areas of the UK's cities generated new fears of civil disorder and unrest. While employment existed for such groups and they were seen to be playing an economic role, the dangers of disorder were, it was argued, mollified. However, in times of recession the value of such communities, it was feared, would decline and the problems associated with their spatial concentration would come to a head. It was this fear, driven by selective imaginations of community balance and (dis)harmony that underpinned the so-called 'anti-ghetto' dispersal strategies of the post-war era. As we will see when we return to contemporary policies on immigration (in Chapter Eight), nothing better illustrates the power-infused tensions surrounding the politics of mobility, fixity, and place.

Notes

[1] The Colonial Dominions were Australia, Canada, New Zealand, Rhodesia (now Zimbabwe), and South Africa.

[2] LAB 8/2736, British Emigration Policy 1961-1967.

[3] Sir Patrick Duff (Foreign Office), Letter on emigration to the Ministry of Labour, BT 193/152 Passenger Travel – Emigration: General, February 1945.

[4] D. Nash, Internal Memorandum for Ministers and Civil Servants on Long Term Balance of Payments Problems, LAB 8/1484 Emigration and Long Term Economic Policy, 1947.

[5] LAB 8/1871 Emigration of Professionals and Skilled Engineers to Commonwealth and USA, 1953-1956.

[6] E. Hitchman, *Our Long Term Balance of Payment Problems*, LAB 8/1484 Emigration and Long Term Economic Policy, 1947.

[7] Lady Smieton, Speech to the House of Lords, LAB 13/281 Review of Emigration Policy in the Light of the Manpower Situtation in the United Kingdom, 22 November 1951.

[8] Lady Smieton, Speech to the House of Lords, LAB 13/281 Review of Emigration Policy in the Light of the Manpower Situation in the United Kingdom, 22 November 1951, p 1.

[9] H. Burness, Ministry of Education, Letter to G. Nash, Ministry of Labour, LAB 8/1871 Emigration of Professionals and Skilled Engineers to Commonwealth and USA 1953-1956, 7 November 1953.

[10] Commonwealth Relations Office, Draft Notes to Home Secretary, LAB 8/2736, British Emigration Policy 1961-1967, 4 October 1962.

[11] Confidential Report by the Inter-Departmental Committee of Officials, LAB 8/2736, British Emigration Policy 1961-1967, 5 December 1961, p 5.

[12] Confidential Report by the Inter-Departmental Committee of Officials, LAB 8/2736, British Emigration Policy 1961-1967, 5 December 1961, p 5.

[13] Confidential Report by the Inter-Departmental Committee of Officials, LAB 8/2736, British Emigration Policy 1961–1967, 5 December 1961, p 5.

[14] Internal Memorandum (no date), LAB 8/2988, Economic Effect of Immigration to the Old Dominions, 1964–1967, p 3.

[15] Internal Memorandum (no date)LAB 8/2988, Economic Effect of Immigration to the Old Dominions, 1964–1967, p 3.

[16] Confidential Report by the Working Party on the Effects on the British Economy of Increased Emigration to Canada, Australia and New Zealand (no date), LAB 8/2988, Economic Effect of Increased Emigration to the Old Dominions, 1964–1967.

[17] Draft of Emigration Policy Speech for Prime Minister at Commonwealth Heads of Government Meeting, LAB 8/2736 British Emigration Policy 1961–1967, 22 June 1964.

[18] Draft of Emigration Policy Speech for Prime Minister at Commonwealth Heads of Government Meeting, LAB 8/2736 British Emigration Policy 1961–1967, 22 June 1964.

[19] Draft of Emigration Policy Speech for Prime Minister at Commonwealth Heads of Government Meeting, LAB 8/2736 British Emigration Policy 1961–1967, 22 June 1964.

[20] LAB 8/2988 Economic Effect of Increased Emigration to the Old Dominions 1964–1967.

[21] LAB 8/2712 Emigration of Skilled Workers from Great Britain – Proposed Approach to White Commonwealth Countries 1962–1964.

[22] H. Jones, Ministry of Labour, Letter to F. Tarrant, Regional Controller for the North West, Manchester, LAB 8/1516 Placing, Dispersal to the Provinces and Other Steps Taken to Deal with the Problem, 27 September 1948.

[23] Ministry of Labour letter to all RCs from W. Hardman, LAB 8/1516 Placing, Dispersal to the Provinces and Other Steps Taken to Deal with the Problem, 1948, p 1.

[24] Ministry of Labour letter to all RCs from W. Hardman, LAB 8/1516 Placing, Dispersal to the Provinces and Other Steps Taken to Deal with the Problem, 1948, p 1.

[25] Ministry of Labour letter to all RCs from W. Hardman, LAB 8/1516 Placing, Dispersal to the Provinces and Other Steps Taken to Deal with the Problem, 1948, p 1.

[26] Sir G. Evans, *The Subject of Immigrants*, LAB 8/1519 Coloured People in the UK: General Policy, Registration and Placing 1948-1949.

[27] Draft Briefing on the Subject of Immigrants, 9 August 1949, LAB 8/1519 Coloured People in the UK: General Policy, Registration and Placing 1948-1949, p 1.

[28] Draft Briefing on the Subject of Immigrants, 9 August 1949, LAB 8/1519 Coloured People in the UK: General Policy, Registration and Placing 1948-1949, p 1.

[29] Ministry of Labour Committee, *Unemployment Amongst Coloured Colonials Resident in Great Britain*, LAB 8/1519 Coloured People in the UK: General Policy, Registration and Placing, 12 September 1949.

[30] Ministry of Labour Committee, *Unemployment Amongst Coloured Colonials Resident in Great Britain*, LAB 8/1519 Coloured People in the UK: General Policy, Registration and Placing, 12 September 1949, p 2.

[31] Note of a meeting held at the Home Office, to discuss the problems of persons from the Colonies and British Protectorates, LAB 8/1519, 18 February 1949.

[32] Lady Smieton, Concluding comments to conference with regional controllers, LAB 8/1519 Coloured People in the UK: General Policy, Registration and Placing, 20 January 1949, p 9.

[33] Lady Smieton, Concluding comments to conference with regional controllers, LAB 8/1519 Coloured People in the UK: General Policy, Registration and Placing, 20 January 1949, p 9.

[34] As with emigration policy, these estimated figures were shrouded in controversy and were deployed for a variety of political ends. There

was no clear system of accounting for those who entered the country and government figures were based on a large element of estimation.

[35] N. Huijman, Home Office Discussion Note, CO 1032/120, 21 June 1955.

[36] Draft Secret Memorandum of the Secretary of State, Home Department, CO 1032/120, no date.

[37] W. Cornish, Home Office, Letter to A. Morley, Commonwealth Relations Office, CO 1032/120, 12 May 1955.

[38] I. Keith, Memorandum on West Indian Immigration, CO 1032/120, 23 November 1954.

[39] Note of a meeting held at the Home Office, to discuss the problems of persons from the Colonies and British Protectorates, LAB 8/1519, 18 February 1949.

[40] G. Osbourne, Question to Prime Minister Anthony Eden, *Hansard*, 21 June 1955, p 1.

[41] Note of a meeting held at the Home Office, to discuss the problems of persons from the Colonies and British Protectorates, LAB 8/1519, 18 February 1949.

[42] Note of a meeting held at the Home Office, to discuss the problems of persons from the Colonies and British Protectorates, LAB 8/1519, 18 February 1949.

[43] Congress Resolution that Entrants Regardless of their Race or Creed be Subject to a Medical Examination Prior to Being Admitted into this Country, MSS 292/805/7/2 Commonwealth Immigration.

[44] MSS 292/805.7/2 Commonwealth Immigration.

[45] MSS 292/805.7/2 Commonwealth Immigration, quoting from 'TUC urged to strive for immigration control – unions fear influx of coloured people', *The Guardian,* 11 July 1957.

[46] General Secretary of TUC to Iain MacLeod, Minister of Labour, 9 May 1956, MSS 292/805.7/2 Commonwealth Immigration.

[47] K. Sheriden, St Pancras North Constituency Labour Party, 23 December 1957, MSS 292/805.7/2 Commonwealth Immigration.

[48] TUC Memorandum of Interview of Meeting with Sir Walter Monckton, Minister of Labour, 1 April 1955, MSS 292/805.7/2 Commonwealth Immigration.

[49] T. Howard–Drake, Letter to M. Johnston, Treasury, HO 376/106, 29 July 1965.

[50] T. Howard–Drake, Letter to M. Johnston, Treasury, HO 376/106, 29 July 1965.

[51] T. Howard–Drake, Letter to M. Johnston, Treasury, HO 376/106, 29 July 1965.

[52] 'Human Rights in the UK' – Background Paper by the Home Office for UN seminar 'The multi-national society', Yugoslavia, May 1965, HLG 118/545 Immigration and Housing Policy.

[53] Ministry of Housing and Local Government, Official Briefing Note for House of Lords debate on 'Commonwealth Immigration', HLG 118/545 Immigration and Housing Policy, 10 March 1965.

[54] Ministry of Housing and Local Government, Official Briefing Note for House of Lords debate on 'Commonwealth Immigration', HLG 118/545 Immigration and Housing Policy, 10 March 1965.

[55] CO 1031/3928 A West Indian Housing Association in the UK, 1960.

[56] R. Brain to M. Waddell, 'The Smethwick case – issues for discussion', HLG 118/545 Immigration and Housing Policy, 19 January 1965.

[57] R. Brain to M. Waddell, 'The Smethwick case – issues for discussion', HLG 118/545 Immigration and Housing Policy, 19 January 1965.

Part Three

Post-war spatial policy, 1979-2006

The reconstruction of regional policy and the remaking of the competitive region

Introduction

The election of the Thatcher government in May 1979 heralded a new era of spatial policy in the UK. The political and economic crises of the mid-1970s and the acceptance of International Monetary Fund loans, under the Callaghan government, had already reduced the scale of support for the Development Areas (DAs). However, from 1979, the rationalities, objectives, and scale of regional policy began to undergo a more significant change. What emerged, as Jones (1997) suggests, was a new strategy of 'spatial selection' in which the needs of growth areas would be prioritised in the drive for greater national economic competitiveness. The old DAs would receive trickle-down benefits from the fast-growing areas in the short term and would be inspired to develop new strategies to match the competitiveness of these stronger regions in the longer term. Regional divergence became a policy aim, rather than a 'problem' to be tackled, as growth places, it was argued, should not be 'held back' through a redistributive spatial policy. In many ways there was, therefore, a return to pre-war agendas in which spatial policy regarded the laggard regions of the UK 'as plague-spots, to be diagnosed by specialists and treated as something apart from the rest of the community' (*The Economist*, 1945b, p 270; see also Chapter Three). As we will see, similar characterisations of spatial policy were to emerge through the programmes of the Major government of the 1990s and the strategies pursued under Tony Blair in the 2000s.

This chapter examines the shift in thinking over the concept of the 'key worker' (KW) within these wider regional policy changes from the end of the 1970s up to the present day. It explores the ways in which new types of creative and entrepreneurial KWs were defined and how their presence and/or creation was seen as essential to the construction of sustainable and competitive places and communities. The absence of such workers was presented as one of the key problems that the DAs faced. In the fast-growing, globally competitive, and economically buoyant regions of the South and East of Britain the situation was very different. The chapter begins by examining the changing rationalities of spatial policy and the wider debates that took place in the late 1970s/early 1980s over its objectives before turning to the changes that have characterised post-Thatcher spatial policy. It focuses on the relationships between the new programmes and labour mobility/fixity and assesses the dominant imaginations over what it is that constitutes a competitive place and how policy programmes can create and sustain them. The discussion draws on archival sources and policy documents to assess the ways in which state strategies and rationalities changed, the shifting politics of mobility that came to dominate development discourses, and the selective imaginations that emerged concerning how places functioned and could be made to function more efficiently.

The changing rationalities of spatial policy

By the late 1970s spatial policy was being subject to a growing critique by policy-makers, businesses, and some academics. Regional assistance was available to over 40% of the population of the UK. The aim of creating self-sustaining and efficient regional economies and places was, it was argued, having a limited effect on the economic geography of the UK, although its genuine achievements were also being discursively downgraded to suit political ends. Evaluations of regional policy in the 1970s indicated that, during the 1960s, 250,000-300,000 jobs were created in or relocated to the DAs through various projects and subsidies (Moore and Rhodes, 1973, 1976). The political dividend of being seen to support the regions was also significant and the philosophy of policy, that it was the responsibility of the state to try to reorganise the spatial economy for the wider benefit of all the UK's citizens, was still embedded in the development frameworks.

However, it was also increasingly clear that there were significant limitations to regional policy. Critics such as Law (1980, p 232) pointed to its failure to 'recreate a self-sustaining economy in the assisted regions so that policies are unnecessary … their rate of indigenous job creation is low and they are poorly equipped to meet the future with the inevitable reduction of job opportunities in certain activities'. Moreover, despite the emphasis on KW support and the wider debates about building new places and communities that would be attractive to a range of workers, it was still argued that by the late 1970s the DAs 'still often lack the cultural facilities which the higher skilled workers require'

(Law, 1980, p 232). There was a general lack of skilled workers and entrepreneurs in these areas and rates of investment within DA firms were still low (see Healey and Ilbery, 1982).

These criticisms of the effectiveness of regional policy went hand in hand with a new set of development philosophies. One of the chief architects of the Thatcher government's reforms, Keith Joseph, succinctly summed up the principles that underpinned the reforms when he told the North West TUC in 1981 that:

> It really does not make sense to operate a regional industrial policy under which an area of the country including well over 40% of the working population is eligible for regional assistance. Moreover, excessive state subsidies have inevitably been among the public expenditure leading to excessive taxation and state borrowing and to inflation. This cannot be the way to bring about industrial regeneration and prosperity to the country as a whole. No region of the country is going to thrive unless the national economy as a whole is healthy ... less government intervention will encourage industry to expand and new firms to start up thus providing a sounder basis from employment in the longer term throughout the country, including the NW [North West]. The government intends to operate a selective and therefore more effective regional industrial policy which will be concentrated on the areas with the severest problems of persistent unemployment.[1]

Labour mobility was conceptualised as being a product of market changes and shifting opportunities for individual workers. The out-migration of businesses and populations away from Britain's major cities in the 1970s was presented as an example of how mobility could not be effectively controlled by interventionist spatial policies. *The Economist* (1977, p 20) noted at the time that:

> The trouble is that the emigration of people and jobs is not and cannot be easily synchronised. Employers move out or close down, skilled workers leave and the top of the labour market becomes tighter. So industry moves to where skilled workers are thicker on the ground.

This 'inability' of policy to synchronise the actions of individual workers and firms was presented as a reason for the adoption of new strategies that would encourage less directed, and more efficient and effective forms of mobility and fixity. For Thatcher it was not:

> governments that create wealth, can create jobs, it's the people. No government on its own can make a country prosperous. Only the people who live in it can do that – by producing and delivering the right products at the right price, at the right time. (1979a, p 1)

This argument represented a clear shift in the objectives of spatial policy and its wider rationality. The state's role was to support economic growth and those entrepreneurs and KWs that made that growth possible. Where they were located was to be *their* decision, based on their own needs and understandings of the best locations for their own enterprises. Individual mobility was something to be freed from the clutches of the state. It was not up to governments to order the movement of labour and capital. Individual actors, it was argued, knew best where they should be located and policy should facilitate their exercising of *choice*.

This extension of choice would bring about a transformation of places and economic competitiveness through two interrelated mechanisms. First, through exercising choice, entrepreneurs and enterprises would be able to optimise their competitiveness within international markets and this, in turn, would lead to the regeneration and enhanced economic and social sustainability of places. Restricting such choices would lead to suboptimal performance. Second, in increasing the mobility of capital and KWs, those responsible for the governance of places within DAs would, it was hoped, change their ways of thinking about their own localities. The extension of choice would force regional actors to take greater responsibility for their own circumstances, with the attraction of entrepreneurs and KWs becoming a core objective of policy. Enhancing mobility through choice would therefore act as a mechanism of place improvement and enhanced competitiveness. If places are attractive to highly skilled workers, entrepreneurs, and investors, it was argued, then they will become the types of places in which people want to live. With the presence of such workers, places would attract further rounds of investment and attract even more. The map of regional policy was 'rolled back' and what was termed 'sensible' regional assistance would become a new vehicle for the restoration of 'the confidence, the cash resources and the vitality of the private sector' (Thatcher, 1979a, p 2; see Figure 6.1).

Within this context, support for entrepreneurs, as the new KWs,

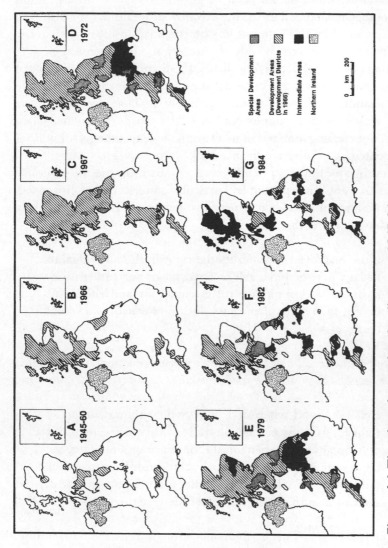

Figure 6.1: The changing regional policy map, 1945-84

Source: Healey and Ilbery, 1992

was seen as a vital dimension of national and regional economic policy. The term 'constructive intervention' was used to summarise the new policy of 'stimulating new industries which do have a future, rather than shoring up lost causes – helping to create tomorrow's world rather than to preserve yesterday's' (Thatcher, 1980a, p 1). The role of industrial subsidies became that of putting 'industries in a position where they can contribute to the creation of wealth rather than be a drain upon it' (p 2). The focus was on the relationships between the wealth-creators and the wealth-consumers, and by extension wealth-creating places and dependent places. Productivity, or the amount of output per worker, was seen as the most important ingredient in the regeneration of regional economies. Again, in Thatcher's words, 'we shall achieve genuine improvements in the job position only when we have increasing numbers of small businesses expanding. Our policies and strategies are directed to that end'.[2]

This shift in thinking placed greater emphasis on the *entrepreneurial subject* and was underpinned by particular conceptions of citizenship as exemplified, in rather extreme terms, by Margaret Thatcher (1979b, p 3) and her belief that:

> If the State usurps or denies the right of the individual to make, where he [*sic*] is able to do so, the important decisions in his life and to provide the essentials for himself and his family, then he is demeaned and diminished as a moral being.

The subsequent logic of this rationality was the emergence of a new set of agendas in which the state should:

> create a mood where it is everywhere thought morally right for as many people as possible to acquire capital; not only because of the beneficial economic consequences, but because the possession of even a little capital encourages the virtues of self-reliance and responsibility, as well as assisting a spirit of freedom and independence. (p 4)

Within this explicitly materialist conception of 'avaricious citizenship', the role of the entrepreneur becomes paramount in any agenda of renewal and regeneration. Again, as Thatcher herself argued:

> Nations depend for their health, economically, culturally, and psychologically upon the achievements of a

comparatively small number of talented and determined people, as well as on the support of a skilled and devoted majority. It was not possible for many of these talented people to believe that we valued them and what they could do for our nation, when we maintained penal tax rates ... in order to please those who seemed to be motivated mainly by envy. (p 5)

Selecting and 'liberating' those who can help deliver a new economic future became the focus of government policy as:

This country depends for its health and strength upon those who produce wealth, raw materials and services, and goods, and this means that although we can idle, strike, or obstruct our way down, we can only work our way up. (Thatcher, 1980b, p 2)

In this shift to a new spatial policy framework we therefore see the fusion of a range of rationalities and ways of thinking about place, mobility, and economic development, all of which, as we will see below, have strong echoes with the agendas of the late 1990s and 2000s. The proposals were constructed out of particular imaginations of the UK economy and ideas of place competitiveness and how this could be nurtured and supported by public policy. Selected forms of mobility for capital and key labour were seen as an essential part of this wider process of change. Rather than directing such mobility, the role of the state was to ensure that mobile actors could take advantage of the differences between places. There was a re-imagining, therefore, of the capacities of the state and the ability of state actors to understand and control processes of economic development. There were also, however, continuities with earlier policy thinking. While the ethos of government had clearly changed, the broader conception that there existed KWs who were essential to the functioning of a spatial economy and community was, in many ways, enhanced and expanded. However, this new emphasis to policy was not without its controversies and inconsistencies and it is the politics through which it was created that the chapter now addresses.

The politics of the new regional policy

The emergence of this new agenda represented a significant shift in the post-war politics of place-building. The new focus on entrepreneurialism and competitiveness was strongly supported at national level by business representatives such as the Confederation of British Industry (CBI) and the Association of British Chambers of Commerce. Both were sceptical about the efficacy of state support for economic projects. Archival evidence shows that the CBI was particularly critical of the ways in which spatial policy had been influenced by 'social reasons such as job creation rather than encouraging greater competitiveness and efficiency'.[3] Spatial policy was blamed for its effect in lowering the competitiveness of the UK economy 'by influencing industry to go to inferior locations',[4] a direct reference to the significance of spatial economies and places in shaping the competitiveness of firms and their production potential. As discussed in Chapter Three, during the 1970s the CBI had increasingly called for regional policy to promote labour mobility as a vehicle for encouraging regional competitiveness, arguing that housing and development policy should prioritise the economic needs of employers who should be able to source their employees from the local area. Similar arguments were increasingly made by other business representatives, such as the Association of British Chambers of Commerce, which pressed for regional policy funds to be concentrated on the labour requirements of firms and how 'the importance of labour mobility must be stressed'.[5]

However, these calls for a new spatial policy and the encouragement of labour mobility were not shared across the business community or even within its national representative bodies. CBI minutes indicate that there was significant unease in the regions over the scaling back of regional assistance and its effects not only on firm competitiveness but also on the places within which businesses operated. Some firms had benefited significantly from regional policy assistance in terms of capital investment or, as Chapter Three showed, in relation to support for KWs. The ending of this support exposed firms to greater competition. In Wales, for example, the regional CBI was inundated by letters of concern from businesses, many of whom had based their expansion plans on the availability of state support. After much internal discussion over how to respond to government policy, the CBI in Wales felt moved to write to the new Secretary of State (Nicholas Edwards) in October 1979 to make it clear that the 'cuts were bound to have an adverse effect ... we wish to be constructive and to try to recommend some policies which we believe will be vital for the stimulation of industrial expansion and development and job creation'.[6] It was a similar story in Northern Ireland and Scotland where meetings were held with government ministers in order to pass on business concerns over the difficulties that firms might face in light of a downscaling of regional policy.

Within the Trades Union Congress (TUC) there were similar discussions over the organisation's stance and how it should best oppose or challenge what the government was doing. An internal memorandum in 1981 noted that regional policy had 'not received enough attention in recent years'[7] and had been rather taken for granted within the movement. In 1981 it established a Regional Policy Working Group to oversee a new strategy that called for the maintenance of regional policy as an 'essential part of national policy for higher rates of economic growth ... not merely as a means of redistribution but a means of improving economic and employment prospects in all regions'.[8] The argument that regional policy should continue to focus on improving the economic conditions and employment prospects of the regions so that they may achieve 'self-sustaining economic growth' continued to be advocated. A core component of this policy was the call for *employment* generation to become a principal objective. The TUC was critical of the tendency of earlier rounds of regional policy to subsidise capital investment, without focusing on job creation, indeed capital subsidies often led to reductions in employment. It recommended that a new regional policy should be overseen by tripartite Regional Economic Planning Councils which could both 'introduce a degree of accountability into the operation of regional assistance and provide a regional plan to guide regional development agencies'.[9] This regional dimension, it was argued, would provide an institutional framework through which better, more accountable, and more efficient decisions could be made over the direction of spatial development policy.

The TUC was also strongly opposed to the new waves of inter-regional migration that would 'inevitably' result from a refocusing of spatial policy. A core policy statement on the subject in 1981, for example, argued that:

> Migration is a very costly social and economic solution,
> not least because migrants, were more often the young and
> skilled ... reducing the labour supply in DAs is unlikely to
> make much immediate contribution [to unemployment

rates] ... and the regions could encounter problems in replacing skilled workers from the unemployed.[10]

The selective and unequal nature of labour migration could, it was argued, make the regions less competitive and generate even greater forms of spatial inequality. There was a concern that this mobility would become less regulated and controlled and in so doing would undermine the skills base and entrepreneurialism of regional economies. Ironically, in this sense, there was some convergence of perspectives between the TUC, business representatives, and the Thatcher government as it was argued that the presence of particular workers in particular places was essential to their economic and social sustainability.

Similarly, the Labour Party argued that any industrial development programme had to be underpinned by a coherent spatial policy agenda that supported the DAs and the jobs of skilled workers. Its Executive Committee, for example, told the Labour Conference in 1981 that:

> An unplanned expansion may create Labour shortages in some areas while other regions still suffer serious unemployment. New public enterprise and public investment must be directed to regions where jobs are most needed and our industrial planning power used to support regional regeneration.[11]

It was argued that the relationships between entrepreneurialism and state support were significantly oversimplified by the Thatcher administration. As a Labour Party (1980, p 5) document noted, 'planners help entrepreneurs' by creating a 'solid and reliable investment environment'. There was a significant internal debate over the best mechanisms for the planning system and how economic programmes could be supported through strong planning frameworks. However, it continued to support the concept of regional policy and argued that resource transfers to assisted areas had been 'highly cost effective and enabled us to influence the plans of companies of all sizes' (Labour Party, 1977, p 5).

However, as with the CBI, there were strong spatial tensions within the labour movement over the efficacy of the regional policy reforms that were taking place. The Southern and Eastern Regional TUC, for example, blamed regional policy for the decline of manufacturing industry in its region and argued, in a somewhat exaggerated way, that the South East was 'unlikely ever again to be in an advantageous position compared to other regions'.[12] While this position statement was rejected by the TUC leadership, it was indicative of wider disagreements within the organisation over the direction of spatial policy and the position that it should take. The needs of the South East were, for SERTUC, being sacrificed in the pursuit of regional development objectives at a time when much of the UK was undergoing significant and serious deindustrialisation (see Law, 1980). The effects of exporting investment, firms, and KWs to the rest of the UK were being felt and SERTUC considered that policy should increasingly look to address the South East's needs, rather than those of the DAs, for the benefit of the whole of the UK. As we will see, it was a prescient argument.

What this discussion of regional policy demonstrates is that perspectives on labour mobility and fixity were intimately linked to wider imaginations about how economies operate and what form spatial policy should take in order to create more balanced and functional spatial economies. The politics of labour mobility was highly contested at a variety of scales because it went to the very heart of arguments over spatial justice, and the responsibilities, roles, and (imagined) capacities of the state. It was increasingly up to individual citizens to take greater responsibility for their own well-being and that of their communities and it was considered that they should become more entrepreneurial and active. However, within this wider vision mobility became something to be simultaneously supported, in the name of greater overall economic efficiency, and something to be limited if DAs were to hold on to their most skilled and talented individuals and sustain their economic competitiveness. This dilemma was to resurface under the succeeding Major administrations and it is to this period that the chapter now turns.

The changing contours of spatial policy: the Major years, 1990-97

Under the Major governments of the 1990s the focus on indigenous regional capacities continued to evolve. In 1994 it became the first government to explicitly refocus development policy on the new, and increasingly popular, concept of 'competitiveness'. Its White Paper entitled *Competitiveness: Helping Business to Win* (DTI, 1995) restructured the civil service to give the then Deputy Prime Minister, Michael Heseltine, a cross-departmental brief, which heralded the development of a new, integrated competitiveness agenda across different government departments. In Heseltine's words, 'the issue that is facing Britain is how we enhance the competitiveness of this nation in order to increase the wealth of this nation in order to meet the aspirations of the people of this country' (p 3). The role of a competitiveness agenda was to help businesses to become more successful. The benefits of this success would trickle down to the national economy and through this process *all* regions of the UK would benefit. The need for a strong redistributive regional policy was still very much off the agenda.

In its place was a new strategy that focused on the power of inward investment to transform the DAs. In Heseltine's words, 'the key to competitiveness is running an economy that enables companies to win and attract people to base their investment here'.[13] Between 1986 and 1994 the UK's stock of Foreign Direct Investment rose from £52 billion to £131 billion (DTI, 1995, paragraph 5.10). The benefits of this investment were seen as not only quantitative (nearly 20% of all manufacturing output and employment in 1994 was provided by foreign-owned manufacturers [DTI, 1995]) but qualitative in that their presence was seen to provide an entrepreneurial spur to existing, indigenous firms and workers. The Department of Trade and Industry (DTI), for example, claimed that these positive impacts were felt in 'the production processes, quality assurance systems, plant and machinery, delivery times, and cost control methods ... and product development' (paragraph 12.37). The emerging strategy was clear. Regional actors needed to develop programmes that enabled them to tap into increasingly mobile flows of capital. In this way they would become cradles of investment and entrepreneurship in ways that did not involve a wholesale redistribution of resources from the more successful and competitive regions of the UK.

At the same time the focus of development policy more broadly was turning to the concepts of knowledge, entrepreneurialism, and creativity. The economic context within which British firms and regions were operating was being re-imagined in terms of enhanced globalisation and new forms of knowledge-based development. In John Major's (1995, p 3) terms, 'we live in an increasingly knowledge-based economy. The education and skills of our people are crucial to our prosperity and national success'. Knowledge-based competitiveness came through 'innovation', or the 'successful exploitation of new ideas' (DTI, 1995, paragraph 11.2). This, in turn, depended upon 'people's ability to embrace new thinking ... stimulated by education, training, and experience' (paragraph 11.2). If competitiveness was increasingly to be found in the 'knowledge sector', then labour market, training, and skills policies had to find new ways to create 'knowledge workers'. Such workers could act as key mediators between flows of capital, innovation, and place competitiveness and it was therefore a priority to create them. In short, knowledge workers became the subjects and objects of policy. Their existence and presence in particular places would generate new forms of innovation, entrepreneurship, and economic activity. Conversely, their absence would undermine regional competitiveness in new and increasingly significant ways.

What took place under the Major administrations of 1990-97 was the gradual acceptance and consolidation of this new regionalism with its enhanced focus on entrepreneurship, regional capacity-building, and local autonomy. There were also moves to redraw the map of regional assistance by creating a Single Regeneration Budget that could be bid for by local communities across England and new areas, such as former coal-mining areas and declining seaside towns (including some in the South East of England, such as Hastings), were reclassified as DAs in an attempt to tackle specific pockets of deprivation linked to the decline of specific industrial sectors. There was also a new emphasis placed on Government Offices for the Regions that were designed to coordinate the cross-departmental activities of government across the country, organisations whose legacies have continued to the present day (Jones and MacLeod, 2004). However, as with many areas of policy, the period of the Major government was characterised by a certain drift and the gradual rolling out of the reforms and philosophies of the Thatcher administration. With the election of Tony Blair in 1997, these evolving philosophies were given a new lease of life.

Spatial policy under New Labour

The transformation of the Labour Party under Tony Blair has been underpinned by the principles of modernisation and reform in the public and private sectors. It has enthusiastically embraced the core features of the so-called 'new regionalism' and its vision of a world characterised by unstoppable globalisation, new forms of technology, and new brutal realities in which people and places must change or perish. For new regionalists the economic and social problems that afflict the regions of the UK are increasingly understood to be a consequence of their internal failures – such as inefficient systems of governance, labour market weaknesses, and/or a lack of 'entrepreneurial spirit' (see Chapter Two). The *inter*relationships between regions are downplayed along with the capacities of the state to redress regional inequalities in a 'new' era of global economic change. For the Blair government this new global economy opens up opportunities in which 'the UK's distinctive capabilities are not raw materials, land or cheap labour. They must be our knowledge, skills and creativity' (Blair, 1998, p 2). Its implications are enormous as, in the words of one former Secretary of State, Stephen Byers (2000, p 1):

> The knowledge economy is bringing about a fundamental change in our country and our economy. The shift from an industrial to a knowledge-based economy at the beginning of the 21st Century is quite as profound as the move from an agricultural to an industrial economy at the beginning of the 19th Century ... there could be more innovation in the next twenty years than at any time in the last 200.

The political justification for new forms of Schumpeterian accumulation (see Jessop, 2002a) could not be clearer.

It is within this wider vision of global change that the Labour Party's focus on knowledge workers and knowledge industries has to be understood. It contains fundamental challenges to wider conceptions of citizenship, responsibility, and state capacities. A new agenda is promoted in which it becomes the:

> responsibility of government to ensure minimum standards of fairness and treatment for all in society; a responsibility on business to work in partnership and ensure that the task of making a reality of the flexible labour market does not fall solely on working people. (Byers, 2000, p 2)

However, it also becomes the responsibility of others, ranging from national, regional, and local planners, and policy-makers to local communities, businesses, workers, and their representatives, to consider how they can contribute to this wider state project and best help themselves. Again in Byers' terms, 'The challenge we face is to both embrace the knowledge economy and to ensure that in the process we avoid widening the inequalities that already exist in our society. The knowledge economy requires the opportunity-rich society – so that all can benefit' (p 3).

This philosophy has been translated into the government's agendas for regional policy. The establishment of nine regional development agencies (RDAs) in England in 1999 represented a clear attempt to encourage a new type of more 'autonomous' spatial policy in which regional actors would be given, albeit limited, responsibility to develop regionally centred programmes of action. The devolution of political power to Scotland, Wales, and (potentially) Northern Ireland was also, in part, based on a belief that regional autonomy could deliver more effective regional development strategies (see Raco, 2003). The RDAs would identify and mobilise regional resources in new ways that would enable regional capacities to be enhanced and sustained in the longer term. RDAs were given the rather small sum of £10 million to 're-focus regional selective assistance on high-quality, knowledge-based projects which provide high value jobs ... [and] promote innovation and competitiveness'. [14] Their core focus was to be on the creation of competitive places to try to ensure that their regions possessed the capacities to engage in global networks and 'fix' new forms of development in their areas.

Within this wider shift towards internally focused regional development strategies, the issue of labour (im)mobility resurfaced as a core consideration. For the government, 'high levels of productivity and employment require efficient matching of workers and jobs at the local and regional level, as well as between regions (and even countries)' (HM Treasury, 2001, p 32). The tendency of workers to move from economically depressed regions with lower wages to those areas with higher wages was increasingly seen as a vital part of the 'regional adjustment mechanisms' that shape the competitiveness of the UK economy. Poor labour mobility, it is argued, 'may result in low productivity as workers are poorly matched ... and may be important in explaining high levels of unemployment in low growth areas and similarly may constrain the economic potential of high growth areas' (HM Treasury, 2001, p 32).

The mobility of highly skilled workers has been elided with that of high-quality investment. It is footloose and less spatially constrained, and workers have become increasingly reflexive and aware of their mobility potential. As the government makes clear, 'high-skilled workers, like firms, are mobile both within the UK and internationally and will seek out the most rewarding employment opportunities wherever they occur' (HM Treasury, 2001, p 18). This notion of 'rewarding' not only relates to wage rates but also to broader quality-of-life issues and therefore it is essential that cities and regions make themselves more attractive to such workers if they are to retain or enhance their prosperity – a point recently echoed by the Urban Task Force among others (see Urban Task Force, 2005). The consequence of this is that 'understanding why regions and localities vary in their skills composition is central to an understanding of regional and local economic performance' (HM Treasury, 2001, p 15), indeed they are the 'major factor in explaining regional variations in productivity' (p 15).

There are strong echoes here of regional policy discourses in the post-war decades. First, the presence of such workers is deemed to have impacts that go beyond their immediate labour market roles as:

> The presence of a high-skilled worker in a region has a beneficial effect on other workers. Relocating that worker does not take into account the detrimental effect this has on those left behind. (HM Treasury, 2001, p 32)

Such workers become essential to the competitiveness of the regions, not only because of their relatively high spending power but also because they have a dynamic, entrepreneurial effect on other, 'less creative' citizens. They are catalysts for innovation, new business growth, and changing aspirations within existing populations (see Miliband, 2005). The absence of entrepreneurs, therefore, has a significant negative impact on place competitiveness and balance as local labour markets become dominated by concentrations of more dependent, less mobile, and less skilled citizens.

Second, skilled workers play an important instrumental/functional role in attracting competitive industries. The perception of a high- or low-quality local labour market, it is argued, influences the locational decisions of firms and reinforces the existing inequalities between regions. It becomes the responsibility of regional development bodies, local communities, and individual citizens to make themselves more 'attractive' to investors. Skilled workers make an important contribution to this process as 'the migration of skilled people will also play an important part in meeting skills and labour shortages' (HM Treasury, 2001, p 32). In short, it is through the development of workers' skills and capacities that the wider objective of marrying economic competitiveness and social cohesion in particular places is to be realised. As Tony Blair et al (2005, p 1) make clear:

> Skills are fundamental to achieving our ambitions, as individuals, for our families and for our communities. They help businesses create wealth, and they help people realise their potential. So they serve the twin goals of social justice and economic success. These goals are at the heart of the government's vision for the future.

In line with wider development initiatives and rationalities, skills policy has become focused on identifying particular groups as both the objects and subjects of policy. It is the responsibility of the state to identify groups in need of support and to provide opportunities through which they can take more responsibility on themselves to ensure that they fulfil their potential in the labour market. It is an example of what Giddens (2005) terms the co-production of policy objectives between the state and empowered, responsible citizens. Again in Tony Blair et al's (2005, p 1) words, the new policy is primarily concerned with:

> replacing the redundant notion of a 'job for life' with our new ambition of 'employability for life', thus helping people and communities meet the challenge of the global economy'.

Within such discourses individuals are encouraged to change their (govern)mentalities and to think about the relationships between their own capacities as workers and the wider competitiveness and well-being of the communities in which they live. A neo-Thatcherite strategy of 'responsibilisation' (see Rose, 1999a) is constructed in which changing the mindsets of individuals is seen as the most effective mechanism through which individuals and communities will become more materially successful. In Blair et al's (2005, p 1) terms, skills policy should be focused on 'raising aspirations by creating a learning culture in each community which breaks the cycle of deprivation passed on from one generation to the next'. Skills 'help individuals achieve their ambitions for themselves, their families and their communities' (DfES, 2005, p 5). The labour market provides a key institutional mechanism through which rewards are allocated to those who have 'achieved' most and it is the state's role to support such aspiring individuals and communities.

This new skills agenda also contains within it a set of spatial premises. The Labour government is explicit about the instrumentalist nature of its reforms in that they are primarily designed to improve the economic capacities of places to meet the new challenges of the global economy. Direct parallels are made between the capacities of workers across the UK and regional and national economic competitiveness. As the Department for Education and Skills (DfES, 2005, p 6) argues, 'lack of skills makes it harder for employers to introduce the innovations, new products and new working methods that feed improvements in productivity'. New threats to the competitiveness of the UK and its regions are identified alongside global economic pressures. An ageing workforce is also raised as a particular concern, with the consequence that 'we cannot rely solely on a flow of better skilled young people entering the labour market' (DfES, 2005, p 6; see also Chapter Eight).

Trades unions and other workers' representatives are called upon to work with employers and government to develop new skills programmes. In this way, it is argued, 'unions can support the long term employment interests of their members, by helping to raise productivity and employability through better skills' (DfES, 2005, p 15).

Through a new National Employment Training Programme the government is committing itself to the delivery of 'publicly funded training and qualifications in a way that is directly led by their needs, that meets their skills priorities, and that is straightforward to use' (p 11). Skills policy is therefore being refocused so that it becomes more employer-led with the recent establishment, for example, of 25 Sector Skills Councils that will develop strategies to meet the specific skills requirements of employers in identified key sectors of the economy (see Table 6.1). The objectives of the network are to 'put employers – working together in industry and public service sectors – centre-stage in meeting their own skills priorities and by doing so drive the agenda we all share in increasing skills productivity to improve industry and public sector performance' (p 15). The Councils will help to create new Skills Academies that will link colleges with dedicated university courses and Vocational Centres of Excellence.

Overall this new emphasis on skills tells us a good deal about the Labour government's wider development philosophies and its imaginations of what it is that makes a sustainable and functioning place. Policy is becoming increasingly concerned with mobilising the capacities and human capital of citizens and businesses. Skills shortages, concentrated in particular places, have increasingly been put forward as the biggest 'impediment' to regional and national economic growth. The corollary of this has been that improvements to the skills base can act as a policy vehicle through which the bridges between enhanced economic competitiveness and social cohesion can be constructed and strengthened. With the new emphasis on Sector Skills Councils it is anticipated that the education system can be increasingly tailored to the needs of economic competitiveness in ways that mirror Jessop's (2002a) observation that the structures of the welfare state are being increasingly turned towards the wider objectives of enhanced capital accumulation through innovation.

Conclusions

This chapter has examined the changing objectives and scale of regional policy in the UK since the late 1970s. It has outlined the changing philosophies of policy and the ways in which dominant imaginations

Table 6.1: The 25 Sector Skills Councils, 2005

Name	Core economic sectors
Asset Skills	Property services, housing, cleaning services, and facilities management
Automotive Skills	The retail motor industry
Cogent	Chemical, nuclear, oil and gas, petroleum, and polymer industries
Construction Skills	Construction
Creative & Cultural Skills	Advertising, crafts, cultural heritage, design, music, performing, literary, and visual arts
Energy & Utility Skills	Electricity, gas, waste management, and water industries
e-skills UK	Information technology, telecommunications, and contract centres
Financial Services Skills Council	Financial services industry
GoSkills	Passenger transport
Government Skills	The Civil Service, non-departmental public bodies, and the armed forces
Improve Ltd	Food and drink manufacturing and processing
Lantra	Environment and land-based industries
Lifelong Learning UK	Community learning and development, further education, higher education, libraries, archives and information services, work-based learning and development
People 1st	Hospitality, leisure, travel, and tourism
ProSkills UK	Process and manufacturing
SEMTA	Science, engineering, and manufacturing technologies
Skillfast-UK	Apparel, footwear, textiles, and related businesses
Skills for Health	Health sector across the UK
Skills for Justice	Custodial care, community justice, court services, prosecution services, customs, excise, and the police
Skills for Logistics	Freight logistics industry
SkillsActive	Sport and recreation, health and fitness, outdoors, playwork, and caravans
Skillset	Broadcast, film, video, interactive media, and photo-imaging
Skillsmark Retail	Retail
Skills for Care & Development	Social care, children, young people, and families
SummitSkills	Building services engineering

Source: Skills for Business Network (2005b, pp 16-17)

have been constructed concerning the form and character of places and the role of policy in making and shaping them. The movement away from donor–recipient models of spatial policy to agendas more focused on indigenous capacity-building within places has been a gradual, but relentless, process. The initial shift to more targeted forms of selection, followed by the emphasis on regional cooperation has evolved into a new concern with regional performance and the ways in which the regional scale provides new opportunities for the bringing together of social cohesion and economic competitiveness.

Labour subsidies for low-skilled workers in DAs and KW programmes to enhance mobility were rapidly removed. Instead, policy focused on a new strategy, in which labour migration was conceptualised as something that should take place 'naturally', without specific measures to assist a specific type of worker. A new market-based approach was adopted with supply and demand driving labour mobility – those areas that were most attractive would attract the right types of worker in response to emerging opportunities. Conversely, those regions that became less attractive would lose highly qualified personnel and would attract different types of lower skilled employment with greater dependency on lower wages. While this trend had existed for some time in the UK, the scaling down of regional policy represented a particular strategy of accumulation. Paradoxically, through deregulation, the state was in fact intervening in the economic geography of the UK in new and more significant ways.

This new approach has had significant implications for the process of sustainable community-building. For, in order for a place to become sustainable, in economic and social terms, it requires the presence of particular groups of skilled entrepreneurs or KWs. Rather than encouraging such workers to move through subsidies, as was the case in the post-war decades, it is up to regional agencies and communities to make themselves attractive locations for such workers. In other words, a very different politics of mobility has been created in which the attraction of mobile workers and investment becomes something that places have to strive for. The state's role is to support such moves and to ensure that the wider competitiveness of the national economy is not damaged by direct interference in the location decisions of business managers and skilled employees. These groups become the 'kingmakers' of regional fortunes, able to make or break the competitiveness of places through their presence or absence. Their mobility is, of course, increasingly global and we will return to migration policy in Chapter Eight.

However, there are also strong continuities with earlier rounds of spatial policy. Contemporary state agencies and planners are, in many ways, drawing on the same conceptualisations of labour markets, social practices, and economic processes as their post-war predecessors. The concern with the *identification* of KWs, whether they be 'new' knowledge workers or the earlier 'essential' managerial and professional workers of relocation programmes is evident across the different periods. Decisions over what types of facilities and environments such workers 'need' in order for them to be present or fixed in a particular place are as politically charged now as they were when Board of Trade civil servants were drawing up definitions of a KW's 'minimum requirements' in the 1940s (see Chapter Three). The contemporary arguments of authors such as Richard Florida (2004) with his passionate plea for a new development politics in which a 'creative class' of KWs is identified and supported is anything but new. Policy-makers and planners have long selected certain groups of workers and given them privileged treatment. Some of these wider points will be developed in Chapter Nine. However, the next chapter now expands on the Labour government's broader conceptions of a sustainable community and examines the ways in which the term 'KW' has been reinvented not to facilitate a redistributive regional policy but to try and ensure that the economic competitiveness of the UK's strongest regions is sustained for the benefit of the whole country.

Notes

[1] TUC Regional Policy Working Groups Minutes, 8 April 1981, MSS 292D/540/12 Regional Policy (Strategy Planning).

[2] Margaret Thatcher, 'Questions on employment and planning regions', *Hansard*, 1979, col 972, p 619.

[3] TUC Minutes of National Economic Development Council Meeting, London, 3 March 1982, MSS 292D/540/14 Regional Policy.

[4] TUC Minutes of National Economic Development Council Meeting, London, 3 March 1982, MSS 292D/540/14 Regional Policy.

[5] Association of British Chambers of Commerce and Regional Policy, 6 August 1979, MSS 292D/540/14 Regional Policy.

[6] Letter CBI Welsh Council to Secretary of State, MSS 200/C/3/ECO/14/5 – CBI Regions 1974-1978, 1 October 1979.

[7] TUC–Labour Party Liaison Committee meeting, 26 October 1981, Labour Research Department, Economic Inequality and Planning 1977-90, People's History Museum Archive, Manchester.

[8] TUC Regional Policy Working Groups Minutes, 8 April 1981, MSS 292D/540/12 Regional Policy (Strategy Planning).

[9] TUC Regional Policy Working Groups Minutes, 8 April 1981, MSS 292D/540/12 Regional Policy (Strategy Planning).

[10] TUC Regional Policy Working Groups Minutes, 8 April 1981, MSS 292D/540/12 Regional Policy (Strategy Planning), p 1.

[11] Association of British Chambers of Commerce and Regional Policy, 6 August 1979, MSS 292D/540/14 Regional Policy, p 4.

[12] TUC Inter-departmental Correspondence – Economic and Social Plan for the South East (Prepared by SERTUC), MSS 292D/520/14 Regional Policy, March 1982.

[13] Michael Heseltine, *Hansard*, 20 July 1994, col 308.

[14] L. Simon, Competitiveness debate, *Hansard*, 16 December 1998, col 1679.

SEVEN

Sustainable community-building under New Labour

Introduction

Chapter Six discussed the evolution of the new regionalism within spatial policy and the ways in which successive administrations have put greater emphasis on policy-makers, communities, and individuals to take greater responsibility for their own well-being. Within this context there has been a growing emphasis on the role that spatial planning can play in delivering the new agendas and how economic and social spaces can be made more balanced and ordered to support wider policy objectives. Since the early 2000s these priorities have been encapsulated in the emergence of sustainable community planning that seeks to create new places in which:

> people want to live and work, now and in the future. They meet the diverse needs of existing and future residents, are sensitive to their environment, and contribute to a high quality of life. They are safe and inclusive, well-planned, built and run, and offer equality of opportunity and good services for all. (ODPM, 2005, p 1)

This chapter examines the form and character of this shift to sustainable community-building through an assessment of the relationships between employment, labour market-building, and (sustainable) spatial communities. It assesses the differences between these policy agendas and those of the post-war period outlined in Chapters Three and Four, and documents the ways in which the sustainable community has become the primary policy vehicle in and through which its wider agendas will be delivered and implemented. It argues that the new agendas are premised on particular conceptions of (im)mobility and the relationships between place, employment, and community-building. In contrast to earlier rounds of spatial policy, the role of the state is relegated to that of an enabler, or in Schuppert's (2005) terms an 'insurer', that guides market processes in ways that fulfil wider policy agendas. State power is not to be used *directly* to create sustainable communities but will instead create the conditions and contexts in which sustainable communities are constructed and developed. The chapter begins by discussing the emergence of the discourse of sustainability and the rise of the sustainable community before turning to contemporary debates over key worker (KW) programmes. It uses these to provide insights into wider questions of labour market-building, citizenship, and state capacities.

The meta-discourse of sustainability and the emergence of the sustainable community

> Sustainable development is the core principle underpinning planning. At the heart of sustainable development is the simple idea of ensuring a better quality of life for everyone, now and for future generations. (ODPM, 2004, paragraph 3)

> Just at a time when philosophers have proclaimed the death of 'meta-narratives' ... international political leaders have come to identify themselves with an ambitious new project intended to act as the focus for human endeavour in the 21st Century. (Meadowcroft, 1999, p 12)

The discourse of sustainable development has become one of the central orthodoxies of planning, not only in Britain but also in Europe and North America (de Roo and Miller, 2000). Planners in a variety of contexts now ostensibly strive to create sustainable places, cities, and regions in which development takes place in ways that can be supported by social, economic, and environmental resources in the long term for the benefit of individuals, communities, and society as a whole. The discourse arose in the 1970s and 1980s with the publication of critical academic work on the limits of growth (see Schumacher, 1973; McRobie, 1990) and environmentally focused reports by global institutions such as the United Nations (World Commission for Environment and Development, 1988), the World Bank (1989), and the World Conservation Union (1991). Collectively, these called for new forms of economic development discourse and practice, which put greater value on environmental resources, extended the time horizons in which actors think and operate, and promoted greater equity between different social groups and communities, primarily through new forms of democratic economic governance (see Pearce et al, 1991; Gibbs, 2002).

In Western countries, sustainability has been increasingly applied to the discourses and practices of urban and regional regeneration as it is in cities and former industrial regions that the negative consequences of globalisation and economic restructuring have been most keenly experienced. In many ways the growing popularity of such discourses represents a cross-fertilisation of ideas and practices that have been introduced in Less Developed Countries and are now finding resonance in the context of declining urban areas of the developed world.[1] The new sustainability agendas call for urban planning that is focused on reversing the negative trends of population and employment loss that cities have been suffering from since the late 1960s (see Pacione, 1998; Turok and Edge, 1999). They, therefore, promote the planning of new and existing urban spaces that: are compact enough to reduce the amount of energy required to transport people from places of residence, work, and leisure (see Jenks et al, 1996; Burton, 2000); draw on efficient technical mechanisms of resource use and recycling (Haughton, 1997); encourage the formation of mixed and diverse communities; promote new mechanisms of urban design that encourage social inclusion and minimise energy use; and establish new forms of civic participation and democratic inclusion (see also Chatterton, 2002).

However, despite being labelled a 'meta-discourse' (Meadowcroft, 1999, 2000), sustainability's widespread acceptance and actually occurring forms in particular places cannot be read off from a wider global logic. The ill-defined and aspirational nature of the term has enabled its meaning to be redefined and reconceptualised in different ways by different groups and deployed for different ends (see Harvey, 1996; Whitehead, 2003). As Maloutas (2003) notes, the term only takes on specific meanings and substance through *processes of recontextualisation* and priority-setting in different local, regional, and national environments. For example, Willers (1994) shows how the term has been taken up with great zeal by big businesses and (neo-liberal) governments intent on promoting agendas of perpetual economic growth, and using sustainability as a discursive cover for their own agendas (see also O'Riordan, 1992).

Decisions over what is sustained and what is not sustained have therefore become politically charged. The diverse and rather chaotic conception of sustainability has enabled governments and other actors to reconceptualise it in their own terms, so that they can promote their own ambitions and broader objectives. In so doing, some of the socially advantageous and democratic aspects of the term have often become subsumed into wider debates over how *economic development* can be made more sustainable, rather than creating a new object of policy that seeks to limit growth. In some cases, the term becomes deliberately confused so that dominant interests are able to 'discursively as well as institutionally manage the heterogeneity of discourses (even those of radical opposition) to their advantage' (Harvey, 1996, p 174). As Counsell (1999, p 46) notes, 'different meanings of the concept result in it being used to support opposite points of view'. It is in this context that the term has increasingly been applied to the Labour government's spatial policy and frameworks and it is to this that the chapter now turns.

New Labour, spatial planning, and the sustainable communities agenda

Since coming to power in 1997 the Blair administration has increasingly embraced the concepts associated with sustainability to the extent that they have gradually come to dominate planning policy guidelines, spatial policy blueprints, and agendas (see Table 7.1 for a summary of the key measures). In 1999 urban sustainability was one of the core themes of the report by Lord Rogers' Urban Task Force with its emphasis on 'liveability' and the 'compact city' (see Lees, 2003; Urban Task Force, 1999, 2005). It was increasingly taken up by government in its planning policy guidelines, culminating in the publication of the *Sustainable Communities: Building for the Future* plan (ODPM, 2003) and *Planning Policy Statement 1: Delivering Sustainable Development* (ODPM, 2004). In combination they establish the principles that should underpin the entire planning process so that local and regional planners are now 'expected' to consider a range of interconnected issues when permitting any development to take place. An, albeit selective, interpretation of sustainability has therefore been placed at the heart of planning reforms.

The *Sustainable Communities* plan, in particular, has had a profound effect on the discourses of spatial planning across the country. It sets out a vision for new-build settlements in the South East of England and the regeneration of urban centres across the UK. Community-building is to be targeted on three growth areas within the South East – Milton Keynes, the Cambridge–Stansted Airport corridor, and Ashford. At least 260,000 homes are to be built in these New Towns (NTs) and, in addition, a minimum of 120,000 homes have been proposed for an area known as the Thames Gateway that stretches along the Thames from East London to the North of Kent. This

Table 7.1: Key moments in the rise of sustainable community planning under New Labour

Initiative/statement	Year	Key dimensions
Urban Task Force Report	1999	• A new vision of urban living • Good quality community design and planning; community empowerment; creation and sharing of prosperity; good quality local services
Sustainable Development Strategy	1999	• Planning should deliver social progress that benefits the needs of everyone • Ensure effective protection of the environment and the prudent use of natural resources • Maintain high and stable levels of economic growth and employment
Greener, Safer Places	2002	• Strong relationships between environmental quality and quality of life; strong communities live in high-quality environments • Building a sense of place and sense of community ownership • Using place to generate new types of social and economic growth
By Design, Urban Design in the Planning System	2003	• Guide for planners for improving the quality of design in their new development • Place-making through design • Focusing on improved practice
Sustainable Communities Plan	2003	• Accelerating the provision of housing and affordable housing • Tackling homelessness and housing abandonment • Tackling empty homes • Encouraging the construction of decent quality homes • Improving liveability in towns and cities • Supporting the development of London and the South East to maintain their status as 'world-class' regions
Planning Policy Statement 1: Delivering Sustainable Development	2004	• Sets out 'guiding principles' for the English planning process • Development plans to ensure that sustainable development is pursued in an 'integrated manner' • Spatial planning approach to be at the heart of sustainable development • Planning policies to promote high-quality and inclusive design • Community involvement as an essential element in creating safe and sustainable communities
Citizen Engagement and Public Services – Why Neighbourhoods Matter	2005	• Strengthening communities and neighbourliness; strengthening community-driven democracy; encouraging local ownership and delivery of public services; developing new relationships between active citizenship and place competitiveness

Sources: Strategies taken from: Urban Task Force (1999); ODPM (2003, 2004, 2005); DEFRA (2005)

Development Area (DA) has been earmarked for large-scale, long-term redevelopment in order to improve the imagined 'balance' in the growth between the west and east of the region. These developments are to be supplemented by the creation of nine Market Renewal Areas in northern cities in which there will be 'sustained action to replace obsolete housing with modern sustainable accommodation, through demolition and new building or refurbishment' (ODPM, 2003, p 24).

Overall, these plans represent a framework for development that ostensibly incorporates the core elements of sustainability planning while facilitating the growth of the UK's cities and regions. The key features of a contemporary sustainable community are outlined in Table 7.2 and contrasted with those of what might logically be termed an unsustainable community.

A sustainable place is one in which a 'balance' of employment, housing, and social facilities are co-present and available to a range of socioeconomic groups. It is populated by *sustainable citizens* who are politically, socially, and economically active and self-reliant. They are 'non-dependent' on the state and provide for themselves through private sector (market) provision. It is argued that with an appropriate mix of different social groups, employment opportunities, and accessible built environments, sustainable communities will play an increasingly significant role in tackling social exclusion at the same time as they underpin new forms of place competitiveness. The Labour government's understanding of a sustainable community represents something of a hybrid between the principles of sustainable development, broadly defined, and a pro-growth strategy of enhanced global economic competitiveness. The role of spatial planning becomes that of 'fixing' imbalances, and ordering space and place so that they become more functional, cohesive, and competitive (see Raco, 2005b).

In essence the concept of the sustainable community is, therefore, an inherently spatial or geographical construct. It involves the integration and co-presence in time and space of a particular type of built environment, a diverse and broad range of employment and employees, and a degree of social cohesion that facilitates a well-functioning social order. The agenda is underpinned by assumptions about how social and economic actors should be ordered in space. It draws upon particular visions of what places could be like in order to be balanced and sustainable and highlights the processes of mobility and fixity through which such places can be made and remade. It is not simply the movement of people that drives the new agendas but the selected mobilisation of diverse social groups by shifting housing development priorities, encouraging the movement of (selected) jobs,

Table 7.2: The core elements of a sustainable community

Criteria	A sustainable community	An unsustainable community
Economic growth	Flourishing economic base; built on long-term commitments; stable; and inclusive of broad range of workers.	Domination by dependent forms of development; lack of employment opportunities; vulnerable; insecure; short-term; and divisive.
Citizenship	Active citizens and communities; long-term community stewardship; effective political engagement; healthy voluntary sector; and strong social capital.	Passive and dependent citizens and communities; lack of community engagement or ownership; low levels of voluntary activity and/or social capital.
Community characteristics	Broad range of skills within workforce; ethnically and socially diverse; mixture of socioeconomic types of inhabitants; balanced community; well-populated neighbourhoods.	Absence of skills within workforce; ill-balanced communities of place; high levels of (physical) separation between groups; lack of diversity; formal and informal segregation; lack of population.
Urban design	Diverse architecture; accessible public spaces; higher urban densities; provision of broad range of amenities; buildings that cater for a range of needs; 'self-contained' communities; the creation of 'place'.	Uniform, zoned architecture; closed, gated, and inaccessible public spaces; absence of community facilities; urban sprawl; 'placeless' suburban development.
Environmental dimensions	Re-use of brownfield sites; minimisation of transport journeys; good-quality public transport.	Expansion into greenfield sites; maximisation of transport journeys; car dependence and the absence of public transport.
Quality of life	Attractive environments; high quality of life; strong pull for a range of social groups.	Low quality of life; strong push for a range of social groups.

Source: Adapted from ODPM (2003, 2005) definitions of a sustainable community

and implementing new, spatially selective priorities for infrastructure investment. Through such measures the *Sustainable Communities* plan explicitly states that its purpose is:

> to accommodate the economic success of London and the wider South East and ensure that the international competitiveness of the region is sustained, for the benefit of the region and the whole country. (ODPM, 2003, p 46)

In short, it epitomises wider shifts in the objectives and practices of spatial policy away from the direct support of producers to the provision of social (and environmental) infrastructure in and through which competitiveness will be sustained and enhanced.

And yet there are also real differences between the plan's grandiose aspirations and its implementation. Existing measures have delivered neither the resources nor the new institutional powers required by local and regional planning agencies to deliver on the proposals. Unlike the state-led agendas of post-war spatial policy outlined in Chapters Three and Four, the mechanisms through which employers will be 'encouraged' to (re)locate in the new areas are largely absent. New types of mobility and fixity will be encouraged through public sector-led investments in existing brownfield sites to make them more attractive but there is little in the way of direct government grants or payments to firms. Instead the sustainable community framework promotes a voluntary mobility in which individuals, investors, and firms make their own decisions with the government's role one of gentle encouragement and aspiration. Choice over when to move and where remains at the heart of the new approach, reflecting a wider shift in the role and function of the state from that of a manager/director to that of a Giddensian-style insurer or enabler.

Sustaining communities: the new politics of spatial development in England

The rise of sustainability has gone hand in hand with a new realisation that some form of spatial planning is essential to ensure that the competitiveness of the UK's regions can be sustained. It became increasingly clear to the Labour government during the early 2000s that spatial imbalances and inequalities were beginning to have a significant impact on the UK's strongest-performing regions and the national economy more generally. The growth in employment, households, and incomes in London and the South East fuelled new levels of demand for social infrastructure such as housing and transport. The supply of housing has not kept pace with these demands, with low-cost housing in particular becoming increasingly scarce. During the 2000s around 25,000 new homes for rent have been built annually by housing associations but there has been a growing shortfall as 50,000 homes have been lost through the government's Right to Buy scheme in which local authority housing is sold off to tenants. At the same time, between 1999 and 2004 household growth in the UK has outpaced housing unit construction by 59,000 per year. This mismatch has been particularly severe in London and the South East where 14,000 fewer houses than the government's target figure were built between 1996 and 2001 (Barker, 2004; see Table 7.3). House-building rates were at their lowest in England since 1924 at a time when economic growth was pushing up demand for a range of housing.

The net effect of these trends has been that so-called 'affordable housing' for a range of social groups has become increasingly scarce, creating labour market shortages in key sectors. In London in 2001 the Greater London Assembly (2001, p 2) reported that each of the city's public sector services 'had a clearly identified recruitment and retention problem, which is severely undermining service delivery'. Some schools in the capital were reporting an annual staff turnover of 30% and other 'essential' public services such as transport companies were reporting turnovers in excess of 70%. In addition, the contracting out of public sector jobs to private sector agencies had been expanding,

Table 7.3: Annualised housing targets for England, 1996-2001

	Current RPG target (per annum)	1996-2001 household projections (average annual increase)	Average past completions 1996-2001	Difference between RPG target and current completion rate
London	23,000	25,200	13,396	−9,604
South East	28,000	35,600	23,680	−4,320
Eastern	20,850	23,600	18,987	−1,863
North East	5,321	3,800	6,995	1,674
Yorkshire & Humber	14,675	12,000	14,041	−634
North West	12,790	12,600	18,652	5,862
West Midlands	16,100	12,200	14,137	−1,963
East Midlands	13,700	15,200	14,680	980
South West	20,200	21,200	16,390	−3,810
England	154,726	161,400	140,958	−13,768

Note: RPG = Regional Planning Guidance

Source: Environmental Audit Committee (2005, p 7)

leaving many lower-skilled public sector workers vulnerable to slashes in their pay and working conditions at a time when housing prices had been rising and the availability of any type of housing had become increasingly scarce. The short-term threats to the social and economic stability of London and the South East were, therefore, becoming apparent.

One of the consequences of these new growth pressures has been that the *politics of regional development* in the 2000s has been very different to that of earlier decades. In Chapter Three we saw that despite there being some disquiet within the South East over the efficacy of regional incentives to companies and the value of KW programmes, the strongest advocates for a coherent spatial policy came from the DAs. Chapter Six showed that during the Thatcher era it was these same regional actors including local government, trades unions, and business interests who challenged the rolling back of regional support. Yet, during the 2000s, in large part due to these perceived threats to labour market sustainability, it has been voices in London and the South East that have been calling for more interventionist and expansive spatial development programmes. The Greater London Assembly (2001, p 25), for example, now forcefully argues that:

> If London is to maintain its relative competitiveness and attract the required labour not only must transport be improved to make commuting easier but the large scale addition of affordable housing must also be addressed.

In 2004 the Mayor of London, Ken Livingstone, similarly called for national government to 'give back' some of the money that the London economy had been generating:

> [London] generates more wealth than any other region in the country, contributes more to national finances, and makes a unique contribution to the nation's prosperity. Sustaining London's progress has to be a national priority. (Livingstone, 2004, p 3)

The emerging regional consensus was that something had to be done to ensure that development pressures did not 'stifle' economic growth in the South East. Organisations such as the South East of England Development Agency (SEEDA, 2004) identified the area as the UK's only '*world-class region*', sentiments echoed by others including the London Development Agency (with its document *Sustaining Success*

[LDA, 2004]), the Greater London Assembly (2004) and the Southern and Eastern TUC. The London Housing Federation summed up this growing consensus by claiming that 'in order to function properly a World Class city needs to be able to house people on a wide range of incomes' (LHF, 2004, p 3).

As a part of the wider discourse in support of more interventionist strategies international comparisons were made with places that had 'failed' to plan for rapid growth and had suffered from potentially catastrophic social and economic breakdown. Aspen in Colorado became a much used exemplar that acted as 'a stark warning as to what could happen in the UK, and in particular London, if nothing is done to create housing for Key Workers' (Salman, 2002, p 1; see Box 7.1). It has become a *cause célèbre* for policy-makers and activists and is cited not only for its alleged parallels with fast-growing areas of the UK but also because it exemplifies what can be achieved once the 'problem' of an unbalanced community is recognised and tackled through coherent (and expensive) state investment programmes.

Box 7.1: KWs and sustainability in Aspen, Colorado

The much publicised case of Aspen has taken on an almost iconic status among policy-makers intent on promoting the needs of fast-growing areas and the specific benefits of KW housing programmes. Aspen is a tourist resort in the Rocky Mountains that for a long period of time has attracted wealthy and high-profile tourists. However, during the 1990s it became a victim of its own success as 'the affluent had been buying up the area's properties as holiday homes, leaving those who actually lived and worked there priced out of the market. Average property prices soared to 12 times the national average, until 70% of all private housing was being used as vacation homes' (Salman, 2002, p 1). It was feared that the place would become 'dysfunctional' as it not only lacked community facilities and social infrastructure but also was losing its status as an attractive venue for holidaymakers, thereby undermining its longer-term competitiveness. The response from the city and state authorities was to develop radical measures through a series of strong and well-resourced *Aspen Area Community Plans* in the late 1990s and 2000s. The plans embodied a commitment to 'open space and the environment and ... preserving and/or providing an appropriate amount of affordable housing' (City of Aspen, 2000, pp 2-3). As part of the proposals the local authority paid direct subsidies to families earning less than $118,000 per annum and developers were forced to set aside up to

70% of new homes at an affordable rate (Salman, 2002). The scheme has been seen as a success and the community has become more balanced and functional, with a wider range of citizens and workers co-present, although some of the structural problems of market inflation are still causing difficulties and the costs of the scheme are being borne by taxpayers outside of the city.

The return of the KW: from the Starter Homes Initiative to the Key Worker Living Programme

It is in this wider context that the 2000s have witnessed the rediscovery of the KW. Chapters Three and Four assessed KW support policies during the post-war period. They examined the ways in which the KW 'problem' first became identified and the strengths and weaknesses of measures taken to support them in the DAs and NTs. KWs were primarily private sector managers or those in specialised, skilled manufacturing professions whose presence or absence in particular places at particular times was seen as critical to the effectiveness of development programmes. They were both the subjects and objects of support programmes and efforts were made to encourage their targeted mobility from areas of economic strength to areas where their presence would engender new forms of development and entrepreneurialism.

During the late 1990s, with the clamour for 'action' to tackle development limitations increasing, the category of the KW was reinvented and redeployed as a spatial policy vehicle. The government's first KW programme was the Starter Homes Initiative (SHI) aimed at a small group of public sector workers in London and the South East. The SHI comprised of two strands. First, it provided £230 million to housing associations to encourage the building of KW homes under shared ownership schemes. Approximately 8,000 homes were offered under the scheme in this way. Second, with a total budget of £20 million, it provided £10,000 interest-free loans to KWs in the health, education, and policing sectors that could be used to purchase property (see Weaver, 2001). Demand for the SHI was strong, demonstrating a clear latent demand within the region's housing and labour markets.

However, as interviewed Office of the Deputy Prime Minister (ODPM) officers now admit, the SHI was plagued with difficulties from the outset. It was not well conceived and there was great difficulty in identifying KWs and tackling the structural problems afflicting housing markets, particularly in relation to the lack of housing supply discussed above. The offer of £10,000 was not enough to make a difference to claimants' decisions and the emphasis on prioritising KW housing at the expense of other building programmes meant that it generated localised pockets of house-price inflation while doing little to tackle wider shortages. It was poorly advertised and awareness among public and private sector players was limited. Despite its limitations the SHI did, however, surpass its original targets. It was designed to assist 4,000 individuals but over four years it paid subsidies to 10,200. It was also popular with regional actors. Local and regional authorities across the South East began to mobilise the object of the KW as a housing priority in a context where the politics of housing was becoming increasingly fractured and tense. It also demonstrated that KW programmes could act as a 'quick fix' to the growing crisis in available and affordable housing. The issue of housing supply is structurally difficult to tackle as it requires the construction of locally unpopular developments and threatens the vested interests that benefit from rapidly increasingly house prices. As one ODPM officer noted in interview there has been a strong push for KW schemes 'across Whitehall' and gradually during the 2000s the issue of KW housing has risen up the political agenda as it is increasingly perceived to be a part of the funding architecture now available for housing development.

In 2004 the SHI was replaced by a much more ambitious and thought-through strategy known as the Key Worker Living Programme (KWLP). The KWLP assists KWs to purchase a property 'suitable for your household's needs and within a reasonable travelling distance of your workplace' (www.communities.co.uk). The KWLP has several dimensions and multiple objectives:

- It can provide a loan of up to £50,000 which only requires repayment when the property is sold or the KW stops being a KW (although for some teachers there is the possibility of £100,000 of assistance [see below]).
- It can help a KW to buy a share of a newly built property with the remainder covered by a Registered Social Landlord. The KW can buy the property gradually.
- The money can be used by existing home owners to upgrade their homes to 'meet your family needs'.

There are a number of rationales that explain its existence. First, it is seen as a compensation mechanism for public sector workers who are unable to access housing through the market. As one ODPM interviewee commented: 'Paying public sector workers an extra ten grand [£10,000] is not going to happen and it wouldn't solve the problem if it did ... the problem is that the private sector can and does pay extra money putting public workers at a disadvantage'. Second, public service managers have increasingly complained about the difficulties of attracting and retaining staff, particularly those at family-rearing age. The programme defines KWs in relation to sectors and these are outlined in Table 7.4. The KWLP differs from the SHI in that assistance is available for new-build as well as equity to support incomes. It aims to assist 35,000 KWs by 2010; by the end of 2005, approximately 10,000 KWs had received assistance. Half of the KW support since 2004 has been spent on the construction of new houses.

The programme is directed by the ODPM and it has taken a binary

Table 7.4: Selection criteria for the KWLP

Employment sector	Criteria
Education*	Must work in Greater London publicly funded school; be unable to buy a suitable home for household needs; be permanent employees; be legal UK residents; household income <£80,000/year.
Health	Must be a permanent NHS employee; household income <£60,000/year; priority for nurses, cancer staff, diagnostic staff, mental health professionals, midwives, GPs in under-doctored areas, chiropodists, physiotherapists, arts therapists, paramedics, radiographers, pharmacists; all assistance dependent on priorities at Strategic Health Authority level according to local vacancies.
Police	Police officers in post >6 months; only those in priority posts of communications officer, scientific support teams, crime analysts, station reception officers, civilian gaolers.
Prison service	Applications must be in one of the following disciplines: prison officer, nursing staff, operational support grades, industrials, or instruction officers. In addition applicants must be working in identified institutions in London and the South East of England.
Probation Service	Permanently employed: senior probation officers, probation officers, probation service officers, trainee probation officers.
Planners	Those in London local authority planning offices from Level I to Level IV.
Social workers**	Fully qualified social workers.
Occupational therapists**	Fully qualified occupational therapists.
Educational psychologists**	Fully qualified educational psychologists.

Notes: * There are two related schemes: the London Challenge Key Teacher Homebuy scheme and the Key Worker Homebuy; ** Local authority employed

role of overseeing the strategic dimensions of the programmes while at the same time taking on, what one respondent referred to as, a 'micro-management' role in which civil servants involve themselves in day-to-day negotiations over particular projects. The *Key Worker Housing Branch* of the ODPM is responsible for the development and implementation of the KWLP and its priorities are reflected in the branch's location in the *Sustainable Communities Directorate* of the ODPM and the *Affordable Housing Division*. It is not a part of the wider *Housing Directorate*. The rationale for this is that KW housing is seen as explicitly being a part of the wider agenda for sustainable community-building as, in the words of one interviewee:

> 'It is no good having a new community with no public sector! You cannot build houses for 30,000 people in the Thames Gateway and have public services like the police living five miles away.'

Public service managers have been at the forefront of demands for their employees to be living within a short distance of their work. Co-presence makes management an easier task and the absence of KWs could undermine the effectiveness of public services and the quality of life and economic sustainability of competitive regions.

The KWLP is being implemented in three regions – London, the South East, and the East. Within these there are 14 identified Action Zones in which the ODPM identifies and works with local stakeholders and project managers. These include individual employers, such as prisons, and local delivery agents, such as local education authorities and local Policing Boards. The deployment of KW housing resources is conditional on Regional Housing Boards (RHBs) requesting the implementation of the programme in their area. Crucially, RHBs have to decide on their own priorities, of which KW housing is a part.[2] Their money is provided by the ODPM on a rolling two-year basis. Where they ask for KW support, this money is directed away from other expenditure programmes so that the contestation over resources comes at the regional level where problems and priorities for action are established and determined. As an ODPM officer stated: 'It is not for us to say they should have KW support ... it is up to them'.

The role of the RHBs was outlined in a letter written by Housing Minister Keith Hill to RHB chairs in February 2004. While RHBs are implored to focus on 'the use of funds within your region ... and on the pattern of needs across these objectives',[3] clear targets for KW housing are laid down, along with associated funding. The funding process for housing in England changed in 2004 with the merging of the existing local authority Housing Investment Programme and the Housing Corporation's Approved Development Programme into a Single Housing Pot. The resources in this pot are allocated by central government to the RHBs and will increase from £2.5 billion in 2005/06 to £2.625 billion in 2006/07 and £2.912 billion in 2007/08. KW housing has been granted an increasingly significant share of this wider allocation as:

> The government is committed to improving the quality of public services and provision of accommodation though [the] Key Worker Living scheme remains a key part of the strategy for achieving this ... it should address areas where there are recruitment and retention problems.[4]

The minimum levels of funding that the government would 'like' the RHBs to allocate for KW housing in London, the South East, and the East are laid out in Table 7.5. The South East RHB plans to spend 25% of its Housing Pot on KW housing in this period and other RHBs have similarly been allocating KWs increased provision (see South East RHB, 2005, p 2).

As such, KW housing has become an increasingly important element of the funding of social housing in the South East of England. It is no longer a small-scale initiative but has taken on a high degree of practical and symbolic/political significance in a context where policies to deal with the lack of housing supply will continue to be relatively slow and dogged by a politics of resistance.

There are signs that the scheme is having some effect on recruitment and retention within key public services. With the increase in available resources, some housing corporations are competitively bidding for the increased money but they need to be able to show that they have a demand to fulfil. The budget for the KWLP has increased from £690 million to £725 million, partly reflecting the continuation of the problem and partly because of an advertising scheme and an

Table 7.5: Minimum levels of funding to be spent on the KWLP (£ millions)

Region	2006/07	2007/08
East of England	31	32
London	199	204
South East	96	99

Source: Hill (2004, paragraph 7)

increasingly high profile – the programme now has its own brand and logo. The KWLP managers are increasingly using Geographic Information System (GIS) technology to 'map' where employers are located and how this relates to the local housing demand. The use of such technologies is indicative of a more resource-intensive and well-organised strategy as well as the wider spatial imaginations that underpin the programme. The ODPM is in the early stages of developing these forms of analysis and it is expected that it will inform the distribution of resources in future policy rounds.

The politics of KW selection

This new scale of KW housing policy has made it, once again, an important focus for public policy. As with the post-war agendas, KW provision requires the creation of relational forms of spatial and socioeconomic selection and boundary drawing to be established and this results from and generates particular forms of spatial development politics. In general terms the new agendas have strong similarities and differences to the earlier rounds of policy. First, the objects of modern KW programmes are public sector workers rather than private sector actors. This is not to say that private sector workers in specialised industries, such as global finance, are not discursively and materially privileged by the Labour government (see Amin et al, 2003; Chapters Six and Eight). Instead, it represents a belated recognition that the wages of public sector workers have been falling behind those of their private sector counterparts and they cannot maintain an 'acceptable' standard of living that matches their aspirations. Second, rather than being in DAs or the NETs, modern KW support is targeted at those in fast-growing regions where housing markets are not able to provide an 'adequate' quality or quantity of housing. This aspect of spatial policy has, therefore, been inverted so that support is now targeted at those areas that are perceived to already be successful. Third, processes of selection have been much more clearly defined than those of the post-war programmes. KW support is only available to a select band of skilled public sector workers in particular places where their absence is construed as a development problem.

However, there are similar problems emerging in other parts of the UK and a new scalar politics of KW recognition is beginning to emerge. In Scotland, for example, the emergence of the sustainable communities agenda has been bound up with the overheating of labour markets in the Edinburgh area and the ways in which spatial policy can ensure that its growth and development will be sustained. Through its new sustainability blueprint, *Building a Better Scotland*, the Scottish Executive (2004) is establishing a new agenda for 'strategic workforce planning in key sectors making sure that we have the right people, with the right skills to deliver the right services' (p 9). Ensuring that these key sectors and key places maintain their competitiveness has become the broad focus of policy with First Minister Jack McConnell (2005, pp 2-3), for example, outlining the basis for sustainable community-building as:

> A strong, stable and sustainable economy [that] will allow us to deliver these goals. Building an economy which provides prosperity and opportunities for all. We need sustained and sustainable economic growth – it is a major priority for us in Scotland as in the rest of the UK, and it will remain so.

The emphasis of this new approach is to encourage private sector managers and those with high levels of administrative and managerial competence to take up work in the public sector and to improve its strategic and delivery capacities. As with the drive towards KWs in parts of England, the Scottish approach is founded on a belief that particular types of workers have the potential to not only transform public sector agencies but also to instil new forms of entrepreneurial working. Within Scotland the theme of sustainable communities has taken a similar course to debates in the rest of the UK.

Across England, there have also been tensions over which areas should be prioritised as being most in need of KW support. The National Housing Federation (2005), for example, has increasingly argued that it is in rural areas across England, not just in the South East, that the problems of sustainable community-building are most acute. The Labour government's unwillingness to restrict or disincentivise the purchasing of second homes, allied to restrictive rural planning and the polarised nature of rural labour markets, has undermined many rural communities. The Federation, along with others, now explicitly calls for an extension of the KW housing scheme to make specific provision for rural workers as their absence both reflects and reproduces reductions in public service provision and community sustainability. In other areas such as North Yorkshire there are also growing calls for KW programmes to be rolled out for similar reasons. This spatial selectivity in the programme reflects the long-standing tension in area-based policies over the drawing of boundaries and the inclusion and exclusion of particular areas. It seems likely that with strong house-price growth across the UK, the political pressure for the spatial expansion of the scheme may build up.

Where the scheme is running, the process of KW selection has been a recurring source of tension and debate. In the words of one ODPM interviewee: 'Everybody is a KW. We don't define who a KW is but we work with stakeholders to identify who, in what circumstances needs assistance as a KW'. The three sectors that have been identified as the central focus of policy have been in the fields of health, education, and 'community safety'. Identifying KWs in these sectors has resulted from discussions between ministers, civil servants, and public sector managers. In healthcare, for example, in the early 2000s London National Health Service (NHS) managers called for extra assistance to be given to cancer specialists as there was a lack of retention in this sector. Similarly, new community safety officers have been identified by the Home Office as KWs as an expanding area of recruitment. As one officer remarked, 'We get lobbied constantly to include new workers from TUs [trades unions], government departments and everybody else ... we've only got so much and we have to make decisions in consultation with others'. At other scales other interests have also been pushing for the boundaries of the KWLP to be expanded. Committee minutes reveal that regional bodies such as the South East RHB have started to consider the processes through which there could be 'a broadening of the definition [of KWs] to include other essential workers according to varying local circumstances' (South East RHB, 2005, p 2). Others such as teaching trades unions have also pushed for the KW scheme to be expanded to include support for classroom assistants who play an increasingly important role in the delivery of education policy (see below).

However, as with earlier rounds of KW policy the categories of a KW and a non-KW are also *ascribed* through a combination of social, political, and economic processes of boundary drawing. The selection criteria within the KWLP also contain pernicious and implicit divisions between different workers, based on their labour market position. For instance, assistance is only available to 'permanent employees', not to workers on flexible, short-term contracts. For those involved in education there is also a competitive, relational 'points system' that allocates points to particular types of worker (see Box 7.2). This system has marginalised particular workers from KW support. For example, the contracting out of public sector employment has changed the modus operandi of public sector labour markets and has created a new class of non-permanent employees. Within the KWLP the restriction on non-permanent staff has, therefore, become critical and

Box 7.2: The Key Worker Living Programme: qualification criteria for those in the education sector

Under the KWLP, assistance of up to £100,000 is available to those who are:

- teachers in Greater London;
- unable to buy a home suitable for their household needs within a reasonable travel-to-work area of their employment;
- permanent employees;
- have indefinite leave to remain (excluding KWs from the European Union);
- have household income that does not exceed £80,000 per annum;
- sell their existing property if they own one;
- work in a school that is in receipt of public funds.

In addition, applicants must score a minimum of seven points to qualify, from the following:

- advanced skills teacher – 5 points
- first grades teacher – 5 points
- commissioner's teacher – 2 points
- fast-track teacher – 2 points
- shortage subject teacher – 2 points
- head teacher, deputy/assistant head teacher – 3 points
- extra responsibilities – 1-3 points
- challenging schools – 1-5 points depending on severity of problems.

Those not receiving enough points may still qualify for £50,000 Open Market Homebuy payments.

Source: ODPM (2006)

restrictive. Not only do contracted-out workers often lose their entitlements to pensions and career progression, but they also fail to qualify for urgently needed housing assistance. In some cases new micro-boundaries on inclusion and exclusion have been drawn with organisations such as the Metropolitan Police even stipulating that its station officers are eligible for support with the exception of those in three London police stations (Sutton, Bromley, and Lewisham) in which the front-desk work has been contracted out. ODPM project managers admitted that the contracting out of staff in the public sector had created a particular difficulty for the KWLP. As one interviewee noted:

> The essence of contracting out is that providers provide the service at a cheaper rate. How they pay their staff and what assistance they give them with housing or transport costs is a matter for them ... there is nothing that we can do about it. It is a cost to be met by the private sector as a part of their contract. Any interference from us would skew the competitive bidding process.

This 'skewing' of the competitive principle would mean, in effect, that public sector resources under schemes such as the KWLP would be used by private sector agencies to subsidise their costs. It is ironic that 'non-intervention' in the case of contracted-out staff, for example, is justified in terms of market 'distortions', whereas the distortions created by support to KWs are justified in terms of wider socioeconomic and community gain.

The focus of such support can also change. In the case of the London NHS the emphasis on cancer specialists has now been renegotiated as the problems with recruitment and retention have become less urgent. Similarly, town planners have become eligible KWs owing to a decline in their numbers in the South East at a time when their professional skills are increasingly in demand. The shortages of qualified planners in London during the 2000s have encouraged London authorities to poach staff from neighbouring areas – the same areas that the government has identified as being at the heart of the sustainable community programme. These 'knock-on' effects have been posing problems both for government and regional and local planning agencies.

It could also be argued that the use of such market-based solutions to the problem of labour shortages is designed to instil market values and a market-driven stakeholder politics into the governmentalities of KWs. Rising house prices are seen as beneficial to individuals and the KWLP encourages workers to become consumers in the housing market – indeed, it offers a vision in which sustainable, active citizenship is closely tied to home ownership, with workers living embedded in their (sustainable) communities. In this sense, KW housing programmes also seek to establish new forms of *fixity* within spatial labour markets in order to help build sustainable communities. As with post-war programmes, KWs are now finding themselves locked into employment positions and de facto become dependent on state support to maintain their quality of life. The KWLP requires KWs to remain in their jobs for a period of time as loan repayments will commence once the value of a property rises or two years after a KW leaves a profession. It is, therefore, being used to deliberately reduce the flexibility of public sector KWs and lock individuals into dependent relationships with their work. This direct linking of employment to quality of life may, over time, alter the balance of the worker–employer relationship, with bargaining power being transferred to the latter.

The attachment of state resources to KWs has also had an effect on the ways in which other actors, such as builders and developers, operate. In the absence of New Town Development Corporations (NTDCs) or strong regional planning bodies, sustainable communities are to be constructed by private developers working in partnership with private sector organisations. There is some early evidence that some developers are seeking to take advantage of the funding opportunities offered by the KWLP at the expense of non-KW affordable housing. The location and scale of house-building in the South East of England has become a fiercely contested political issue at the local and regional scale (see Pacione, 2004). Despite the government's emphasis on 'balancing housing supply and demand', the construction of new houses has generated significant levels of protest on environmental, social, and economic grounds (see English Heritage, 2004; Council for the Protection of Rural England, 2006) and rates of house-building have remained relatively low. As a number of interviewees admitted, constructing homes for KWs has been less controversial and has represented a mechanism through which developers and state agencies have been able to promote house-building while limiting criticism. As one KW project manager noted (emphasis added):

> 'The type of people who are KWs are those who are seen as "good" people. For the mortgage companies and development industry they are safe bets with steady incomes and they are unlikely to lose their jobs. For developers and planners they are good because they are popular with existing residents – you know they are "good" people who deserve assistance and can help raise the profile of the neighbourhood – *they are everybody's idea of successful mixed housing and are a part of any community.*'

KWs, therefore, represent the politically acceptable face of social housing in a context where developers and house-builders are being forced to provide more mixed housing in their developments. By creating units for KWs, developers are able to claim that they are providing 'social' housing and are creating spaces for citizens who are essential to the functioning of communities and places. Other research has shown that there is a strong tendency for house purchasers to choose locations in which their neighbours possess similar class backgrounds and aspirations to themselves (see Butler and Robson, 2003; Savage et al, 2005). Selling developments on the basis that their social housing residents will consist of professional KWs is likely to improve their market value.

On a broader canvass, ODPM respondents suggested that thus far the KWLP had not generated significant regional tensions across the public sector. In some sectors of the labour market, it is argued, there is now a significant regional turnover of younger staff for whom a period of employment in London or the South East is seen as a part of a career-cycle move, in which they move back to the regions once experience has been gained. But as an ODPM officer commented in interview, 'The fact that it is the RHBs that request KW support and that the resources are not coming out of other budgets, there is lack of argument between regions'. There is also some evidence that the programme is being considered in other parts of the country where spatial inequalities have grown rapidly since the mid-1990s and public services are coming under staff recruitment and retention pressure. In some places outside of the East and South East, local agencies are taking it upon themselves to build KW homes. In Bath, for example, a local housing association has recently started selling off some of its expensive town flats in order to raise money for KW housing so that the community can become more balanced and functional (see Box 7.3). Such local initiatives provide evidence that the concept and delivery of KW policy looks set to remain high up the housing agenda.

Box 7.3: KW housing in Bath

In February 2005, the housing association Somer Housing, in Bath, embarked on a scheme to sell off some of its most expensive properties and use the proceeds for a programme of KW house-building. Housing markets in Bath and neighbouring Bristol have been subject to rapid increases in the 1990s and 2000s and 'the situation has become particularly acute with even directors in the health service finding they cannot afford to live in the city and having to look to homes further afield' (Morris, 2005, p 1). As Morris recounts, the housing association responded to this increasingly ill-balanced situation by selling expensive properties and using the money to attract further grants to be able to afford to buy land and develop 22 new KW homes. The local hospital has also launched initiatives to try to expand the number of available homes for its workers, many of whom cited accommodation difficulties as their main reason for leaving.

KW housing and the wider politics of state selection

As we saw in Chapter Three, the notion of spatially or socially targeted policies creates particular tensions as it necessitates the *institutionalisation of divisions* between different groups of interests. For instance, there are clear parallels between the ways in which the trades union movement was divided over post-war KW schemes and the ways in which the current TUC leadership is seeking to mediate between the voices of different unions and develop a consistent and coherent policy. As one TUC official noted in interview:

> 'The TUC is not strong on regional policy and regional jealousies are currently up the agenda ... but as a movement we fight for fair pay and against bad practice wherever it takes places, not just in particular regions.'

The TUC is officially opposed to the concept of the 'key' worker and argues that rather than creating particular groups and supporting them through housing subsidies, more affordable, public sector housing should be made available for the benefit of all workers. A representative commented in interview:

> 'The fundamental root of the KW debate is about housing and good quality and available public housing should be a right of all workers ... the KWLP is just a sticking plaster, what is required is more supply in the housing market.'

However, for different unions representing different groups of workers there is not so much unanimity. Interviews with unions that represent low-paid public sector workers, for example, revealed a high degree of hostility to the discourses and practices of KW programmes. As one prominent representative of one of the UK's biggest trades unions argued:

> 'We simply do not accept the concept of the key worker for four reasons: it creates divisive definitional problems; vital jobs are excluded; it frames debates over housing and worker support; and it is based on a series of assumptions about what workers do.'

Others highlighted the relatively arbitrary nature of KW selection and pointed to anomalies in which district nurses and teachers qualify for support but healthcare and teaching assistants do not, even though their roles have become increasingly intertwined. In addition, some sets of workers, such as home care workers (who are often female), are so poorly paid that schemes to assist with the purchase of a house are unrealistic in the absence of significant pay rises. Other union representatives highlighted some of the practical problems that have beset the KWLP. It was considered that the schemes are inherently divisive and there was evidence that this was causing feelings of resentment among workers excluded from assistance. There was also a confusing diversity of information and misinformation concerning complex questions over eligibility and accessibility. There were also concerns raised over the transparency of the support being given to some groups of workers and which state agencies are responsible for its implementation.

However, this scepticism over KW policy was not shared by all trades unions. Some teaching unions' representatives, for example, expressed qualified support for KW definitions and programmes. There was an instrumental rationality to this support – that KW programmes can assist in the retention and recruitment of staff in the London area. However, there was also a clear social/cultural rationale in that, in one respondent's words:

> 'When you become a teacher you have an expectation of
> good housing and that you will have a sufficient income
> for a good quality of living and a reasonable lifestyle ...
> you need a place to relax and to go home and work ...
> teachers need this in a way that other groups of workers
> do not, it is all about aspirations and teachers' aspirations
> are higher than other groups and this needs to be reflected
> in government policy.'

It was argued that without such support, teachers, as skilled individuals, will find themselves other jobs, particularly in a context where the costs of housing have increased. Owner-occupation is still cited as a minimum requirement for teachers as 'council housing is not what a teacher aspires to', as one interviewee commented. Some of the teaching unions have, therefore, called for the programme to be extended, particularly at the top end of the scale for head teachers whose skills are needed in 'problem' areas such as inner cities and whose presence in such places the state should seek to support and encourage.

What is of particular interest here is the way in which relational

classifications of citizenship, underpinned by resource transfers between
different groups, institutionalise and reinforce divisions between types
of workers in different places. Workers and worker representatives are
asked to justify why their workers should be entitled to specific forms
of support at the same time as others are excluded from it. This political
process of inclusion/exclusion has taken on both a social and spatial
character with tensions arising over the different 'needs' of different
classes of workers and different regional and local circumstances. One
teaching union representative, for instance, noted:

> 'You just don't get problems filling classes with classroom
> assistants or getting secretaries. These people are local, they
> are happy with their lot and happy to do a local job, there's
> never a problem filling vacancies. For teachers coming into
> an area from outside it is a different story. They expect and
> deserve a house of their own and their skills are needed in
> these localities.'

In a context of increasingly scarce housing resources in the London
area the relational divisions between different groups take on even
more significance. Low-skilled, often part-time workers are being
ascribed with particular roles, needs, and aspirations. These, it is argued,
are relationally different from those of more 'professional' citizens whose
expectations and importance to the functioning of communities are
greater.

Within the interviews it was also noted that there were growing
spatial divisions that were impacting on the efficiency of particular
spatial economies and sustainable communities. For example, London-
based representatives of some trades unions explicitly argued for extra
provision to be made for London-based KWs. As one local activist
noted: 'It is simple – there simply is no cheap housing anywhere in
London, period. It is just not the same elsewhere and I'm delighted
that something is being done about it'. However, others noted that
the issue of KW assistance was creating some tensions across the union
movement, particularly in relation to the boundaries where KW
programmes start and end. As one interview noted: 'It is at the cliff
edges that we have problems, with those on the wrong sides of the
divide being unhappy about what London-based workers are getting'.
Others referred to the regional differences that were emerging over
what was perceived as favouritism on the part of government to the
issues affecting public sector workers in the capital. In other 'hotspots'
of development, such as North Yorkshire and some parts of the M4

corridor, the absence of a KW support programme has been criticised for being unfair.

Business community representatives in London and the South East have in general been supportive of the rolling out of the KWLP. The Confederation of British Industry's (CBI's) official policy on KW housing is that it represents a 'key business issue' and that labour markets are becoming increasingly uncompetitive and dysfunctional owing to a lack of housing supply. Digby Jones (2005), the Director General, for example, told the CBI Congress in 2005:

> 'I want a society where the lower-paid postal workers, nurses, and teachers, especially south of Birmingham can afford a house. They can't at the moment ... we are going to have people not being able to live in a home of their own in Great Britain.'

This focus on the needs of lower-paid, public sector workers is presented as a problem for the efficient functioning of businesses as public and private sector labour markets are fundamentally interrelated. At the same time, it was further argued that:

> 'We are not going to be a place where overseas investors are going to want to invest. We've always been the location of choice in Europe for the Boardrooms of Detroit, Tokyo, Johannesburg, Frankfurt, to create the wealth, pay tax, build schools and hospitals. I want that to continue. But if they can't get the labour because there's nowhere to live they won't come.'

The CBI's focus however, is on a more holistic agenda in which the planning system is freed up and made less restrictive in order to allow the house-building industry to deliver all the homes required. Notwithstanding the environmental tensions that such an agenda would create (see Environment Agency, 2005), the expectation is that the law of supply and demand will work if government provides the right incentives and opportunities. The apparent tensions involved in supporting market-based solutions, while at the same time backing direct public intervention through programmes such as the KWLP, are not readily acknowledged. Both the TUC and CBI do, however, see KW housing programmes as a short-term solution for wider market and planning failure, even if the former also sees the policy as part of a wider social housing programme.

However, within the social housing sector there is evidence of growing disquiet over the potential knock-on effects of KW housing support. During the mid-2000s organisations such as the Association of London Government were arguing that there needed to be a new balance between the needs of KWs and other social housing projects. As one of the Association of London Government's statements succinctly puts it:

> Although we are seeing a welcome increase in government investment in housing, this is limited and mainly targeted at homeless households and certain public sector workers. It is unlikely to make a significant difference to the average London worker. (ALG, 2004a, p 3)

Its own surveys of those involved in the social housing sector in London indicated, for example, that in many communities 'there is a risk of key workers and those needing social housing being perceived as 'deserving' and 'undeserving' respectively' (ALG, 2004a, p 5). Because of this divisiveness, social housing policy should therefore 'prioritise social rented housing and increase the proportion of social rented rather than key worker homes' (p 2). In terms of the delivery of the KWLP there are also growing complaints that it helps those who are best able to help themselves – a criticism common to the post-war KW programmes discussed in Chapter Four. Once again the Association of London Government (ALG, 2004b, p 3) argue that 'the current definition of key workers is too narrow, and should be expanded to recognise the many groups of workers who find it hard to access housing'. They go on to argue that the scheme should be linked to specific employment centres and a closer understanding of the needs and priorities of KWs.

Overall, then, the re-establishment of KW support programmes has been enmeshed within a wider politics and this section has highlighted some of the political debates that the KWLP has stirred both within and outside of government. As schemes have become more important in discursive and material terms, so debates at different scales and in different places have intensified and, in many ways, become more divisive. This politics exemplifies the wider processes inherent in the sustainable communities agenda and the form and character of contemporary spatial policy agendas. Its attempts to generate selective forms of mobility and, perhaps more importantly, fixity have been partial and relatively voluntaristic, reflecting wider state objectives and forms of regulation.

Conclusions

This chapter has examined the relationships between sustainable community-building, KW support programmes, and the changing form and character of British spatial policy under New Labour. It has illustrated the close interrelationships that exist between imaginations of competitive places, labour markets, and functioning communities and the types of policy initiatives that have been developed to bring communities somewhere closer to these imagined norms. These new imaginations are in turn constructed upon specific understandings of the concepts and practices of sustainable development, the capacities the state now possesses to bring to fruition a coherent spatial development strategy, and how the competitiveness of places is to be sustained. The priority for policy is to ensure that within new sustainable communities particular types of workers are present, as their absence would undermine their broader efficiency and functionality. Conceptions of balance and harmony have taken on a particular, politically constructed form with significant consequences for those who are included and excluded from the new arrangements. Whatever the strengths and weaknesses of the KW programmes it seems likely that they will remain a policy priority in the medium to long term.

The chapter has also demonstrated that such programmes are inherently divisive. KW definitions require relational distinctions to be made between different groups of citizens whose 'value' to community-building and economic sustainability is politically defined in relation to spatial policy priorities and objectives. Boundaries of entitlement have to be drawn between different citizens based on often loosely articulated definitions of individual and community need. Assistance for KWs acts as a politically legitimate form of state intervention. In line with wider Blairite and Third Way thinking it is a form of government expenditure that helps those who have already helped themselves, while at the same time playing a pivotal role in sustainable community-building and the enhancement of spatial economic competitiveness in an increasingly global world. For a place to 'function' in social and economic terms, it is argued, it requires the presence of such workers even if this comes at the expense of other, less qualified and less well-paid workers and residents. As discussed above, one consequence of this is that social housing priorities are being skewed towards these 'deserving' cases. A politics of aspiration has been mobilised and developed to legitimate this new agenda of inequality so that direct support becomes a legitimate and acceptable government activity.

The comparisons between these contemporary programmes and their earlier spatial policy precedents also reveal much about the continuities and changes in the form and character of state intervention. One continuity relates to the policies' emphasis on voluntarism and the boundaries of rights and responsibilities between the state and KWs. Governments have not seen it to be in their power to compel workers to move. The right to mobility is instead channelled through market provision and the choices of citizens to act as consumers of places. Through the planning system and public sector employment, governments have some direct and indirect capacity to influence spatial patterns of employment and this process of shaping and influencing has been at the heart of rationalities and objectives of spatial policy since the end of the Second World War. However, where the absence of particular types of workers has become a 'problem', state agencies have sought to encourage their mobility and fixity, often with limited success. There are also clear similarities in the imaginations of places that are called upon to justify and shape labour mobility programmes with the post-war notions of balance and harmony being integrated into contemporary discourses of the sustainable community.

In other ways there are significant differences. The new agendas look to sustain and enhance the growth of the core regions of the UK in the belief that the benefits of their globally oriented growth will trickle down to the rest of the country. The post-war concept of donor–recipient regions has been turned on its head so that the development needs of the core regions take precedence. The targeting of programmes such as those for KWs reflects and reproduces these new rationalities. As inequalities have increased between different segments of spatial labour markets, so new planning strategies have had to be adopted to try to ensure that the broader needs of capital accumulation are sustained. In this way the notion of sustainability has been interpreted and deployed to meet particular ends. There has also been a greater emphasis on the extent to which the provision of social infrastructure and the availability of the means of social consumption and reproduction both *sustain and enhance* modern forms of economic competitiveness. This concern with the relationships between production and consumption is not new, in and of itself (see Chapters Three and Four), but it has taken on a different form with less direct support to producers and more to the provision of social and environmental infrastructure. There has also been a renewed interest in the ways in which the movements of people can also tackle the socioeconomic problems of the spatial economy and it is to these that the next chapter now turns.

Notes

[1] In many ways sustainable development reflects the globalisation of development discourses. It has become ubiquitous in both developed and developing countries. This owes much to the ways in which powerful institutions, from the World Bank to the European Union, have pushed the term as a conditional requirement for local projects to adopt.

[2] RHBs were established as part of the *Sustainable Communities* plan in 2003 to ensure that housing policies would be better integrated with the regional, spatial, transport, economic, and sustainable development strategies.

[3] Letter to Regional Housing Boards from Rt Hon Keith Hill MP, ODPM, London, February 2004, paragraph 3.

[4] Letter to Regional Housing Boards from Rt Hon Keith Hill MP, ODPM, London, February 2004, paragraph 4.

EIGHT

Managed migration, sustainable community-building, and international labour movements

In short, we're trying to get the right people with the right skills in the right place at the right time. (Skills for Business Network, 2005a, p 1)

Immigration and politics do not make easy bedfellows. They never have. We need few reminders of what can happen when the politics of immigration gets out of hand. (Tony Blair, 2004, p 2)

Introduction

The discourse of globalisation is inherently bound up with the increased mobility of information, capital, and people (see Arte-Scholte, 2003). It is presented by some as representing a new era in which such flows are becoming quantitatively and qualitatively more significant and in which there is a new freedom of movement (see Ohmae, 1997; Gogia, 2006). However, within this wider discourse the movement of labour between countries has been anything but free and the whole question of labour mobility has become one of the most politically contentious aspects of change. Critics of globalisation point to its inconsistencies. On the one hand its advocates celebrate (and pursue) a vision of transnational capital mobility and freedom, the benefits of which are experienced by a wider cross-section of the world's population in the 2000s than at any time in the past (see Giddens, 2002b). On the other hand, however, the same governments and thinkers that champion the mobility of capital have placed new restrictions and limitations on international labour and population mobility (see Klein, 2002; Bauman, 2005). The era of globalisation has seen the creation of new barriers and mechanisms of control that seek to strengthen the borders between areas of labour availability and those areas where jobs are in short supply. Despite this, processes of globalisation have also indirectly created the conditions through which new forms of legal and illegal cross-border movements of people take place. The labour markets of cities such as London and New York are now characterised by a remarkable diversity of communities and workers from a variety of destinations (see Sassen, 1999b). With the growth in modes of connection between places and an enhanced awareness of the 'opportunities' available in different parts of the world, new forms of migration have emerged and are becoming stronger.

For governments in countries such as the UK, this mobility of workers, particularly when viewed as an externally generated phenomenon, has been perceived as a threat by many policy-makers and others (Sassen, 1999a; see Chapter Two of this book for an extended discussion). It represents an imagined 'influx' of workers that has the potential to 'overwhelm' state services and lead to the destabilisation of economic and social harmony and order. However, the argument is also increasingly made that if such mobility is effectively controlled, managed, and regulated and if cross-border movements are seen as a logical and rational response to identifiable shortages of labour, then the movement of workers becomes a more legitimate policy goal that can help to tackle particular problems of government.

At the same time, wider trends are having an impact on policy thinking. Across the European Union (EU) demographic changes are putting new pressures on the sustainability of socioeconomic systems. Significant labour mobility provides perhaps the only realistic mechanism through which this demographic decline is realistically going to be tackled. The Office of National Statistics (ONS, 2005) predicts that the UK population, for example, is expected to increase by 7.2 million between 2004 and 2031 *but* this growth will be primarily caused by immigration, not natural increase. At the same time, global populations are rapidly expanding and average ages across the less developed world are falling.

In addition, the unbalanced economic development of countries like the UK has created particular labour market problems in particular areas. As Chapter Seven demonstrated, the debate around key workers (KWs) and sustainable communities agendas has been driven by the problems of sustainability now faced in faster-growing parts of the country. There are new demands for public sector workers, at a variety of levels, to maintain public services. At the same time, the presence of (increasingly mobile) entrepreneurs and knowledge workers, particularly in high-tech industries, has been increasingly presented as a vehicle for new forms of economic growth. Controlled and managed labour migration provides one mechanism through which public and private sector labour vacancies can be filled, with the additional bonus that the significant costs of training such workers have, in large part, been met elsewhere (see Hutton, 2003). For Sassen (1999a) it exemplifies new conceptions of the role of national borders that are no longer sites for imposing levies but rather transmitting membranes guaranteeing the free flow of goods, capital, and information. In short, 'since the start of the new century immigration has been recognised as part of the solution to many issues in the political economy of First World states, as well as a problem for them' (Jordan and Duvell, 2002, p 154).

This chapter explores these issues through a discussion of the relationships between (im)migration policy under New Labour and its wider strategies for spatial development and social cohesion. It examines the ways in which the government has sought to address these problems and what its strategies have been. No issue exemplifies the guiding themes of this book in a more direct way, as any understanding of the government's approach requires an explanation of its imaginations of places and spaces, the politics of mobility, and the dilemmas and possibilities it faces in the operationalisation of spatial policy in a context of changing modes of state regulation and control. The chapter argues that policy has been directly linked to conceptions of what constitutes a functioning, balanced, and efficient labour market in the regions of the UK and the relationships between the spatial location of different forms of work and worker. It begins by discussing the recent shift to a so-called 'managed migration' policy, before turning to the example of the National Health Service (NHS) to exemplify wider philosophies and strategies of action. It also discusses the growing role of the EU and the wider politics of immigration and (sustainable) community-building.

Globalisation, sustainable community-building, and managed migration

The roots of contemporary policies need to be explored in relation to the experiences of earlier programmes and the changing perceptions of social and economic processes outlined in earlier chapters. Chapter Five examined the ways in which immigration policy was increasingly tightened in the inter-war decades as governments sought to take more control over the mobility of workers. The 1971 Immigration Act further tightened the regulations and was particularly aimed at controlling flows of Ugandan Asians to the UK who were expelled by the dictator Idi Amin.[1] Mrs Thatcher's 1981 British Nationality Act introduced a Primary Purpose Rule that forbade the entry of spouses of migrating workers to the UK in an attempt to restrict non-essential immigration. The Act also forced elderly dependants to show that they had no relatives in their countries of origin and that they were wholly dependent on their children living in the UK. And yet, despite this tightening of restrictions a new emphasis on selective *types* of labour mobility gradually became not only acceptable but also increasingly desirable. During the 1980s and early 1990s the emphasis on 'knowledge workers' and 'entrepreneurs' went hand in hand with a celebration of the benefits of overseas investment into the UK and the forging of economic links between different countries (see Chapter Six).

This acceptance of the important role that highly skilled labour migrants could play in economic modernisation was taken up with enthusiasm by the Blair government. Ever since coming to power in 1997 it has argued that social and economic contexts within which the UK is competing are changing rapidly and that in order for the UK to maintain its competitiveness its socioeconomic systems need to adapt (see Raco, 2002; Brown, 2006). New migration policy measures have, therefore, sought to simultaneously restrict (or forcibly remove) so-called 'economic' or 'bogus' migrants on the one hand, and encourage the selective in-migration of KWs on the other. This 'managed migration' strategy is unequivocally based on the wish 'to manage legal migration in the interests of the UK economy' (Home Office, 2005a, p 1). Labour migration is to be used to further the competitiveness of the UK economy and its regions, particularly those that require an expansion of labour availability and where 'there are opportunities for people with very different types and level of skill' (Home Office, 2005a, p 1). As with other labour market-building strategies examined in the book, the new policies are primarily concerned with particular, selective imaginations of places, how they function, and how their competitiveness and cohesion can be sustained in the longer term.

As justification for its new strategies the government points to international research and 'good practice' that demonstrates the scale of the benefits that can now be accrued from a highly skilled labour migration policy. For example, the Organisation for Economic Co-operation and Development's (OECD's) study of the US calculates that approximately 900,000 professionals entered the North American labour market between 1990 and 2000 and that in 2000 such individuals accounted for approximately one-sixth of the country's total information technology (IT) workforce (Guellec, 2003). During the second half of the 1990s the number of researchers grew by 5% per year in the OECD and 7% in the US (Guellec, 2003, p 2). The advantages for the host economy of such movements, the OECD argues, are numerous as many skilled migrants have gone on to become high-tech entrepreneurs. Other evidence for this trend comes from the Silicon Valley where in 1998 one-quarter of hi-tech firms were headed by immigrants from China and India, collectively generating almost $17 billion in sales and more than 50,000 jobs (Guellec, 2003). This 'demonstration effect', it is argued, underpins a regional culture of entrepreneurialism and dynamism. Migrants also tend to become more involved in international business and information networks. These in turn enable firms and regions to tap into new sources of innovation and trade, thereby boosting their economic competitiveness.

Just as the presence of such workers represents a vehicle for economic growth, so their absence, and presence elsewhere, has the potential to destabilise established spatial economies. In Meyer's (2003, p 1) terms:

> In the global knowledge-based economy, the international mobility of skills-holders has become viewed as a natural extension of the traditional cosmopolitan character of the world's scientific community. At the same time since research and development has become a major source of wealth and of socioeconomic development, there is intense competition between nations to attract qualified scientists and technologists.

In short, many economists and policy-makers argue that globalisation makes the enhanced mobility of skilled workers inevitable and that states should seek to identify the policies they can pursue that would make their cities and regions more attractive and accommodating (see, in particular, Florida, 2004). If these ways of characterising labour markets and global economies are accepted then strategies that attract these KWs become a priority. And yet, the focus on such workers is underpinned by particular, politically charged definitions of who does and who does not constitute a KW and how their needs can be identified and 'satisfied'. It conveniently focuses on the needs of those who are already materially and discursively privileged in the global economic system, while excluding those in the weakest positions (see Peck, 2005). There are close parallels here with the ways that post-war policy-makers sought to define the needs and aspirations of KWs within UK regional policy and the types of imaginations, dilemmas, and inequalities that such programmes involved (see Chapter Three).

One of the problems facing policy-makers is that the movement of skilled workers between places is, in practice, a highly complex and multidirectional process. Such workers often 'do not arrive at their destination alone ... and seldom break all ties with their country of origin' (Regets, 2003, p 1). Greater freedom of mobility enables skilled migrants to adopt mobility patterns that are less predictable and stable than those whose movement is restricted and controlled (Duleep and Regets, 1998). The longer-term implications of this may be that 'countries on the receiving end may find their 'brain gain' more short-lived, as highly mobile and educated individuals find alternative options' (Regets, 2003, p 2). As with other aspects of global investment, enhanced mobility has many dimensions and implications. Reducing barriers to mobility for certain groups not only generates and reinforces new labour market inequalities but also increases the prospects for zero-sum territorial competition between places in their anxiety to ensure that enough key or essential workers are present. As Amin and Thrift (1995) argue, holding on to any form of mobile production asset in the medium term becomes increasingly difficult as countries develop new ways of encouraging selected forms of mobility and immobility.

The movement of skilled workers into and out of the UK represents one of the best examples of these multiple processes in action. In 2005 the World Bank claimed that the UK lost more skilled workers to the global 'brain drain' than any other country. More than 1.44 million graduates (16.7%) left the UK to look for more highly paid employment, primarily in anglophone countries such as Canada, the US, and Australia – a legacy of the colonial emigration policies outlined in Chapter Five (see also Thornton, 2005). In-migration rates have not matched these outflows with only 1.26 million graduates entering the UK during the same period. For the World Bank this reflects 'an economic problem for developed countries. For countries such as the UK, a brain drain is clearly a loss. It may impact on the rate of growth and the number of innovations that create growth in the long run' (F. Docquier, quoted in *The Independent*, 2005, p 5).

However, this focus on skilled workers and 'brain drains' at the top end of the labour market shifts attention away from the wider problem of underemployment of less skilled workers across the UK economy. The Equal Opportunities Commission (2005), for example, has highlighted the 'hidden brain drain of 5.6 million part-timers in Great Britain who are working below their potential, one in five of the working population' (p 5). Other writers speak of brain 'gains' associated with recipient areas and the spatial patterns of flows of skilled workers between different places. The emphasis on skilled workers and their 'brains', therefore, reflects and reproduces a wider politics of place-building in which the needs of lower-skilled workers receive much less attention that those of so-called 'wealth creators'. As KWs, skilled professionals are portrayed as the prized assets of the modern global economy (see Nunn, 2004). Expanding and enhancing the skills of 'non-essential' workers has become less of a priority particularly in a context where the focus is increasingly on what places 'have to do' to make themselves attractive investment sites in the new global economy.

Making migration work: the new migration policies

It is within this wider context that the UK government has pursued a series of programmes to attract skilled migrants. Its most significant statement was the publication in 2005 of *Controlling Our Borders: Making Migration Work for Britain* (Home Office, 2005b). The strategy explicitly calls for new forms of migrant selection and represents a clear example of the differential porosity of the UK's borders to different types of workers. Skilled migrants are presented as KWs who play an essential social and economic role. In Blair's (2005, p 5) terms:

> Our vital public services depend upon skilled staff from overseas. Far from being a burden on these services, our expanding NHS, for example, would have difficulty meeting the needs of patients without foreign-born nurses and doctors. The expertise of IT and finance professionals from India, the USA and the EU help maintain London as the financial centre of the world.

The emphasis is, therefore, on 'managed migration' as 'good for this country'. Indeed, Blair goes on to state that 'it is essential for our continued prosperity' (p 5). Or in the words of the Chancellor, Gordon Brown (2006), policy needs to ensure that Britain becomes 'the location of choice' for businesses and skilled workers.

The argument is expanded throughout *Controlling Our Borders*. Migrants, for example, 'have brought dynamism to the economy, the most successful of them have created many jobs for others' (Home Office, 2005b, p 17). Skilled migrants are said to bring new ideas and new ways of working that are essential ingredients to the competitiveness of the UK economy. They instil new attitudes and, in so doing:

help meet labour shortages, easing inflationary pressures and increasing productivity. They make an important contribution to our broader government objectives to increase innovation to respond to the challenges of global economic change, to shift towards a high-skill economy and to deliver high-quality public services. (pp 17-18)

There is, therefore, a 'good economic case for allowing certain skilled workers to stay. Research shows that their economic contribution grows the longer they stay as they acquire increased UK specific skills and experience' (p 21). This wider rationality is reflected in the government's core principles of immigration policy, as outlined in Box 8.1.

Box 8.1: Immigration policy principles under New Labour

The Labour government's principles for an immigration policy are:

(1) A recognition of the benefits that controlled migration brings not just to the economy but also to delivering the public and private services on which we rely.

(2) Being clear that all those who come here to work and study must be able to support themselves. There can be no access to state support or housing for the economically inactive.

(3) We will continue to tackle abuses in the asylum system, including through the legislation currently before parliament which will establish a single tier of appeal and clamp down on asylum seekers who deliberately destroy their documents and lie about their identity.

(4) Action on illegal immigration through the introduction of ID cards and millions invested in strengthening border controls.

(5) Celebrating the major achievements of migrants in the country and the success of our uniquely British model of diversity. But alongside that an explicit expectation that rights must be balanced by responsibilities. That there are clear obligations that go alongside British residency and ultimately citizenship – to reject extremism and intolerance and make a positive contribution to UK society.

(6) An acknowledgement that there is no longer a neat separation between the domestic and the international. In a world of global interdependence our policies on migration cannot be isolated from our policies on international development or EU enlargement.

Source: Adapted from Blair (2004, p 2)

In order to facilitate this functionalist–instrumentalist approach to immigration the government has set up 'independent', business-led quangos to advise it on the needs of particular sectors and the categories that should underpin citizen selection procedures. As former Home Secretary Charles Clarke (2005, p 7) makes clear, 'We will set up an independent body to advise us on labour market needs. The system will be flexible and employer-led. This is what our economy needs, not a rigid, arbitrary quota'. The prioritisation of employer-led advice in this way represents an attempt to demonstrate the government's commitment to wider questions of economic competitiveness. It has sought to legitimate its migration programmes through the deployment of the combined discourses of sustainability, globalisation, and labour market-building. Economic competitiveness, it is argued, is premised upon the presence of particular actors who not only tap into broader networks of knowledge, expertise, and resources but also may foster new types of entrepreneurialism in host populations and firms.

These stated principles illustrate the dominant imaginations of places, communities, and economic processes that underpin the Labour government's policies towards migration and economic development. They highlight the relationships between rights and responsibilities and call for migrants to take more responsibility for their own prospects and well-being (see Giddens, 2005). In Blair's own words (2004, p 1):

> British residency and eventually citizenship carries with it obligations as well as opportunities ... the obligation to pay taxes and pay your way. To look after your children and other dependents. The obligation to learn something about the country and culture and language that you are now part of.

If migrants are to be welcomed then, according to government policy, they must act as responsible, active citizens, able to look after themselves, their families, and their wider communities. The links are explicitly made between their presence and the construction of communities of trust and self-reliance. In short, they represent essential building blocks of new, sustainable communities. The right to migration is therefore dependent upon an individual's employment capacities and their desire to become a good British citizen.[2] This rights and responsibility agenda also presupposes that migrants are entering communities that are already balanced and harmonious as it focuses on their direct and indirect obligations and contributions. In Kymlicka's (2003, p 205) terms, 'Native born Britons do not need to change their own habits, practices, or identities ... [the new agendas] expect nothing from them in terms of adaptation'. Instead, the onus is on incomers to adapt to the communities into which they are settling.

There is also a clear attempt to legitimate policy by recourse to economic arguments. In the same way that post-war governments used instrumentalist arguments for immigration to try to quell opposition to their policies, so the Labour government has been keen to highlight the 'contribution' that in-migrants make in economic terms. It claims, for example, that economic growth would be 0.5% lower per annum in the absence of net inflows of people. Tony Blair (2004, p 2) has directly appealed to this individual and community self-interest by stating: 'Lower growth means less individual and family prosperity, and less revenue to spend on public services'. Earlier rounds of workers are credited with 'fuelling the post-war economic boom' and since the late 1980s 'it is the IT and finance professionals from the US, India, and the EU and elsewhere who have driven London's growth as the financial centre of the world in a highly competitive global economic market for services'. The message is clear. In a new global context, controlled migration can help to deliver new forms of economic growth and, in so doing, underpin new forms of community cohesion and sustainability. As Blair (2004, p 1) observes, without immigrants 'our public services would be close to collapse', a point re-emphasised by Lord Dholakia who told the House of Lords in 2005 that:

> Immigration should be looked at on the basis of huge economic benefits for the UK if we are able to adapt to the new environment of the global economy....The stark reality is that if we fail to produce wealth, and it is people who produce wealth, this country cannot sustain health, education, pensions and service provision for future generations.[3]

There is an explicit geography to these agendas. The most cited economic 'sector' that benefits from this inflow of workers is consistently the City of London-based IT and financial sector. In-migration policy has not been embedded into a comprehensive spatial development framework for the whole of the UK. Instead, the emphasis has been on ensuring that globally successful economic sectors, and the increasingly stretched public services that support them, are sustained and their labour requirements satisfied. In this sense it represents an extension of the KW and sustainable communities strategies outlined in earlier chapters.

Policy in practice: the Highly Skilled Migrant Programme

These wider policy objectives and discourses are best exemplified by the introduction in 2002 of the Highly Skilled Migrants Programme (HSMP). Its aim was 'to strike the right balance between enabling employers to recruit or transfer skilled people from abroad and safeguarding the interests of the resident workforce. This assists employers in their business development and helps them to overcome short-term skill shortages that it would not be feasible to meet by training resident workers' (McLaughlin and Salt, 2002, p 3). The HSMP introduced a single points-based migration scheme based upon the criteria laid out in Table 8.1. Applicants are divided into four principal categories:

(i) highly skilled individuals;
(ii) skilled workers with a specific job offer;
(iii) temporary low-skilled worker schemes; and
(iv) specialist and temporary workers, trainees and students.

The treatment of individuals in the different groups varies significantly, reflecting a core concern with economic considerations. For category (i) applicants, the existence of a specific job or position will not be a necessary precondition for entry as it is for the other categories. However, for category (iii) migrants, the government expects to impose future controls:

> In light of EU enlargement it seems unlikely that there will continue to be a case for specific low skills schemes. They will be phased out over time, in consultation with the sectors concerned. If it is agreed that there is a case for any new scheme, it would be on condition that it is ... managed, quota-based, not open to nationals without satisfactory return arrangements, time-limited and subject to review. (Home Office, 2005b, p 38)

Such migrants would also be banned from bringing dependants with them as their presence would not be seen as conducive to balanced communities and spatial economies. The maximum score for an

Table 8.1: Characteristics of the points system for the HSMP

Points criteria	Characteristics	Points
Young person assessment	The dividing line for a 'young person' is 28. Applicants below this age qualify for 5 extra points.	0-5
Qualifications	Points are gained for one of the following: PhD	30
	Masters Degree	25
	Vocational/professional qualifications	15
	Separate provision for MBA graduates	
Relevant work experience	*For those over 28:*	
	5 years + experience of graduate level job	25
	PhD + 3 years in graduate level job	25
	5 years + experience in graduate level job including 2 years in high level management position	35
	10 years + experience in graduate level job including 2 years in high level management position	50
	For those under 28:	
	2 years + work experience in a graduate level job	25
	4 years + work experience in a graduate level job	35
	4 years + work experience in a graduate level job including 1 year in high level management position	50
Earning power	General expectation that highly skilled people earn more than average in *relative* terms. Countries divided into 5 categories (A-E) each with different criteria for what constitutes above average.	25-50
Achievements in your field	(i) Applicants should show 3 examples of significant or outstanding achievement from the following: Industry Prize; published work; peer group reviews; academic references; industry reference; ownership of intellectual property rights; published testimonials; scholarship/research awards; or press articles. (ii) Examples of outstanding achievements including: receipt of a Nobel Prize; an Oscar, BAFTA or Palme d'Or; winning an Olympic medal; achievement of a major sporting world record; election to the premiership or headship of a country or international organisation; establishing a significant company; designing an internationally recognised building.	25
	(iii) Examples of significant other achievements	25
		15
Partner's achievements	Bachelors degree	10
	Vocational/professional qualification equivalent	10
	Current/previous graduate level work	10
Priority application	Limited to doctors who are legally entitled to work as General Medical Practitioners in the UK	50 max.
Other requirements	Proficiency in English language; can continue to work in chosen field; can support oneself without recourse to public funds; intend to make UK main home; no criminal offences.	N/A

Source: Compiled with information from Home Office (2005c) and workpermit.com (2005)

individual is 215 points and the heaviest scoring categories are awarded to experienced entrepreneurs, those with significantly above-average incomes in their home countries, and healthcare workers whose skills are desperately needed by the UK's NHS.

The HSMP's selection criteria are therefore based on a complex set of perspectives, imaginations, and interrelationships between a migrant's value and how they can be embedded into existing communities. These judgements stem from particular ways of viewing people and places and it is to the politics of migration that the chapter now turns.

The scheme was introduced as part of a wider attempt to make migration policy 'work' for the UK economy. Critics in the business community have been pressing the government to introduce such measures to alleviate their own skills shortages and tap into international pools of highly skilled labour. In reference to the HSMP, one prominent business leader, for example, argued strongly that 'if the UK economy is to attract and retain talented and experienced workers from overseas, there has never been a more urgent time to act' (Jackson, 2005, p 1). Without such a scheme the government would be 'closing a door on overseas nationals with skills valued by UK business ... [that] benefits day in-day out from the skills and experience brought to the UK by overseas nationals' (p 1). Such protestations reflect and reproduce the wider concern with ensuring that skilled, creative workers are present in the UK. Again, as Jackson (2005, p 4) notes in her support for the programme:

> Consider the knock-on effects of a delayed response to an HSMP application from a businessperson in New York earning £100,000 a year – just the type of person the HSMP aims to attract. While their application remains in a [processing] queue ... they continue to work in their home country and the UK economy loses the tax on the income they would have earned in the UK had their application been approved, the increased company profit (and consequent tax) that their activities in the UK could have generated, and also their own personal spending power.

Nothing better illustrates the rationality that underpins the new programmes and their explicit support for the attraction of a new, Richard Florida style, globally creative class (Florida, 2004). The implication for policy-makers is clear: attract such KWs or lose your economic competitiveness.

At the time of writing in March 2006 the immigration system was being further reformed and a new five-tier system introduced 'to make it easier for highly-skilled workers to enter the UK, but more difficult for those with fewer or lower skills' (workpermit.com, 2006, p 1). It was proposed that all the different work permit and entry schemes will now be replaced by a single points system in which 'the more skills you have, and the more those skills are in demand, the more points you will gain, increasing your likelihood of entry to the UK' (BBC News Online, 2006b, p 1). It will enable 'UK employers to recruit or transfer people from outside the European Economic Area while safeguarding the interests of resident workers in the UK' (Home Office, 2006, p 1). Details of the five tiers are outlined in Table 8.2.

Such a scheme is indicative of the political pressures associated with labour mobility and boundary crossing. It represents a much-trumpeted but in practice rather limited set of proposed changes that seek to defuse the political tensions of immigration. In *The Economist's* (2006a, p 30) terms, 'By subjecting the huddled masses to a more rigorous-seeming system, the government hopes to calm Britons' nerves'. However, it is also an implicit recognition that the economic sustainability of the very regions that the *Sustainable Communities* plan is seeking to support is being threatened by labour mobility boundaries and the potential immobilisation of particular types of KW. Making those boundaries more selectively permeable is being directly related to these wider regional and national development agendas. In crossing boundaries individual workers are being ascribed with particular attributes and capabilities and individual worth is being categorised in relation to the wider objectives of policy and imaginations of a functioning economy and society.

The politics of managed migration

> Migration policy is concerned not only with the needs of the labour market but also with social cohesion, public protection, international development goals, and human rights. The challenge for migration policy is getting the balance right both within and between these objectives. (Kleinmann, 2003, p 67)

As with debates in the post-war period, outlined at length in Chapter Five, immigration raises a whole set of political tensions and dilemmas at a variety of scales. The government argues that its new policy represents a 'consensus', or 'common-sense' approach. A MORI poll in 2005 (MORI, 2005), for example, found that 87% of Labour

Table 8.2: The proposed five-tier immigration system

Tier	Categorisation of workers
1 – Highly skilled	Workers will be considered for Tier 1 status if they are in the following categories (employers are not required to provide documentation that a shortage exists for these workers): • inter-company international transfers; • board-level workers – senior posts of equivalents; • inward investment – cases involving an overseas company making a substantial investment in a UK company; • shortage occupations – cases where the occupation is recognised by the UK government as being in acute short supply in the UK and the European Economic Area; • sponsored researchers.
2 – Skilled with job offer if working in a 'shortage area' such as teaching or nursing	For Tier 2 applications employers need to prove that a vacancy exists and are required to make a recruitment search from the resident labour market. Individual workers must possess one of the following: • a UK equivalent degree level qualification; • a Higher National Level qualification that is relevant to the post on offer; • a HND Level qualification that is relevant to the post on offer, plus 12 months of relevant full-time work experience; • at least 3 years' relevant experience at NVQ level 3 or above.
3 – Low skilled	A small number of workers to fill specific (often temporary) labour shortages. Particularly relates to workers from the expanded EU.
4 – Students	Students paying for tuition fees at UK higher education institutions.
5 – Temporary workers, youth mobility	Young people entering to work in specific events such as sporting events or cultural exchanges.

Source: Adapted from information from Home Office (2006)

213

Members of Parliament (MPs) agree that economic migration should be used to plug skills shortages in the UK. It is a policy that has been supported by politicians across the political divide, with the Conservative Party, for example, stating that it 'want[s] hard working people [to be present] in this country' (Green, 2006, p 1). According to Blair, this consensus is based on a sense of fairness and legitimacy. As he told the Confederation of British Industry (CBI):

> The vast bulk of the British people are not racist.... They can accept migration that is controlled and selective. They accept and welcome migrants who play by the rules. But they will not accept abuse or absurdity and why should they? (2004, p 1)

The instrumentalist argument is presented as the acceptable face of migration policy in a context where community and labour market change is politically controversial (see Box 8.2 for a discussion of the particularities of Scottish policy on in-migration).

Box 8.2: The politics of migration in Scotland

The politics of migration has taken a particular turn in the case of Scotland. Of all the regions in the UK, it is in Scotland that demographic trends threaten to do most damage to long-term economic prospects and the balance of local communities. Scotland's current population is relatively stable at 5,062,000 but changing fertility rates since the 1980s means that although the population is likely to peak at 5.1 million in 2019, it will then slowly decline, reaching 4.86 million by 2044 (see McNiven, 2005). Moreover, between 2004 and 2031 it is anticipated that the number of people of working age will fall by 7% (from 3.18 million to 2.96 million) and the number of people of pensionable age will rise by 35% (from 0.97 million to 1.31 million). Scotland's population is declining faster than anywhere else in Europe and its longer-term welfare is being sustained by what has traditionally been one of the UK's least prosperous regional economies, albeit with areas of relative prosperity mainly in and around Edinburgh and Grampian.

The Scottish Executive and the ruling Labour–Liberal Group argue that these demographic trends may lead to severe long-term damage to the sustainability of the Scottish economy. Labour markets will become tighter, entrepreneurial workers will become thinner on the ground, and KW positions in industry and the public sector will become increasingly difficult to fill. As First Minister Jack McConnell (2004, p 1) made clear in a speech to the Scottish Parliament, population decline represents 'the most serious long-term issue facing our country'. It is so significant that it presents:

> the greatest threat to Scotland's future prosperity. Tax revenues will fall. Falling school rolls mean local schools will close, other local services will become less sustainable, communities will become weaker. The labour market will contract and there will be fewer consumers to underpin a domestic market. Our economy will be less dynamic and likely to contract. (pp 1-2)

The solution to this 'problem' is presented as the selective in-migration of skilled workers whose presence within the country will not only provide additional resources to meet growing (older) population demands but also give the economy new entrepreneurial dynamism. The new approach has been strongly supported across the political spectrum, although there also exist tensions at a variety of levels over the 'threat' of in-migration to community 'harmony'. The influx of asylum-seekers in some of the poorest parts of Glasgow in the early 2000s, for example, generated significant tensions with local populations which culminated in social disturbances in 2001.

It is estimated by the Scottish Executive that 8,000 in-migrants per annum are required between 2005 and 2009 in order to rebalance the country's economy and social mix. Its population strategy emphasises the place-promotion of Scotland as a destination to live and work. It is going beyond the common focus of promotional strategies that focus on inward investment and short-term tourist visits to attract would-be migrants to go and live in Scotland. In October 2004 a *Relocation Advisory Service* was established that consists of teams of advisers who offer help to would-be immigrants on the possibilities and practicalities of moving to Scotland. The scheme is a part of the wider Work Permits UK system and between October 2004 and January 2005 the scheme gave information to approximately 1,000 clients. The service is part of a so-called *Fresh Talent* programme that also includes a *Challenge Fund* that is open to Scottish universities to help them to attract overseas graduates. Other existing institutions are being re-energised as a part of this wider programme. For example, the *Friends of Scotland* and the *Global Scots* networks have been mobilised to target ex-Scots and those of Scottish ancestry to think about relocating. The Executive has been keen to emphasise its devolved powers in relation to immigration policy, arguing that 'it is a flexibility that allows the management of migration into the UK to respond to local requirements' (McConnell, 2004, p 4). It is perhaps in Scotland that the tensions, possibilities, and paradoxes of migration policy will be best exemplified.

There is evidence of this wider consensus in action. Trades unions, for example, in contrast to their post-war reticence over immigration, have taken a lead role in supporting migrants and helping them to become established in communities and labour markets. There have been few of the tensions with existing workers that have emerged in other countries, such as Ireland, where, in sectors such as transport and construction, immigrants have become increasingly unwelcome and blamed for cuts in wages and conditions (see *The Economist*, 2006b). In 2005 the Trades Union Congress (TUC) committed itself to providing migrants with information about their legal rights, drawing on its 2002 publication *Migrant Workers: A TUC Guide* (TUC, 2002). There has been less tension within the wider movement over the 'threat' posed by incomers, particularly as many of the strongly unionised industries of the post-war period have gone into decline and unions now represent some of the lowest-paid workers in the labour market, many of whom are migrants. Migrant workers, in many ways, provide trades unions with new opportunities to expand their role and significance. The UK's largest union, UNISON, for instance, sees its role as one of 'promoting equality of pay and conditions for migrant workers and harmonious relations between workers from different countries of origin and protecting migrants from exploitation' (UNISON, 2005, p 2).

National business representatives have also welcomed the government's wider economic objectives in its migration policies and have tried to ensure that the instrumental/economic focus of policy is sustained. The CBI's Director General, for example, argues that 'using controlled migration to help reduce skill gaps and stimulate economic growth in geographical areas that might otherwise have problems is nothing more than common sense' (Jones, 2005, p 1). This utilitarian attitude towards in-migrants is partly explained by the poor levels of training that exist in both the public and private sectors in the UK and the benefits for businesses in transferring costs onto public and private sector institutions in 'donating' countries. In a joint statement with the TUC and Home Office (Home Office, 2005c) entitled

Managed Migration: Working for Britain, the CBI declares that it will actively:

> promote the case for legal and managed migration, support measures to eradicate illegal working to help companies and employees move away from the illegal economy to the legal economy; promote integrated and diverse workforces, including migrant workers; ... encourage the provision of English teaching; [and] consult with members. (p 1)

The possibilities inherent in attracting a new set of skilled workers are clearly attractive to many businesses.

Indeed, for some authors, it has been the political pressure exerted by business representatives that has had the most significant impact on government thinking and policy. Spencer (2003, p 2) argues that since the mid-1990s there have been relentless and 'growing demands by employers for overseas workers ... there is a global market for the highly skilled, and employers competing to attract them find the bureaucracy of visa controls and work permits an unwelcome regulatory burden'. More broadly the politics of the new migration is, of course, closely connected with other political movements operating at a variety of scales. Thus, for some interests, migration policy is still too restrictive. The European Commission has, for example, long promoted labour migration as a core feature of the European Single Market (see section below). Other interests in the public and private sectors have also been active supporters of a more open-borders policy and concerned that limits on mobility will limit their effectiveness.

However, as with the post-war period, immigration, particularly of identifiable groups from the New Commonwealth, has also generated political tensions. At a national scale, organisations such as *Migrant Watch* constantly challenge the government to justify its migration policies and are critical of the social, cultural, and economic impacts of an expanded migration policy. In a direct parallel from earlier eras of debate, the focus has primarily been on the *numbers* of migrants entering the UK and the accuracy of official statistics produced by the state. The British National Party and other groups also oppose immigration for a variety of ideological reasons. They draw on selective imaginations of places and communities to engender a particular type of, in this case reactionary, politics. The racially motivated resistance that was evident in places such as Notting Hill and Smethwick during the 1950s and 1960s has found new expression in the contemporary politics of globalisation.

It is partly in response to such challenges that the Labour government has maintained a cautious approach to immigration. As Spencer (2003, p 5) observes, 'Governments [in the UK] are unwilling to lead an open debate on migration options for fear of provoking public hostility. The real decisions are ... [therefore] taken behind closed doors'. The emphasis on 'management' implies that the process is being controlled, targeted, and regulated. Even the approach to skilled workers has become 'timid and cautious ... as if the government were terrified of provoking a backlash against even the modest affirmations of immigration and multiculturalism, and hedged them with multiple qualifications and safeguards' (Kymlicka, 2003, p 205).

The added dimension to these debates is the growing significance of *illegal* migration to the UK's economy. Some pressure groups claim, for example, that between 310,000 and 570,000 illegal immigrants have not been registered in official government statistics (BBC News Online, 2005c). Globalisation has not only encouraged the movement and mobility of skilled and knowledgeable workers but has also opened new opportunities for the dispossessed to find their own methods of migration. It is this duality in global processes that has been at the heart of the government's 'managed migration' policy. Borders are to act as selectively permeable filters that facilitate the 'right' types of immigration. However, there is a paradox at the heart of these debates. On the one hand, illegal immigration is presented by government, the CBI, and others as an evil that is undermining the legitimacy of 'genuine' migrants, particularly those entering the country for economic reasons or to escape political persecution. On the other hand, however, a number of industries increasingly rely on the cheap wages that such workers are prepared to work for. Low pay is endemic within migrant communities who, in faster-growing regions such as London and the South East, play an essential role in facilitating economic growth and the sustainability of social and economic systems (see Wills, 2001; Peck, 2005). These 'KWs' are, of course, not defined as such given the wider politics of development, community-building, and welfare that has been outlined in the discussion above. The next section of the chapter turns to the NHS as an example of a (public) sector of the labour market that has increasingly relied upon immigrants and the effects and implications of these processes.

Skilled foreign workers and the sustainability of the NHS

No example better illustrates the close relationships between globalisation, conceptions over the value of skilled labour, and processes of state selection than that of foreign workers and the NHS. As Chapter Five illustrated, skilled and unskilled migrants played a significant role in the development of the UK's post-war public services. Many of the debates that took place during this period were focused on questions such as: whose labour is 'necessary' to the functioning of sections of the UK economy and its public services? How should decisions over the perceived supply and demand of labour be negotiated? What mechanisms of state selection should be established? And what would be the impacts of (im)migration on existing communities and places? The restrictions imposed by the 1962 Commonwealth Immigrants Act shifted policy towards an explicit concern with skills and the 'values' attributed to individual citizens and workers. Throughout this period the need to supply the NHS with KWs represented one of the core objectives of policy and one that was used to 'disarm' anti-immigration critics.

The NHS was established in 1946 and represented perhaps the most significant manifestation of the Attlee government's commitment to a national welfare state system (Mohan, 1995). It embodied the core values inherent in the new social contract with all citizens automatically entitled to free healthcare at the point of delivery. Access was governed only by national citizenship with healthcare services provided through the stewardship of local authorities (see Cochrane, 1993). The political symbolism of the NHS ensured that it has withstood wider cuts to public services since the 1980s, although as with every other public sector it has been exposed to swingeing administrative and managerial reforms. Within recent planning discourses, good-quality healthcare is also presented as a core element of any sustainable community. Local healthcare agencies have found themselves at the forefront of new development partnerships across the UK as the impetus towards sustainable community-building has brought into focus the relationships between the presence of efficient public services, spatial planning, and functioning places.

During the 1990s and 2000s the problems of understaffing have, however, become critical. Healthcare services require the presence of staff at all times and this creates particular managerial difficulties. As Chapter Seven showed, health workers have, therefore, become KWs as their presence represents a necessary element in the functioning not only of healthcare systems but also of sustainable communities as a whole. And as with other KWs it is their absence in faster-growing areas that has become a core problem for governments and NHS managers. Thus far, programmes like the KWLP have failed to tackle the difficulties that lower-paid NHS staff face in accessing housing; nearly 5,000 nursing students in 2004 alone decided to quit the profession altogether (BBC News Online, 2005a, 2006a). In 2004 approximately 50,000 UK-trained nurses left or retired from the NHS, with only 20,000 new UK recruits joining (BBC News Online, 2005b). At the same time the government's expansion programme for the NHS has fuelled the demand for healthcare staff. Between 1997 and 2004, for example, there was a 23% increase in the number of nurses working in England, from 246,000 to 301,000 (RCN, 2005).

The response from NHS managers has been to look to international immigration to fill the gaps. According to the British Medical Association, in 2003 two-thirds of newly registered doctors and more than 40% of new nurses in the UK came from abroad. In one year, 2000-01, there was an increase of 41% – approximately 8,000 – nurses recruited from outside the EU and they made up more than half of the Nursing and Midwifery Council's 29,602 new additions (RCNS, 2004). About 12,500 doctors currently registered to work in the UK are migrants from sub-Saharan African nations that face serious staff shortages themselves. In 2003 it was estimated that the region as a whole was short of one million healthcare workers, with countries like Ghana running healthcare systems for 20 million people with only 1,500 doctors (BBC News Online, 2005c). In Zambia only 50 out of 600 doctors trained since independence are still practising in the country, while in Uganda there are only 10 nurses for every 100,000 people – 10 times less than in the UK. The shift of skilled migrant workers in this way represents an indirect subsidising of the NHS by poorer nations who have to bear the significant costs of healthcare training. Save the Children (2006) estimates that it has cost African nations £270 million to train the doctors and nurses who have migrated to the UK. In the case of one country alone, Ghana, this has saved the UK £65 million in training costs.

There is also a geography to the settlement patterns of health worker in-migrants that closely reflects wider KW and sustainable communities policies and strategies. The NHS has established a target of recruiting 35,000 more nurses by 2008 with priority given to areas where the retention of existing staff is proving to be a significant problem. London is the primary location, with Royal College of Nursing (RCN, 2003) figures showing that in 2003 a quarter of all nurses working in its

NHS hospitals were recruited from overseas. In 2004 14% of nurses based in London had qualified outside of the UK, compared with just 4% in the UK as a whole. One London NHS trust employs nurses of 39 different nationalities (*Health Service Journal*, 2004).

This taking of KWs from Less Developed Countries has been criticised by development agencies. In 2003 the World Health Assembly called for developed countries to mitigate the adverse effects of migration on poorer countries. In response, in 2004 the UK government significantly updated its *Code of Practice for the International Recruitment of Healthcare Professionals* (DH, 2004) that was originally published in 2001. The Code claims to be underpinned by the principle 'that any international recruitment of healthcare professionals should not prejudice the healthcare systems of developing countries' (p 4). It is only in cases where government-to-government agreements exist that NHS managers should be allowed to recruit particular workers. The Code is designed to 'supply international healthcare professionals in an ethical and managed way' (p 4). It is underpinned by seven core principles, as outlined in Box 8.3.

Box 8.3: The core principles of the Department of Health's *Code of Practice for the International Recruitment of Healthcare Professionals*

(1)   International recruitment is a sound and legitimate contribution to the development of the healthcare workforce.

(2)   Extensive opportunities exist for individuals in terms of training and education and the enhancement of clinical practice.

(3)   Developing countries will not be targeted for recruitment, unless there is an explicit government-to-government agreement with the UK to support recruitment activities.

(4)   International healthcare professionals will have a level of knowledge and proficiency comparable to that expected of an individual trained in the UK.

(5)   International healthcare professionals will demonstrate a level of English language proficiency consistent with safe and skilled communication with patients, clients, carers, and colleagues.

(6)   International healthcare professionals legally recruited from overseas to work in the UK are protected by relevant UK employment law in the same way as all other employees.

> (7) International healthcare professionals will have equitable support and access to further education and training and continuing professional development as all other employees.
>
> *Source:* DH (2004, pp 7-9)

Such codes of practice are designed to give order to this labour mobility in ways that make them calculable and regulated. As with other forms of labour mobility policy documented in earlier chapters, what we see here is an attempt to ensure that the needs of operational efficiency and the striving to create balance within (in this case) segments of the labour market in specific areas, are privileged over and above wider concerns. The implication is that it is not the structural deficiencies in the training and retention of UK staff that is the core problem to be addressed. Instead, it is the unregulated mobility of workers that is the target for action, with proposals seeking to identify and construct clear channels through which individuals' movements can be calculated and directed in order to fulfil wider policy agendas.

Finally, as with all KWs, their current 'mooring' (see Urry, 2003) in the UK may only be temporary. The impacts of globalisation on healthcare recruitment are multidirectional. It is estimated, for example, that the US health system requires an additional three million skilled workers by 2010 (*Health Service Journal*, 2004) and staff within the UK sector represent a primary target. In addition, countries such as Australia and Canada have launched international recruitment strategies, directly aimed at UK workers. The difficulties in finding quality accommodation and a quality of life in many parts of the UK make it a particularly vulnerable target for such poaching. As with the politics of post-war emigration, the dynamism of the labour market in this sector makes its governance and management a particularly difficult problem.

Labour mobility, the EU, and new scales of regulation

One additional factor in the regulation of labour markets in the UK has been the growing significance of legislation at the European level. As Chapter Five showed, emigration and immigration policy in the post-war decades was dominated by views of the Commonwealth, with some even advocating that the former Empire territories become an integrated and free-flowing space of regulation. However, following the UK's accession to the European Economic Community (EEC) in 1973 this geographical imagination has shifted significantly as the role and significance of the EU and European labour markets have grown inexorably. Article 39 of the founding 1957 Treaty of Rome established a freedom of international mobility within the EEC's borders for the citizens of member states (see Box 8.4). Its unambiguous contents graphically illustrate the ways in which geographical mobility for workers was, and remains, a core element of the wider European project.

Box 8.4: Article 39 of the Treaty of Rome

All European citizens have the right to:

- Look for work in another member state
- Work in another member state
- Reside there for that purpose
- Remain there
- Equality of treatment in respect of access to employment, working conditions, and all other advantages which could help to facilitate the worker's integration in the host member state.

The stipulations of the original treaty have been expanded and developed through case law within the European Court of Justice and through the regulatory powers of the European Commission. As the Commission makes clear, 'The right of free movement within the Community ... is perhaps the most important right under Community law for individuals, and an essential element of European citizenship' (EC, 2002, p 4). In line with other place- and labour market-building strategies, worker mobility is presented as a vehicle for the balancing of labour demands and supply across the European spatial economy. For the Commission:

> It is common ground that labour mobility allows individuals to improve their job prospects and allows employers to recruit the people they need. It is an important element in achieving efficient labour markets and a high level of employment. (EC, 2002, p 4)

The objectives of labour market policy being elaborated here are both economic and socio-political. Mobility is closely linked to the concept of European citizenship, with the experience of living in another country acting as a mechanism of cultural learning and exchange.

At the same time, economic growth and labour market expansion have been key elements of the European project. The 1997 Amsterdam Treaty endorsed an ambitious European employment strategy that tried to lay the foundations for a new, integrated, single European space. It saw the flow of workers across national labour market boundaries as a vehicle for ensuring greater economic efficiency. The 2000 Lisbon Agreement also set targets for employment rates of 70% across the EU by 2010. The problem of unemployment and underemployment across the EU has taken on greater salience in a context where 9% of workers were unemployed in 2004 with strong international and interregional differences (Poland's unemployment rate, for example, in 2003 was 19%, compared to just under 4% in the Netherlands [see Eurostat, 2005]). Enhanced worker mobility, therefore, provided one obvious mechanism through which spatial labour market differences could be reduced.

And yet, even within this wider citizenship-building strategy, an individual's capacity to *work* is presented as the key determinate of mobility. Article 39 of the Treaty of Rome is concerned with the freedom of mobility of workers between countries and how they should be allowed to access EU-wide labour markets and reside in other member states for '*that purpose*'. Work acts as a gateway to mobility for individuals as they fulfil the wider strategic objective of balancing labour markets and making them operate in a functional and efficient manner. This principle has been consistently supported by the institutions of the EU that have tried to expand the numbers and types of citizens who should be allowed to migrate. So, for example, the European Parliament's (2001) definitions of economically active citizens have been expanded to cover categories such as students, persons undergoing training, volunteers, teachers, and trainers. New rules have been applied that increase the residency rights of workers' spouses and families in order to make labour mobility more attractive to skilled workers.

However, the politics of mobility surrounding this European project has, as with other programmes discussed in the book, been the subject of much argument and debate. The European Court of Justice has been called upon to define a 'worker' in relation to EU and member state EU laws. Its working definition is: 'any person who (i) undertakes genuine and effective work (ii) under the direction of someone else (iii) for which he [*sic*] is paid' (EC, 2006, p 5). For the Commission such categorisations are essential 'as the definition of worker defines the scope of the fundamental principles of freedom of movement' (p 5). Thus, national governments have been criticised for failing to open up their public sector labour markets to workers from across the

EU and a series of legal actions have been taken in cases where it is argued restrictive practices still operate.

For example, under EU law a member state is allowed to bar certain jobs within the public sector to foreign nationals if they can be shown to be 'responsible for safeguarding the general interest of the state' (Article 39, clause 4 of the Treaty of Rome). The exact definitions of which types of employment and workers come under this category and which do not have been the subject of much wrangling and argument. National public sector employers are accused of not treating, for example, workers' skills as comparable and using this as a bar to employment and promotion. This re-ascription of workers' capacities and citizenship rights once they have crossed boundaries is a recurring feature of labour migration processes. At the same time, the logic of a single labour (and exchange) market has generated other tensions. It has become apparent to European policy-makers that, for example, 'social security is a key issue for persons exercising their right to free movement' (EC, 2002, p 4). A failure to address the wider social needs of workers will 'stand in the way of the full benefits and potential of geographical mobility for workers and employers' (p 4). Measures are called for through which there should be a harmonisation of social and welfare systems to enable greater flexibility and movement as and when required by the market. In short, the new agendas promote greater marketisation, through enhanced mobility, and paradoxically seek to apply greater state power (through regulation) to enhance the competitiveness and 'freedom' of labour markets.

The accession of the 10 new member countries to the EU (following a treaty signed on 16 April 2003) brought many of these tensions to the fore. Within many existing member states concerns were expressed that the free movement of labour would encourage massive levels of in-migration. It was agreed that there would be a period of seven years (up to 2011) in which member states could continue to exercise strong controls over which workers could migrate from the new, primarily Eastern European countries. The UK, Ireland, and Sweden decided on an open-borders policy from the outset. For the EU the benefits of a more integrated labour market on a European scale have been exemplified by the experiences of these countries that have seen a major influx of workers to take up positions that otherwise would not be filled (see Langescu, 2006). The European Commission (EC, 2006) has been keen to emphasise that this influx has been 'measured' and has not led to an undermining of a sense of community balance or harmony in the receiving countries. Nowhere have these new member states' nationals represented more than 1% of the working-age population, other than in the small countries of Ireland (3.8% in 2005) and Austria (1.4%). There has been 'no evidence of a surge in welfare expenditure following enlargement' (p 1) and the new workers contributed to strong economic performance in Ireland and the UK by alleviating 'skills bottlenecks'. National governments that adopted a more positive attitude to labour market integration experienced significant economic benefits as a consequence with little 'threat' to their socio-cultural balance and the harmony of communities.

Conclusions

The dimensions of UK migration have been subject to rapid change during the 2000s. Office of National Statistics (ONS, 2005) figures show that in 2004, a record 582,000 people migrated into the UK with a net balance of 223,000. At the same time, there was a net outflow of existing British citizens of 120,000, with a total of 208,000 leaving the UK for a variety of reasons. There was a net gain of 72,000 migrants from EU countries, 48,000 of whom were from the new accession states. It is under these circumstances that the Labour government's management strategies need to be understood. A managed migration policy is presented as a vehicle through which individuals can bring new forms of entrepreneurialism, skills, and energies to the UK, all of which can be used in the pursuit of wider social and economic development objectives. The regulatory and socioeconomic contexts within which policy decisions are made have undoubtedly shifted and the chapter has given some insights into the new imaginations that are drawn upon by different actors to underpin their perspectives and policy programmes. The shift in emphasis from the Commonwealth to the EU in relation to migration policy is indicative of a wider set of changes in the relationships between the UK and the wider world. The expanding borders and powers of the EU mean that its policies towards borders, mobility, and migration are becoming more significant all of the time, with implications for economic development and community change in the UK.

There are clear parallels with earlier eras. The politics and practices of migrant mobility and fixity have continued to draw upon particular imaginations of how places and spatial economies function. While these imaginations have clearly been subject to change there is still a core emphasis on the question of whose presence and absence is necessary, legitimate, and desirable. Economic rationalities play an important part in these wider debates as governments are keen to ensure that their wider competitiveness strategies are successful.

Increasing the limitations on labour mobility has the capacity to undermine wider efforts to modernise the UK economy. However, discussions around immigration are always bound up with other socio-political processes of place-building and sustainability such as broader concerns with imagined community 'harmony' and 'balance'. Governments and others, such as trades unions and business leaders, have long wrestled with these diverse and all too often competing objectives.

The chapter has also shown that there are strong links between sustainable community-building agendas and immigration policy. The problems of recruitment and retention in public services in the South East and East of England have meant that the concept of the KW has been expanded to include those from overseas. At the same time, the emphasis on skilled migrants has been focused on the needs of those industrial sectors that support the same fast-growing, globally competitive regions. This new manifestation of spatial selectivity (see Jones, 1997) represents a particular response to globalisation and the chapter has shown how international workers and communities are being drawn upon to fuel the continued growth of the South East and East. As Massey (2004b) argues, this exploitation of wider resources often goes unacknowledged. There is a lack of responsibility on the part of policy-makers and planners as they strive to build new, 'sustainable' communities of their own.

Notes
[1] It is worth noting that suggestions were even made in the early 1970s to ship all Ugandan immigrants to a British-owned island, such as the Falkland Islands, to prevent them from settling in the UK (BBC News Online, 2003a).

[2] In 2005, for example, new migrants were required to sit a 'Britishness Test' that they had to pass before being accepted as 'proper' citizens (see *The Economist*, 2006a, b, c).

[3] Lord Dholakia (2005) 'House of Lords debate on immigration', *Hansard*, 23 February, col 1260.

NINE

Spatial policy, sustainable communities, and labour market-building: towards a new research agenda

Introduction

Never has Claus Offe's (1985) observation that modern policy-making involves a 'restless search' for new and better ways of doing things seemed more apt or appropriate (see Healey, 1997). The combination of a modernising Labour government, ongoing globalisation, the growing importance of new technologies and virtual spaces, and changing imaginations about how economies and societies function, has produced a dynamic and rapidly changing policy environment. Modernisation, change, and fluidity have become the new mantras of governance, with citizens and communities given the increasingly blunt message that changes in the regulation and organisation of the welfare state and labour markets are inevitable and that they have no alternative but to adapt to the new realities. The recent emergence of the sustainable communities agenda ostensibly represents a modernisation of spatial planning that will make it more responsive to these wider changes. Its 'new' vision of mixed, diverse, and balanced communities, underpinned by strong and globally competitive labour markets, is presented as an original and innovative way forward. It is a vision that seeks to engender a sense of both ordered fixity and fluidity to places, citizens, and communities caught up in the uncertain and threatening instabilities of global change.

And yet, as this book has argued, the core principles that underpin these new agendas have a long history within the discourses of post-war spatial planning. The conviction that the economic and social characteristics of places and communities can be ordered and harnessed in the pursuit of wider policy objectives has been reproduced throughout the decades. Spatial planning policy becomes 'successful' if it is able to engineer and take control of the complex and tangled relationships between the mobility and fixity of people and investment. As such it is the *continuities* in the discourses, objectives, and practices of spatial policy that are striking, rather than the much-cited 'newness' of contemporary policy. The latter represents an extension of existing principles and ways of doing things rather than a major step change.

This concluding chapter draws together the key findings under each of the four themes that have shaped the analysis: (i) imaginations of place and space; (ii) the processes, practices, and politics of mobility; (iii) the engendering of particular forms of citizenship and subjectivity; and (iv) the changing perceptions and realities of state capacities and modes of regulation. It argues that in each case a historical narrative has enabled new insights to be developed and the continuities and changes in policy emphasis to be established and contextualised. It then turns to a discussion of the avenues and directions that future research on spatial policy and governance might take and the key questions that could inform such research.

Spatial policy and imaginations of place and space

The chapters in this book have demonstrated that the concept of the balanced, mixed, and what is now termed 'sustainable' community is an inherently political construction underpinned by dominant imaginations over what constitutes a functioning place, and how it can be shaped to become both an object and subject of policy. This is in marked contrast to the ways in which the 'balanced place' is often represented in policy discourses as a 'common-sense', politically uncontroversial objective that policy-makers, planners, developers, and communities should prioritise in the drawing up of their development blueprints. This process of interpretation has, in turn, been dependent on wider conceptions of how economies and societies function, what types of citizens are essential to the functioning of a place, and how their needs and priorities can be identified and supported.

The research has shown that a search for 'balance' is often used to discursively legitimate measures that prioritise those whose subjectivity is seen as essential to community 'well-being', such as key worker (KW) managers and skilled workers in Development Areas (DAs) and New Towns (NTs) after the Second World War or essential public sector and knowledge workers in London, the South East, and other development hotspots during the 2000s. The need to support such individuals and to enable them to meet their higher aspirations is presented as being in the best interests of *all* members of a community, even those who do not directly qualify for selective forms of social or economic assistance. As we saw in Chapter Five, conceptions of 'balanced places' also relate to broader social and community imaginations. National and local debates over the so-called 'over-concentration' of minority ethnic groups in some areas, for example, highlighted the selective nature of imaginations that existed over what a 'balanced community' should consist of in terms of ethnic diversity.

These conceptions have become increasingly important and the book has argued that spatial policy has to be conceptualised as an *active social policy* developed in and through changes to the wider welfare state (see Cochrane, 2003). It has involved a shift in emphasis from the provision of direct support to producers to a broader concern with how the conditions for economic competitiveness can be sustained and enhanced through welfare policy interventions in fields such as housing, skills development, and health service provision. Providing the means of consumption to a broad range of workers and citizens has, at different times, underpinned spatial policy discourses and practices. Once again, this is not an entirely new phenomenon, as the discussion of the 'needs' of KWs in the post-war decades suggests. However, it has become increasingly important as the character of the economy and flows of capital have been subject to change.

The chapters have also highlighted the role of context-dependent *geographical imaginations* in shaping and defining particular policy problems, responses, and solutions. Identifying fields of action and policy subjects and objects always requires the mobilisation of particular imaginations of *scale*. For example, Chapter Two examined the argument that the dominant scale of spatial policy intervention in the UK has shifted from a post-war, Keynesian concern with the *national* economy to a more targeted emphasis on the needs of selected, fast-growing *regions* and their competitiveness within global markets. Subsequent chapters have empirically assessed the ways in which these processes have worked in practice and charted the discourses and debates that have underpinned broader policy changes. Chapters Six and Seven, for example, examined the recent rise of new regionalist thinking and the sustainable communities agenda and documented some of the changes that have taken place in policy thinking and practice.

The analysis has documented how, during different eras of spatial policy, the socioeconomic *connections* between different scales have been re-imagined and the impacts this has had on the objectives and priorities of policy. There has been a particular concern with the interrelationships between the (imagined) characteristics of the local scale and communities and wider regional and global development processes. Chapters Three and Four demonstrated that, for policy-makers and planners after the Second World War, the poor quality of life to be found in many urban and DA communities acted as an impediment to regional and national economic development priorities. Long before the emergence of modern 'entrepreneurialist' and place-marketing strategies, policy-makers were expressing concern that unless the places in which social reproduction took place were attractive to the right types of people and investors, development would be constrained. The KW housing programmes of the 1940s and 1950s, for example, were premised on particular understandings of what places in DAs lacked, by way of 'high-quality' amenities and infrastructure for the 'better class' of person. In other words, without changing the character, perception, and make-up of the places/communities within which migrating workers would live, wider policy objectives could not be met. Similar imaginations characterise the contemporary shift towards sustainable community-building and the skewing of spatial policy objectives towards the needs of a 'creative class' of mobile and entrepreneurial subjects (see Florida, 2004; Peck, 2005). A failure to do this, it is argued, will limit the longer-term competitiveness of both the South Eastern and, ultimately, the UK economy.

These geographical imaginations also relate to the connections between global economic processes and the objectives of spatial policy. Various chapters have shown that there have been marked changes in how governments have perceived economies to function at a variety of scales. Thus, earlier chapters pointed to the importance that was given to manufacturing industries after the Second World War and the ways in which the transfer of jobs to DAs could turn them into exporters and 'contributors' to national wealth. Later chapters explored the ways in which dominant discourses, or ways of writing about the economy (see Thrift, 2005), became increasingly focused on the broader concepts of technology, entrepreneurialism, and knowledge in which service sector and the so-called 'knowledge industries' have taken centre stage. As has been shown, this has had a significant impact on the rationalities and objectives of spatial policy.

The processes, practices, and politics of mobility

The chapters have demonstrated that the effectiveness of any spatial policy is in large part dependent on the *mobility* of people, jobs, and investment. Encouraging the right types of inter- and intra-regional mobility (and fixity) could help to solve the spatial and social problems of the UK's most deprived places and make the national economy more competitive. Inter- and intra-national migration and movement has repeatedly been used to change the composition and characteristics of places. Throughout the post-war period controversial decisions have been taken over *whose* movements should be promoted and supported and *where* migrants should go in order to meet the wider objectives of policy. Earlier chapters demonstrated how time and again immigration policy focused less on the needs of migrants as citizens, and more on what their labour and knowledge could 'contribute' to the overall efficiency of local, regional, and national labour markets. At the same time, the movement of people has not always been welcomed and the politics of mobility and settlement continues to generate heated debate at a variety of scales.

The research has also drawn attention to the rights and responsibilities associated with mobility and the ways in which these processes are directly linked to wider forms of *social and economic power*. One recurring theme through the analysis, for example, has been the unwillingness of governments to restrict the mobility of more privileged workers and citizens. Thus, in Chapter Five we saw that little was done to stop the emigration of UK citizens if they had the capacity and desire to move abroad, whatever the social and economic impacts on the spatial economy. Indeed, for political reasons efforts were made during the 1950s and 1960s to actively support them. In Chapter Eight we saw that similar trends are evident today in relation to the so-called 'brain drain'. In addition, the policy objective of enticing KWs to move (or not to move) has also been underpinned by a politics of 'encouragement', rather than compulsion. Governments have consistently taken the view that they have little or no right to interfere with the location decisions of those who, through their own actions and skills, have made themselves into valuable, sustainable, and self-reliant citizens. For those with the resources and skills, mobility is a fundamental right that has been earned. This celebration of mobility for some citizens has, of course, been contrasted with the erosion of mobility rights for other groups. Chapters Five and Eight examined the ways in which UK migration policy has become gradually more restrictive, a process that has culminated in the explicit 'managed migration' policies of the Blair government.

One additional finding has been that processes of mobility have been and continue to be extremely difficult for states to manage and control at local, national, and even supranational scales. A variety of policy programmes have been examined and in each it has been the *limitations* of state management that have been evident, rather than the exercise of firm control. So, for example, even in the relatively ordered building of communities in the NTs in the 1950s and 1960s a bureaucratic programme such as the Industrial Selection Scheme was unable to control the movement of people and jobs in a coordinated and effective manner (see Chapter Four for an extended discussion). As economic and social trends become increasingly global in scale, control over processes of mobility may become increasingly limited, and yet more significant, in the future. It is this lack of control, or the inability to order socioeconomic processes, that has in large part contributed to the political controversies surrounding migration and movement.

Citizenship and subjectivity

Debates around spatial policy, labour markets, and community-building have also reflected and reproduced particular conceptions of citizenship or the relationships between citizens, communities, and the state. Ostensibly, there are clearly definable shifts over time in these relationships with post-war governments exercising greater control over the life-worlds of their citizens (see Habermas, 1976). With the arrival of the Thatcher government in 1979 and the erosion of universalist principles of welfare support, it is commonly argued, the state has come to play a more hands-off and enabling role with citizens and communities expected to take greater responsibility for managing their own circumstances (see Imrie and Raco, 2003). In the analysis presented in this book there are clearly echoes of these wider simplifications. The moral and practical rationalities that were used to justify the scale and legitimacy of the spatial policy programmes outlined in Chapters Three and Four were very different to those of the post-Thatcher regimes, with their emphasis on global competitiveness and the counterproductive impacts of too much government 'interference'.

However, there are also strong continuities during these different eras, particularly in relation to processes of *boundary drawing* between citizens and the *ascription* of characteristics to different types of citizen. As discussed above, imaginations of balanced places have tended to assume that different classes of people exist with very different needs and aspirations. Boundaries are drawn between different types of citizens and these not only determine their access to welfare entitlements but also shape the ways in which their broader subjectivities and social status are defined. In large part, they reflect and reproduce state-driven, bureaucratic ascriptions of the characteristics of particular groups. Citizenship has, therefore, been defined in relational terms (see Rose,

1999b), with one group's characteristics and needs defined in and through their relationships with others. This principle has been evident throughout the empirical discussion, whether it be in relation to KWs, the politics of labour market-building, conceptions of (un)sustainable communities, or the selection of 'good' and 'bad' migrants.

The chapters have also highlighted the key connections between citizenship, subjectivity, and *place politics*. The bitterness with which battles over place imaginations, mobility, and individuals' rights and responsibilities have been fought out is indicative of the close interrelationships between places, identities, socioeconomic opportunities, and perceptions of social justice. Imaginations over who should and who should not be co-present in a particular place underpin wider debates over issues such as the in-migration of minority ethnic groups, the relocation of skilled workers, or the location of social housing. This politics of place has also been bound up with particular conceptions of the labour market and how it should redistribute the risks and rewards associated with different types of work. Place-based labour markets are very much a 'lived experience' for citizens and communities (see Jonas, 1996; Peck, 1996). They play a critical role in shaping the latter's identities, social status, and material well-being and these are directly connected to conceptions of place.

The findings also shed light on the future of community-building agendas in the UK and what the implications of ongoing forms of modernisation and reform might be for different socioeconomic groups. For example, the Blair government's recent focus on a politics of *aspiration* is being promoted as a way forward for the welfare state. According to the government's former Minister for Communities, David Miliband (2005, p 1):

> We know that all people aspire to living not just in decent homes but in decent communities, bound together by shared values, supported by sense of neighbourhood, inspired by high quality design, and of course free from anti-social behaviour.

These aspirations reflect and reproduce some of the core principles of the new sustainable communities agenda. They have also been directly linked to the increasingly used concept of *personalised welfare* (see Brown, 2006) in which the state's priority becomes the extension of consumer-style welfare choice to individuals in ways that better reflect, in relational terms, the different needs of different citizens. The historical narrative developed here has shown how such processes operate in practice and highlighted their often divisive implications.

State capacities and modes of regulation

The study illuminates a range of wider theoretical points concerning the relationships between citizens and states and the types of state regulation that came to dominate spatial policy discourses and agendas in the post-war period. The regulationist conception of 'strategic selectivity' provides an insightful starting point for understanding how and why states select (and seek to reproduce) particular types of subjects. The chapters have demonstrated that processes of selection are inherently politicised with different institutions of the 'state' often possessing very different interpretations and conceptions 'about the kinds of problems that can and should be addressed by various authorities' (Miller and Rose, 1990, p 2). This represents more than a simple implementation deficit but is indicative of the fractured and contested nature of modern governance. Privileging some actors, some interests, and some types of citizen above others has been a recurring feature of modern government but one that has also been subject to debate and re-articulation over time. State-centred theoretical approaches are particularly effective in identifying the rationalities and objectives of policy programmes and how states (re)organise their territories of action in order to develop and implement policy programmes.

However, such accounts are on less firm ground in explaining the form and character of actually occurring policy programmes in specific contexts and how these are shaped by a range of interrelated factors. State 'strategies' cannot simply be read off from wider policy statements but must be subject to empirical scrutiny of the specific contexts and circumstances through which political strategies emerge. While it is relatively simple to label eras as consisting of specific types of regulation, the ways that these broader contexts are embedded in policy programmes is erratic and contested. For example, as noted above, the evidence in earlier chapters highlights the limited *ordering capacities* on the part of the state and its inability to control wider processes of mobility and change. Such limitations should call into question simple characterisations.

Within such approaches there is also insufficient attention paid to the *politics of scale* and how the politics of place can help to shape the objectives, rationalities, and actually occurring character of state regulation. Throughout the discussion we have seen examples of how local political action has helped to redraw the boundaries of policy at wider regional, national, and international scales. In Part Two we saw that the form and character of government programmes such as KW housing support, NT-building, and migration policy were forged not only through top-down policy decisions but also through the contested politics of places. Policy outcomes were the result of dynamic processes. Similarly in Part Three, the evidence has shown that spatial policy priorities have, in part, been shaped by the politics of place and shifting perceptions of spatial policy priorities. State regulation and practices have to, therefore, be understood as the outcome of contested forms of politics operating across different spatial scales.

New directions for spatial policy research

This final section expands on the discussion thus far and draws out some possible directions for future research on spatial policy.

Population and labour market changes

The new emphasis on the knowledge economy and sustainable communities has drawn attention to the needs of young, mobile, and skilled workers in the public and private sectors. And yet, over the coming decades it is at the other end of the age-scale that population and labour market changes will be most profound. *The Economist* (2006c) notes that by 2013 the number of workers aged between 50 and 64 in Europe will grow by a quarter, while those aged 20-29 will decrease by 20%. In some industries, such as aerospace and defence, 'as many as 40% of the workforce in some companies will be eligible to retire within the next five years' (p 75). There will be significant implications for firms and other institutions to ensure that workers possess the appropriate skills and knowledge and that that knowledge is passed down to new workers before the older ones retire (see Dychtwald et al, 2004). At the same time, the quantitative and qualitative character of the global labour market is changing at a rapid rate. The inclusion of China, India, and the Soviet bloc into the global trading system in the mid-1990s has increased the supply of global labour by 1.47 billion workers, 'effectively doubling the size of the world's now connected workforce' (Freeman, 2006, p 2; *Corriere Della Sera*, 2006). This has the potential to transform the position of labour in countries such as the UK, across the skills spectrum.

Such changes raise significant questions for policy-makers and open up new avenues for research. For example, what will be the core features and future definitions of what are currently termed 'functioning' labour markets? What types of skills and knowledge will be prioritised in the future and how will KWs and entrepreneurs be defined in a context where the very nature of communities and work is subject to change? On what grounds will definitions be made and whose interests will be prioritised? Moreover, how will these processes of selection and identification operate and be institutionalised and what will be the wider politics through which these changes will be made? As the availability of skills and knowledge changes it seems likely that governments and others will find very different answers to these questions as they strive to tackle emerging problems and their capacities to develop solutions are subject to change.

Migration, mobility, and community change

With the abundance of global labour and the declining fertility of EU populations it seems likely that governments will increasingly turn to international migration as a way of sustaining the economic and social vitality of communities and broader spatial economies. The scale of this migration could have significant implications, for, as the Office of National Statistics (ONS, 2005) notes, on current trends the UK alone would have to import at least 125,000 migrants per annum in order to avoid long-term population ageing. This in turn raises a series of questions over the rationalities and objectives of policy. What shape, for example, will dominant conceptions of balanced communities take in the future in a context of rapidly changing populations? If population movements and 'turnover' become more rapid, what effect will this have on the character of places and place politics? In the new sustainable communities frameworks the government is clear that population stability is essential to the fostering of active citizenship and communities (see ODPM, 2005). The constant turnover of population groups in many UK cities is currently presented as an obstacle to the creation of balanced and harmonious communities. And yet, at the same time, the diversity and fluidity of places is also presented as an economic and social asset that helps engender creativity, vibrancy, and entrepreneurialism. The successful bid for the 2012 London Olympics, for example, was in large part based on selective imaginations of the city as a hub of creativity forged through its social diversity and the mobility of its population (see Livingstone, 2004; London Olympic Bid Team, 2004). There is a tension here that may act as an interesting focus for further work.

There are also research avenues to be explored in relation to mobilities. Across the social sciences there now exists a growing body of important work in this area (see Urry, 2003; Sheller and Urry, 2006). However, less research has thus far been carried out on the links between mobility politics and the broader rationalities and practices of spatial policy. Such an approach could examine broader questions concerning citizenship, state capacities, and rights and responsibilities. Do states, for instance, have the right to promote particular forms of mobility and community-building? Should citizens, in making their location decisions, take into account the 'well-being' of the wider community and what scales does this wider community encompass? In other words should KWs and others be 'responsibilised' (see Rose, 1999a) as subjects and objects of wider efforts to enhance social cohesion and economic competitiveness?

Such questions are pertinent to both inter- and intra-regional mobility in the UK and, of course, international migration. They also relate to the socioeconomic programmes of other Western countries. The fierce debates currently raging in the US over Hispanic immigration and its geographically diverse economic, social, and political consequences for communities across the country engages with similar themes. The recent pleas of the New Zealand government for its emigrated skilled citizens and entrepreneurs to return reflect particular imaginations in that country over the socioeconomic effects of the absence of skilled subjects. Their attraction has become a priority for policy-makers.

Methodological approaches to spatial policy research

This research also demonstrates the value of *empirically grounded accounts* of state programmes and grounded politics. Recent debates within geography and sociology over the extent to which places are 'relationally constructed' (see Amin and Thrift, 2002) or the ways in which policy is shaped by particular, accumulation-based logics (Jessop, 2002a; Brenner, 2003) have been characterised by conceptually heavy interventions often supported by the thinnest of empirical evidence. Within whole sections of the discipline of geography, in particular, the value of empirical research has been challenged in the wider pursuit of abstract truths and a broader critique of so-called 'representational theory' (see Thrift, 2003). At the same time, paradoxically, policy-makers and government funders are increasingly demanding that the work of social scientists becomes more 'evidence-based', with a greater emphasis on context-free, uncritical, and limited empirical studies that aim to produce 'best practice guidelines' and 'transferable policy models'.

Future research projects based on theoretically informed, empirically thorough research will have to steer a tight line between these wider trends.

On a related point, the study has also argued that a historically grounded focus can provide a platform from which further research can be developed to provide a historical inflection on contemporary policy. The extent to which, what Dodgshon (1999, p 615) terms, 'a principle of persistence' is evident in policy agendas is essential for any assessment of its originality and effectiveness. There is a tendency in some contemporary work to write in a rather ahistorical manner so that the advocacy of change, newness, and difference is simplistically elided with the nebulous concept of 'originality'. This is a trait shared with politicians, particularly those intent on promoting 'modernisation' strategies, sometimes for the sake of being seen to be doing something 'new'. Research should be more sensitive to the continuities within policy discourses in order to situate and better understand the changes that are taking place and what their impacts might be.

Characterising sustainability

Within development discourses the term 'sustainability' has increasingly become a 'chaotic concept' (Sayer, 1992) that has been deployed differentially by different interests in the pursuit of selective socio-political objectives. The emergence of the discourse of sustainability in UK spatial policy thus far has been defined primarily in economic and social terms, rather than environmental terms (see Raco, 2005b). Indeed, the latter is becoming less and less significant as the programme is being rolled out, particularly in the South East. Whatever the outcome of this wider politics, it seems likely that the relationships between resource exploitation, production, and consumption will have a greater and greater influence over spatial policy programmes in the future. For example, the availability of land and water resources, in a context of climate change, is already beginning to have an effect on the planning of sustainable communities and could set the limits to further growth and development in the South East (see Environment Agency, 2005; Council for the Protection of Rural England, 2006). The relationships between spatial policy and the discourse of sustainability are clearly a research direction to pursue both within and outwith the UK.

The future of spatial policy

The scale of the social, economic, and political changes now taking place raises important questions about the form and character of spatial policy in the future. Will governments still see spatial policy as having a significant role in ordering spaces and places or will efforts to order mobility and change become less significant over time? It could be argued that the emergence of the sustainable communities agenda challenges policy-makers, planners, citizens, and communities to think more positively about desired futures and what role the planning process should have in creating 'better places' (Meadowcroft, 2000). It could encourage new governmentalities to emerge in which planning either comes to be seen as more significant to people's lives or is perceived to be a growing irrelevance in the face of wider, 'unstoppable' changes. This tension lies at the heart of the Blair government's modernisation agenda. On the one hand, reform promises to increase the relevance, legitimacy, and effectiveness of state systems. The introduction of blueprints, such as *Planning Policy Statement 1* (ODPM, 2004) and the *Sustainable Communities* plan, are ostensibly designed to legitimate the planning system and ensure its longer-term survival. On the other hand, modernisation also threatens the very existence, structure, and purpose of such systems and paradoxically calls into question the wider rationalities and desirability of 'restrictive' state regulation. Examining how such tensions will be played out in the coming decades will tell us much about the restlessness and direction of policy-making processes.

References

ALG (Association of London Government) (2004a) *Through the Eyes of Londoners: Housing and Communities*, ALG, London.

ALG (2004b) *Response to the London Housing Strategy Consultation*, 22 July, ALG, London.

Allen, J. and Pryke, M. (1999) 'Money cultures after Georg Simmel: mobility, movement and identity', *Environment and Planning D: Society and Space*, 17, pp 51-68.

Amin, A. and Thrift, N. (eds) (1995) *Globalisation, Institutions and Regional Development in Europe*, Oxford University Press, Oxford.

Amin, A. and Thrift, N. (2002) *Cities: Reimagining the Urban*, Polity, Cambridge.

Amin, A., Thrift, N. and Massey, D. (2003) *De-centering the Nation: A Radical Approach to Regional Inequality*, Catalyst, London.

Arte-Scholte, J. (2003) *Globalisation – a Critical Introduction* (2nd edition), Palgrave, London.

Atkinson, R. and Wilks-Heeg, S. (2001) *Local Government From Thatcher to Blair: The Politics of Creative Autonomy*, Polity Press, Cambridge.

Australian, The (1964) 'Immigration stop! Workers urged to stay away', 9 December, p 4.

Barker, K. (2004) *Delivering Stability: Securing Our Housing Needs*, HMSO, London.

Barlow Commission (1940) *Report of the Royal Commission on the Distribution of Industrial Labour*, Cmnd 6153, HMSO, London.

Barr, J. (1965) 'New towns as anti-ghettos?', *New Society*, April, pp 2-3.

Bauman, Z. (2005) *Liquid Life*, Polity Press, Cambridge.

BBC News Online (2003a) 'UK "did not want Ugandan Asians"', 1 January.

BBC News Online (2005a) 'Nurses "quitting to buy houses"', 19 June.

BBC News Online (2005b) 'Recruits to nursing "must double"', 25 April.

BBC News Online (2005c) 'Warning over healthcare migration – increasing migration of healthcare workers has resulted in an emergency in the developing world, doctors say', 11 May.

BBC News Online (2006a) 'Many student nurses quit course', 15 February.

BBC News Online (2006b) 'Migration: How points would work', http://news.bbc.co.uk/1/hi/uk_politics/4244707.stm, 7 March.

Beck, U. (1992) *Risk Society*, Polity Press, Cambridge.

Bentley, T. and Halpern, D. (2005) '21st century citizenship', in A. Giddens (ed) *The Progressive Manifesto: New Ideas for the Centre Left*, Polity Press, Cambridge, pp 73-96.

Berman, M. (1982) *All that is Solid Melts into Air*, Verso, London.

Blair, A. (1996) *My Vision for a Young Country*, Verso, London.

Blair, A. (2000) 'The knowledge economy – access for all', Speech to the conference 'Knowledge 2000', London, 7 March.

Blair, A. (2004) *Prime Minister's Speech to the Confederation of British Industry*, Cabinet Office, London, 27 April .

Blair, A. (2005) 'Foreword', in *Controlling Our Borders: Making Migration Work for Britain*, Home Office, HMSO, London, pp 4-5.

Blair, A., Kelly, R., Hewitt, P., Brown, G. and Johnson, A. (2005) *Skills: Getting on in Business, Getting on at Work; Part 1*, HMSO, London.

Bolsover, P. (1955) *No Colour Bar for Britain*, The Communist Party of Britain, London.

Bourdieu, P. (1998) *On Resistance*, Polity Press, Cambridge.

Bowlby, S., Lloyd-Evans, S. and Roche, C. (2004) 'Youth employment, racialised gendering, and school-work transitions', in M. Boddy and M. Parkinson (eds) *City Matters*, The Policy Press, Bristol, pp 323-48.

Bradley, H., Erickson, M., Stephenson, C. and Williams, G. (2000) *Myths at Work*, Polity Press, Cambridge.

Braverman, H. (1977) *Labour and Monopoly Capital: The Degradation of Work in the Twentieth Century*, Monthly Review Press, New York.

Brenner, N. (2003) 'Glocalisation as a state spatial strategy: urban entrepreneurialism and the new politics of uneven development in western Europe', in J. Peck and H. Wai-chung Yeung (eds) *Remaking the Global Economy: Economic-Geographical Perspectives*, Sage, London, pp 197-215.

Brenner, N. and Theodore N. (eds) (2002) *Spaces of Neoliberalism*, Blackwell, Oxford.

Briggs, A. (1979) *Victorian Cities*, Penguin, London.

British Colonial Office (1958) *Community Development*, HMSO, London.

Brooke-Taylor, G. (1951) 'Hemel Hempstead', *Town & Country Planning*, XIX, pp 11-13.

Brown, G. (2006) *Budget Statement 2006*, Speech to the House of Commons, www.hm-treasury.gov.uk/budget/budget_06/bud_bud06_index.cfm, 22 March.

Burton, E. (2000) 'The compact city: just or just compact? A preliminary analysis', *Urban Studies*, 37, pp 1969-2006.

Butler, T. and Robson, G. (2003) 'Negotiating their way in: the middle classes, gentrification, and the deployment of global capital in a globalising metropolis', *Urban Studies*, 40 (9), pp 1791-810.

Byers, S. (2000) 'The knowledge-based economy', Speech to the conference 'Knowledge 2000', London, 7 March.

Calder, A. (1994) *The People's War, Britain 1939-1945*, Pimlico, London.

Carrier, N. and Jeffrey, J. (1953) *His Majesty's Report on External Migration*, HMSO, London.

Carson, H., MP (1952) 'Emigration on a bigger scale', Letter to *The Daily Telegraph*, 27 March.

Carter, E. and Goldfinger, E. (1945) *The County of London Plan*, Penguin, London.

Central Intelligence Agency (2005) *The World Fact Book 2005*, www.cia.gov/cia/publications/factbook/index.html

Chatterton, P. (2002) 'Be realistic, demand the impossible: moving towards strong sustainable development in an industrial region', *Regional Studies*, 36, pp 552-62.

Chick, M. (1998) *Industrial policy in Britain, 1945-1951: Economic Planning, Nationalisation, and the Labour Governments*, Cambridge University Press, Cambridge.

City of Aspen (2000) *Aspen Area Community Plan*, Aspen City Council, Aspen.

Clarke, C. (2005) 'Introduction', in *Controlling Our Borders: Making Migration Work for Britain*, The Stationery Office, London, p 7.

Clarke, J. (2005) 'New Labour's citizens: activated, empowered, responsibilized, abandoned?', *Citizenship Studies*, 25, pp 447-63.

Cochrane, A. (1993) *Whatever Happened to Local Government?*, Harvester/ Wheatsheaf, Buckingham.

Cochrane, A. (1999) 'Just another failed urban experiment? The legacy of the Urban Development Corporations', in R. Imrie and H. Thomas (eds) *British Urban Policy – An Evaluation of the Urban Development Corporations*, Sage Publications, London, pp 246-58.

Cooke, P. (1989) 'Locality, theory, and the poverty of spatial variation', *Antipode*, 21, pp 261-73.

Corriere Della Sera, La (2006) 'A Bangalore le cure per il benessere degli occidentali', 19 February, p 27.

Council for the Protection of Rural England (2006) 'CPRE asks: growth at what price in the South East?', www.cpre.org.uk/news-releases/news-rel-2006/news-briefing-growth-in-south-east.htm, 29 March.

Counsell, D. (1999) 'Sustainable development and structure plans in England and Wales: operationalising the themes and principles', *Journal of Environmental Planning and Management*, 42, pp 45-61.

Cresswell, T. (2001) 'The production of mobilities', *New Formations*, Spring, pp 11-25.

Cruikshank, B. (1999) *The Will to Empower: Democratic Citizens and Other Subjects*, Cornell University Press, London.

Cullingworth, J. (1975) *Environmental Planning 1939-1969, Volume I, Reconstruction and Land Use Planning*, HMSO, London.

Davis, M. (2003) *Dead Cities*, The New Press, London.

De Brunhoff, S. (1976) *The State, Capital and Economic Policy*, Pluto Press, New York.

De Roo, G. and Miller, D. (2000) *Compact Cities and Sustainable Urban Development: A Critical Assessment of Policies and Plans from an International Perspective*, Ashgate, London.

Dean, M. (1999) *Governmentality: Power and Rule in Modern Society*, Sage, London.

DEFRA (Department for the Environment, Food and Rural Affairs) (2005) *The UK Government Sustainable Development Strategy*, Cm 6467, HMSO, London.

DfES (Department for Education and Skills) (2005) *Skills: Getting on in Business, Getting on at Work; Part 1*, Cm 6483-1, HMSO, London.

DH (Department of Health) (2004) *Code of Practice for the International Recruitment of Healthcare Professionals*, HMSO, London.

Dixon, S. (2004) 'Migration within Britain for job reasons', *Office for National Statistics Labour Market Trends*, April, pp 191-201.

Dodgshon, R. (1999) 'Human geography at the end of time? Some thoughts on the notion of time–space compression', *Environment and Planning D: Society and Space*, 17, pp 606-20.

Dorling, D. and Rees, P. (2003) 'A nation ever more divided', *Town and Country Planning*, 72, pp 270-85.

DTI (Department of Trade and Industry) (1995) *Competitiveness: Helping Business to Win*, HMSO, London.

DTI (2004) 'History of the Board of Trade – Introduction', www.dti.gov.uk, accessed 20 February 2006.

Du Gay, P. (1996) *Consumption and Identity at Work*, Sage, London.

Duleep, H. and Regets, M. (1998) 'Immigrants and human capital', *American Economic Review*, 89, p 2.

Duncan, S. and Savage, M. (1989) 'Space, scale and locality', *Antipode*, 21, pp 183-201.

Dychtwald, K., Erickson, T. and Morison, R. (2004) *Workforce Crisis: How to Beat the Coming Shortage of Skills and Talent*, Harvard Business School Press, Harvard.

EC (European Commission) (2002) *Communication 694 Final: Free Movement of Workers: Achieving the Full Benefits and Potential*, Commission of the European Communities, Brussels.

EC (2006) *Free Movement of Workers Since 2004 Enlargement had a Positive Impact – Commission Report Finds*, Press Release IP/06/130, European Commission, Brussels.

Economist, The (1945a) 'The distribution of industry', 3 March, pp 270-2.

Economist, The (1945b) 'The reallocation of labour', 3 February, p 139.

Economist, The (1947) 'Policy for the development areas', 27 November, p 514.

Economist, The (1969) 'The regional trough', 21 July 21, p 75.

Economist, The (1972) 'Blank cheque', 13 April, pp 104-7.

Economist, The (1977) 'London – moving out', 1 January, p 20.

Economist, The (1979) 'No charity, no tax', 14 July, p 107.

Economist, The (2006a) 'Immigration – pick and mix', 11 March, pp 28-30.

Economist, The (2006b) 'Europe's labour mobility – when East meets West', 11 February, p 41.

Economist, The (2006c) 'Turning boomers into boomerangs', 11 February, pp 75-8.

Ehrenreich, B. (2001) *Nickel and Dimed: Undercover in Low Wage USA*, Granta Books, London.

English Heritage (2004) *A Welcome Home: A Sense of Place for a New Thames Gateway*, English Heritage, London.

Environment Agency (2005) *Creating a Better Place: The Environment Agency's Assessment of the Environment in South East England*, Environment Agency, London.

Environmental Audit Committee (2005) *Housing: Building a Sustainable Future*, HMSO, London.

Equal Opportunities Commission (2005) *Britain's Hidden Brain Drain: Final Report*, EOC, London.

ESRC (Economic and Social Research Council) (2005) *Wages and the Distribution of Wealth in the UK*, www.esrcsocietytoday.ac.uk/ESRCInfoCentre/facts/index41.aspx?ComponentId=12619&SourcePageId=12700#footnote

European Parliament (2001) *Recommendation of the European Parliament on Mobility Within the Community for Students, Persons undergoing Training, Volunteers, Teachers, and Trainers*, European Commission, Brussels.

Eurostat (2005) *Europe in Figures: Eurostat Yearbook 2005*, European Commission, Brussels.

Fabian Society, The (1968) *Immigration Facts versus Myths*, The Fabian Society, London.

Fabian Society, The (1970) *Immigration and Race Relations: A Study by David Stephen*, Fabian Research Series 291, The Fabian Society, London.

Field, A. and Crofts, C. (1977) *Some Aspects of Planned Migration to New and Expanding Towns*, GLC Research Memorandum 527, GLC, London.

Financial Times (1955) 'Peopling the Commonwealth', 7 October.

Florida, R. (2004) *Cities and the Creative Class*, Routledge, New York.

Florio, S. and Brownill, S. (2000) 'Whatever happened to criticism? Interpreting the London Docklands Development Corporations' Obituary', *City*, 4, pp 53-64.

Forrest, R. and Kearns, A. (2001) 'Social cohesion, social capital and the neighbourhood', *Urban Studies*, 38, pp 2125-43.

Freeman, R. (2006) *China, India and the Doubling of the Global Labor Force: Who Pays the Price of Globalisation?*, JapanFocus.org, accessed from www.japanfocus.org

Frogner, M. (2002) 'Housing tenure and the labour market', *Labour Market Trends*, Office for National Statistics, London, pp 523-34.

Fuller, S. (2004) 'Intellectuals: an endangered species in the twenty-first century?', *Economy and Society*, 33, pp 463-83.

Galbraith, J. (2004) *The Economics of Innocent Fraud*, Penguin, London.

Gamble, A. (1988) *The Free Economy and the Strong State*, Polity Press, Cambridge.

Gee, F. (1972) *Homes and Jobs for Londoners in New and Expanding Towns*, HMSO, London.

Gibbs, D. (2002) *Local Economic Development and the Environment*, Routledge, London.

Giddens, A. (1995) *A Contemporary Critique of Historical Materialism*, Polity Press, Cambridge.

Giddens, A. (2002a) *Where Now for New Labour?*, Polity Press, Cambridge.

Giddens, A. (2002b) *Runaway World*, Polity Press, Cambridge.

Giddens, A. (2005) 'Neoprogressivism: a new agenda for social democracy', in A. Giddens (ed) *The Progressive Manifesto: New Ideas for the Centre Left*, Polity Press, Cambridge, pp 1-35.

Gogia, N. (2006) 'Unpacking corporeal mobilities: the global voyages of labour and leisure', *Environment and Planning A*, 38, pp 359-75.

Gordon, I. and Buck, N. (2005) 'Introduction: cities in the new conventional wisdom', in N. Buck, I. Gordon, A. Harding and I. Turok (eds) *Changing Cities: Rethinking Urban Competitiveness, Cohesion and Governance*, Palgrave, London, pp 1-24.

Gordon, I. and Turok, I. (2005) 'How urban labour markets matter' in N. Buck, I. Gordon, A. Harding and I. Turok (eds) *Changing Cities: Rethinking Urban Competitiveness, Cohesion and Governance*, Palgrave, London, pp 242-64.

Gough, I. (1979) *The Political Economy of the Welfare State*, Macmillan, Basingstoke.

Greater London Assembly: Affordable Housng Scrutiny Committee (2001) *Key Issues for Key Workers: Affordable Housing in London*, Greater London Assembly, London.

Greater London Assembly (2004) *The Case for London: London's Loss is No-one's Gain*, Greater London Assembly, London.

Green, D. (2006) *Scrap EU Worker Registration Scheme: Statement on the EU Worker Registration Scheme*, The Conservative Party, London.

Guardian, The (1955) 'Squalor pays dividends in Wolverhampton – the new slums of Wolverhampton', 28 November.

Guardian, The (1965) 'Smethwick still to buy up homes – loan from the Ministry sought', 24 February.

Guellec, F. (2003) 'Introduction', *Brain Drain Dossier*, wwwSciDev.Net.

Habermas, J. (1976) *Legitimation Crisis*, Heinemann, London.

Hall, P. (1998) *Cities in Civilisation*, Weidenfeld and Nicolson, London.

Hall, P., Gracey, H., Drewett, R. and Thomas, R. (1973) *The Containment of Urban England: The Planning System: Objectives, Operations and Impacts*. Allen & Unwin, London.

Hall, T. and Hubbard, P. (1998) 'The entrepreneurial city and the new urban politics', in T. Hall and P. Hubbard (eds) *The Entrepreneurial City: Geographies of Politics, Regime and Representation*, Wiley, New York, pp 1-23.

Hannington, W. (1937) *The Problems of Distressed Areas*, Gollancz Press, London.

Hansen, R. (2000) *Citizenship and Immigration in Post-War Britain*, Oxford University Press, Oxford.

Harvey, D. (1989) 'From managerialism to entrepreneurialism: the transformation in urban governance in late capitalism', *Geografiska Annaler B*, 71, pp 3–17.

Harvey, D. (1994) *The Urban Experience*, Blackwell, Oxford.

Harvey, D. (1996) *Justice, Nature and the Politics of Difference*, Blackwell, Oxford.

Harvey, D. (2000) *Spaces of Hope*, Edinburgh University Press, Edinburgh.

Harvey, D. (2005) *A History of Neoliberalism*, Blackwell, Oxford.

Hastings, A. (1999) 'Discourse and urban change: introduction to the special issue', *Urban Studies*, 36, pp 1–17.

Haughton, D. (1997) 'Developing sustainable urban development models', *Cities*, 14, pp 189–95.

Haughton, G. and Peck, J. (1996) 'Geographies of labour market governance', *Regional Studies*, 30, pp 319–22.

Hayes, N. (2005) '"Humanising" construction? The languages of industrial relations reform, full employment and productivity after 1945', *Contemporary British History*, 19, pp 3–26.

Healey, M. and Ilbery, C. (1992) *Location and Change*, Oxford University Press, Oxford.

Healey, P. (1997) *Collaborative Planning: Shaping Places in Fragmented Societies*, Macmillan, Basingstoke.

Health Service Journal (2004) 114 (5914), pp 30–1.

Hennessy, P. (1993) *Never Again*, Vintage, London.

Heseltine, M. (1995) Interview, *On the Record*, BBC Centre, London, 9 July.

HM Treasury (2001) *Productivity in the UK 3 – The Regional Dimension*, HMSO, London.

Hogwood, B. W. and Gunn, L. (1984) *Policy Analysis for the Real World*, Oxford University Press, Oxford.

Holmes, R. (1999) *The Great War*, BBC Books, London.

Home Office (1955) *Working Party Report on the Socio-Economic Problems Arising From the Growing Influx into the UK of Coloured Workers From Other Commonwealth Countries, Draft Report*, HMSO, London.

Home Office (1968) *Voluntary Dispersal of Commonwealth Immigrants*, Draft Working Paper No. 53, HMSO, London.

Home Office (2005a) *The Highly Skilled Migrant Programme Points System*, HMSO, London.

Home Office (2005b) *Controlling Our Borders: Making Migration Work for Britain*, HMSO, London.

Home Office (2005c) *Managed Migration: Working for Britain: A Joint Statement from the Home Office, CBI, TUC,* Home Office Press Release, 5 September.

Home Office (2006) *An Overview of the Work Permit Arrangements,* HMSO, London.

Houlihan, B. (1988) *Housing Policy and Central–Local Government Relations,* Avebury, Aldershot.

Howard, E. (1902) *Garden Cities of Tomorrow,* Faber and Faber, London.

Hutton, W. (2003) *The World We're In,* Vintage Press, London.

Ignatieff, M. (1991) 'Citizenship and moral narcissism', in G. Andrews (ed) *Citizenship,* Lawrence & Wishart, London, pp 26–36.

Imrie, R. and Raco, M. (1999) 'How new is the new urban governance? Lessons from the UK', *Transactions of the Institute of British Geographers,* 24, pp 45–64.

Imrie, R. and Raco, M. (2003) *Urban Renaissance? New Labour, Community and Urban Policy,* The Policy Press, Bristol.

Jackson, J. (2005) *The Highly Skilled Migrant Programme: A Review,* Magrath & Co, London.

Jay, D. (1947) 'Policy for the development areas', *The Economist,* 4 October, p 558.

Jefferys, M. (1954) *Mobility in the Labour Market: Employment Changes in Battersea and Dagenham,* Routledge, London.

Jenks, M., Burton, E. and Williams, K. (ed) (1996) *The Compact City: A Sustainable Urban Form?,* E & F Spon, London.

Jessop, B. (1990) *State Theory: Putting Capitalist States in their Place,* Princeton University Press, Princeton, NJ.

Jessop, B. (2002a) *The Future of the Capitalist State,* Polity Press, Cambridge.

Jessop, B., Bonnett, K., Bromely, S. and Ling, T. (1988) *Thatcherism: A Tale of Two Nations,* Polity Press, Cambridge.

Johnson, J., Salt, J. and Wood, P. (1974) *Housing and the Migration of Labour in England and Wales,* Saxon House Press, London.

Jonas, A. (1996) 'Local labour control regimes: uneven development and the social regulation of production', *Regional Studies,* 30, pp 323–39.

Jones, B. and Keating, M. (1985) *Labour and the British State,* Clarendon Press, Oxford.

Jones, D. (2005) *Speech to CBI Congress, Birmingham,* cited on Channel 4 News, 4 October.

Jones, M. (1997) 'Spatial selectivity of the state: the regulationist enigma and local struggles over economic governance', *Environment and Planning A*, 29, pp 831-64.

Jones, M. (1999) *New Institutional Spaces: TECs and the Remaking of Economic Governance*, Jessica Kingsley, London.

Jones, M. and MacLeod, G. (2004) 'Regional spaces, space of regionalism: territory, insurgent politics and the English question', *Transactions of the Institute of British Geographers*, 29, pp 433-52.

Jordan, B. and Duvell, F. (2003) *Migration: The Boundaries of Equality and Justice*, Polity Press, Cambridge.

Keegan, J. (1999) *The First World War*, Pimlico Press, London.

Kenny, M. and Meadowcroft, J. (eds) (1999) *Planning for Sustainability*, Routledge, London.

Kesselring, S. (2006) 'Pioneering mobilities: new patterns of movement and mobility in a mobile world', *Environment and Planning A*, 38, pp 269-79.

Klein, N. (2002) *Fences and Windows: Dispatches from the Frontlines of the Globalisation Debate*, Flamingo, New York.

Kleinmann, M. (2003) 'The economic impact of labour migration', in S. Spencer (ed) *The Politics of Migration: Managing Opportunity, Conflict, and Change*, Blackwell, Oxford, pp 59-74.

Kymlicka, W. (2003) 'Immigration, citizenship, multiculturalism: exploring the links', in S. Spencer (ed) *The Politics of Migration: Managing Opportunity, Conflict, and Change*, Blackwell, Oxford, pp 195-208.

Labour Party (1943) *Housing and Planning After the War*, The Labour Party, London.

Labour Party (1968) *Citizenship, Immigration and Integration*, The Labour Party, London.

Labour Party (1977) 'Minutes of Cabinet/NEC Working Party on Industrial Policy', 16 November, Labour Party Archive of the Planning Working Group, Manchester.

Labour Party (1980) 'Home Policy Committee – Enterprize Zones', 16 June, Labour Party Archive of the Planning Working Group, Manchester.

Langescu, O. (2006) *EU Call to Life Labour Barriers*, BBC News, 8 February.

Larner, W. and Craig, D. (2003) 'After neoliberalism? Community activism and local partnerships in Aotearoa New Zealand', *Antipode*, 35, pp 403-24.

Larner, W. and Walters, W. (2006) *Global Governmentality*, Taylor & Francis, London.

Law, J. (1994) *Organising Modernity*, Blackwell, Oxford.

Law, C. (1980) *British Regional Development since World War I*, Methuen, London.

Lawless, P. (1989) *Britain's Inner Cities*, Paul Chapman Publishing, London.

LDA (London Development Agency) (2001) *Annual Report, 2000/ 2001*, LDA, London.

LDA (2004) *Sustaining Success: Developing London's Economy*, LDA, London.

Lees, L. (2003) 'Visions of the urban renaissance: the Urban Task Force report and the Urban White Paper', in R. Imrie and M. Raco (eds) *Urban Renaissance? New Labour, Community and Urban Policy*, The Policy Press, Bristol, pp 61-82.

Levitas, R. (1998) *The Inclusive Society? Social Exclusion and New Labour*, Macmillan, Basingstoke.

LHF (London Housing Federation) (2004) *Homes for London's Workers*, LHF, London.

Linehan, D. (2000) 'An archaeology of dereliction: poetics and policy in the governing of depressed industrial districts in interwar England and Wales', *Journal of Historical Geography*, 26, pp 99-113.

Linehan, D. (2003) 'Regional survey and the economic geographies of Britain 1930-1939', *Transactions of the Institute of British Geographers*, 27, pp 96-122.

Little, K. (1972) *Negroes in Britain: A Study of Racial Relations in English Society*, Routledge & Kegan Paul, London.

Livingstone, K. (2004) 'Foreword', in Greater London Assembly, *The Case for London: London's Loss is No-one's Gain*, GLA, London, pp 3-4.

Lloyd, C. and Payne, J. (2003) 'On the political economy of skill: assessing the possibilities for a viable high skills project in the UK', *New Political Economy*, 7, pp 367-95.

London County Council (1961) *The Planning of a New Town*, London County Council Publications, London.

London Olympic Bid Team (2004) *London 2012 Candidate File*, www.london2012.org

Lovering, J. (2006) 'Regionalism and the neo-liberalisation of governance', Paper presented at the ESRC Research Seminar 'The Rise of Multi-level Governance and Meta-governance in an International Context', Sheffield, 2-3 March.

Lowanthal, D. (1997) *The Heritage Crusade and the Spoils of History*, Cambridge University Press, Cambridge.

McConnell, J. (2004) 'First Minister's statement on fresh talent', *Scottish Executive News*, 25 February, pp 1-5.

MacFadyen, E. (1951) 'Letchworth', *Town & Country Planning*, XIX, pp 16-18.

McLaughlin, G. and Salt, J. (2002) *Migration Policies towards Highly Skilled Foreign Workers: Report to the Home Office*, HMSO, London.

MacLeod, G. and Goodwin, M. (1999) 'Reconstructing an urban and regional political economy: on the state, politics, scale and explanation', *Political Geography*, 18, pp 697-730.

McNiven, D. (2005) *Registrar General's Report on Scottish Population*, Scottish Executive, Edinburgh.

McQuaid, R. and Lindsay, C. (2005) 'The concept of employability', *Urban Studies*, 42, pp 197-219.

McQuaid, R., Green, A. and Danson, M. (2005) 'Introducing employability', *Urban Studies*, 42, pp 191-5.

McRobbie, G. (1990) *Small is Possible*, Abacus Press, London.

Major, J. (1995) 'Foreword', in Department of Trade and Industry, *Competitiveness: Forging Ahead*, Cm 2867, HMSO, London.

Maloutas, T. (2003) 'Promoting social sustainability: the case of Athens', *City*, 7, pp 165-79.

Marx, K. (1974) *Capital: A Critical Analysis of Capitalist Production*, Lawrence & Wishart, London.

Massey, D. (1994) *Space, Place and Gender*, Polity Press, Cambridge.

Massey, D. (1995) *Spatial Divisions of Labour* (2nd edition), Macmillan, London.

Massey, D. (2004a) *For Space*, Sage, London.

Massey, D. (2004b) 'Geographies of responsibility', *Geografiska Annaler B*, 86, pp 5-18.

Matless, D. (1993) 'Appropriate geography: Patrick Abercrombie and the energy of the world', *Journal of Design History*, 6, pp 167-78.

May, T. (1997) *Social Research*, Sage, London.

Meadowcroft, J. (1999) 'Planning for sustainable development: what can be learnt from the critics?', in M. Kenny and J. Meadowcroft (eds) *Planning for Sustainability*, Routledge, London, pp 12-38.

Meadowcroft, J. (2000) 'Sustainable development: a new(ish) idea for a new century?', *Political Studies*, 48, pp 370-87.

Megoran, N. (2005) 'The case for ending migration controls', *Antipode*, 37, pp 638-42.

Meyer, J.-P. (2003) 'Policy implications of the brain drain's changing face', Science and Development Network, July, www.sciDev.net

Miliband, R. (1968) *The State in Capitalist Society*, Weidenfield & Nicholson, London.

Miliband, D. (2005) 'Allies of aspiration', Speech to the National Housing Federation Annual Conference, 16 September, www.communities.gov.uk/index.asp?id=1122748

Miller, J. (1998) 'Jobs and work', in N. Smelser (ed) *Handbook of Sociology*, Sage, London, pp 327-59.

Miller, P. and Rose, N. (1990) 'Governing economic life', *Economy and Society*, 19 (1), pp 1-31.

Mohan, J. (1995) *A National Health Service? Restructuring Health Care in Britain since 1979*, Macmillan, Basingstoke.

Moore, B. and Rhodes, J. (1973) 'Evaluating the effects of British regional policy', *Economic Journal*, pp 87-110.

Moore, B. and Rhodes, J. (1976) 'Regional economic policy and the movement of manufacturing firms to development areas', *Economica*, 43, pp 12-31.

MORI (2005) *Survey of Britain's Members of Parliament*, MORI, London.

Morris, S. (2005) 'Sale of premium flats in Bath will house key workers', 28 February, www.SocietyGuardian.co.uk, p 1.

Mueller, C. (1982) *The Economics of Labour Migration: A Behavioural Analysis*, Academic Press, New York.

Mulgan, G. (1998) *Connexity: Responsibility, Freedom, Business and Power in the New Century*, Vintage Press, London.

Mullan, B. (1980) *Stevenage Ltd: Aspects of the Planning and Politics of Stevenage New Town 1945-78*, Routledge & Kegan Paul, London.

National Archives (2004) 'Ministry of Housing and Local Government and predecessors: regional offices: registered files', www.catalogue.nationalarchives.gov.uk/displaycataloguedetails.asp?CATID=7493&CATLN=3&Highlight=&FullDetails=True

National Housing Federation (2005) 'Evidence to the Affordable Rural Housing Commission', *BBC News*, 27 November.

New Statesman (1958) 'The hooligans of Notting Hill', 58, 9 June, p 3.

Nunn, A. (2004) *The Brain Drain: Academic and Skilled Migration to the UK and its Impacts on Africa*, AUT and NATFHE, London.

ODPM (Office of the Deputy Prime Minister) (2003) *Sustainable Communities: Building for the Future*, HMSO, London.

ODPM (2004) *Planning Policy Statement 1: Planning for Sustainable Development*, HMSO, London.

ODPM (2005) *Sustainable Communities*, www.communities.gov.uk

ODPM (2006) *The Key Worker Living Programme: Qualification Criteria*, HMSO, London.

Offe, C. (1985) *Disorganised Capitalism*, Polity Press, Cambridge.

Ohmae, K. (1997) *The Borderless World*, Collins, London.

ONS (Office of National Statistics) (2005) *Migration to the UK*, HMSO, London.

O'Riordan, T. (1992) 'The environment', in P. Cloke (ed) *Policy and Change in Thatcher's Britain*, Pergamon Press, Oxford, pp 297-324.

Orlans, H. (1953) *Stevenage: A Sociological Study of a New Town*, Routledge & Kegan Paul, London.

Paasi, A. (1991) 'Deconstructing regions: notes on the scales of spatial life', *Environment and Planning A*, 23, pp 239-56.

Pacione, M. (1998) *Britain's Cities*, Routledge, London.

Pacione, M. (2004) 'Where *will* the people go? Assisting the new settlement option for the United Kingdom', *Progress in Planning*, 62, pp 73-129.

Pahl, J. and Pahl, R. (1971) *Managers and their Wives: A Study of Career and Family Relationships in the Middle Class*, Allen Lane, London.

Pahl, R. (1988) *On Work: Historical, Comparative and Theoretical Approaches*, Blackwell, Oxford.

Parsons, W. (1988) *The Political Economy of Regional Policy*, Routledge, London.

Paul, K. (1997) *Whitewashing Britain: Race and Citizenship in the Postwar Era*, Cornell University Press, New York.

Pearce, D., Markandya, A. and Barbier, E. (1991) *Blueprint for a Green Economy*, Earthscan, London.

Peck, J. (1996) *Work-Place: The Social Regulation of Labor Markets*, The Guilford Press, New York.

Peck, J. (2005) 'Struggling with the creative class', *International Journal of Urban and Regional Research*, 29, pp 740-70.

Peck, J. and Theodore, N. (2000) 'Beyond employability', *Cambridge Journal of Economics*, 24, pp 729-49.

Peck, J. and Tickell, A. (2002) 'Neo-liberalising space', in N. Brenner and N. Theodore (eds) *Spaces of Neoliberalism: Urban Restructuring in North America and Western Europe*, Blackwell, Oxford, pp 33-57.

Phillips, M. (2004) 'Immigration legislation in Britain', www.movinghere.org.uk, accessed 20 November 2005.

Picchio, A. (1992) *Social Reproduction: The Political Economy of the Labour Market*, Cambridge University Press, Cambridge.

Plant, R. (1991) 'Social rights and the reconstruction of welfare', in G. Andrews (ed) *Citizenship*, Lawrence & Wishart, London, pp 50-64.

Powell, D. (1992) *British Politics and the Labour Question, 1868-1890*, MacMillan, Basingstoke.

Prime Minister's Office (1965) *Immigration from the Commonwealth*, Cmnd 2739, August, HMSO, London.

Pringle, R. (1989) *Secretaries Talk: Sexuality, Power and Work*, Allen & Unwin, London.

Raco, M. (2002) 'Risk, fear and control: deconstructing the discourses of New Labour's economic policy', *Space & Polity*, 6, pp 25-47.

Raco, M. (2003) 'Subject-building, and the discourses and practices of devolution in the UK', *Transactions of the Institute of British Geographers*, 28, pp 75-95.

Raco, M. (2005a) 'A step change or a step back?: The Thames Gateway and the re-birth of the Urban Development Corporations', *Local Economy*, 20, pp 141-53.

Raco, M. (2005b) 'Sustainable development, rolled-out neo-liberalism and sustainable communities', *Antipode*, pp 324-46.

Raco, M. (2006) 'Moving workers with the work: state selection, key workers and spatial development policy in post-war Britain', *Geoforum*, 37, pp 581-95.

Raco, M., Henderson, S. and Bowlby, S. (2006) 'From trickle-down economics to aspirational politics: the new politics of sustainable city-building in the UK', Paper presented at the Association of American Geographers' Conference, Chicago, 7 March.

RCN (2005) *Past Trends, Future Imperfect? A Review of the UK Nursing Labour Market in 2004/2005*, RCN, London.

RCNS (Royal College of Nursing Scotland) (2004) *Nurses Recruited from Overseas*, RCNS, Edinburgh.

Regets, M. (2003) 'Impact of skilled migration on receiving countries', *Policy Briefs – Science and Development Network*, May, pp 1-7.

Reith Committee (1946) *Second Interim Report of the New Towns Committee*, Cmnd 6759, HMSO, London.

Reith Committee (1947) *Report on the New Towns*, HMSO, London.

Rose, N. (1999a) *The Powers of Freedom*, Cambridge University Press, Cambridge.

Rose, N. (1999b) 'Governing cities, governing citizens', in E. Isin (ed) *Democracy, Citizenship and the Global City*, Routledge, London, pp 95-109.

Rose, N. (2000) 'Community, citizenship and the Third Way', *American Behavioural Scientist*, 43, pp 1395-411.

Salman, S. (2002) 'Looking abroad for the solution', *The Guardian*, 20 February.

Sassen, S. (1999a) *Globalisation and its Discontents: Essays on the New Mobility of People and Money*, The New Press, New York.

Sassen, S. (1999b) *Guests and Aliens*, The New Press, New York.

Saunders, P. (1995) *Capitalism: A Social Audit*, Open University Press, Buckingham.

Savage, M., Bagnall, G. and Longhurst, B. (2005) *Globalisation & Belonging*, Sage, London.

Save the Children (2006) *One Million More: Mobilising the African Diaspora Healthcare Professionals for Capacity-Building in Africa*, Save the Children, London.

Sayer, A. (1992) *Method in Social Science: A Realist Approach*, Sage, London.

Sayer, A. (1994) 'Cultural studies and the economy stupid', *Environment and Planning D: Society and Space*, 12, pp 635-7.

SCDI (Scottish Council of Development and Industry) (1962) *Inquiry into the Scottish Economy 1960-61: Report of a Committee under the Chairmanship of J. Toothill*, SCDI, Edinburgh.

Schaffer, (1970) *The New Town Story*, Paladin, London.

Schneider, A. and Ingram, H. (1997) *Policy Design for Democracy*, Kansas University Press, Kansas.

Schoon, N. (2002) *The Chosen City*, Spon, London.

Schumacher, E. (1973) *Small is Beautiful: A Study of Economics as if People Mattered*, Blond and Briggs, London.

Schuppert, F. (2005) 'The ensuring state', in A. Giddens (ed) *The Progressive Manifesto: New Ideas for the Centre Left*, Polity Press, Cambridge, pp 54-72.

Scotsman, The (1953) 'The White Paper on emigration', 25 June.

Scott, A. (2005) *Global City-regions: Trends, Theory, Policy*, Oxford University Press, Oxford.

Scott, P. (2000) 'The state, industrial migration and the growth of new industrial communities in inter-war Britain', *English Historical Review*, 115, pp 329-53.

Scottish Executive (2004) *Building a Better Scotland: Efficient Government – Securing Efficiency, Effectiveness and Productivity*, Scottish Executive, Edinburgh.

SDC (Stevenage Development Corporation) (1949) *The New Town of Stevenage*, SDC, Stevenage.

SEATO (South East Asian Trading Organisation) (1966) *Proceedings to the SEATO Conference on Sustainable Development*, SEATO, Bangkok.

SEEDA (South East England Development Agency) (2003) *Board Meeting Wednesday 11 June – Item 8 Housing*, SEEDA, Guildford.

SEEDA (2004) *Regional Economic Strategy for South East England, 2002-2012*, SEEDA, Guildford.

Sennett, R. (1998) *The Corrosion of Character: The Personal Consequences of Work in the New Capitalism*, Norton Press, New York.

Sennett, R. (2003) *Respect: The Formation of Character in an Age of Inequality*, Penguin, London.

Sharma, S. (2002) *A History of Britain: Volume 3*, BBC Books, London.

Shaw, E. (1996) *The Labour Party Since 1945: Old Labour and New Labour*, Blackwell, Oxford.

Sheller, M. and Urry, J. (2006) 'The new mobilities paradigm', *Environment and Planning A*, 38, pp 207-226.

Skeldon, R. (1997) *Migration and Development: A Global Perspective*, Longman, New York.

Skills for Business Network (2005a) 'Mission Statement', www.ssda.org.uk

Skills for Business Network (2005b) 'Employers – you have new power. Use it', *The Times – Skills Supplement*, 29 November, pp 16-17.

South East RHB (Regional Housing Board) (2005) *South East Regional Housing Strategy, 2004/05, 2005/06*, Government Office of the South East, London.

Spencer, I. (1997) *British Immigration Policy since 1939: The Making of Multi-Racial Britain*, Routledge, London.

Spencer, S. (2003) 'Introduction', in S. Spencer (ed) *The Politics of Migration: Managing Opportunity, Conflict, and Change*, Blackwell, Oxford, pp 1-24.

Spirings, N. and Allen, C. (2005) 'The communities we are regaining but need to lose – a critical commentary on community building in beyond-place societies', *Community, Work and Family*, 8, pp 389-411.

Swenarton, M. (1981) *Homes Fit for Heroes: The Politics and Architecture of Early State Housing in Britain*, Heinmann, London.

Taylor, P. (1999) 'Places, spaces and Macy's: place-space tensions in the political geography of modernities', *Progress in Human Geography*, 23, pp 7-26.

Thatcher, M. (1979a) Speech to the Scottish Conservative Party, Perth, 12 May, Thatcher Archive CCOPR 820/79.

Thatcher, M. (1979b) Speech to the Conservative Political Centre Summer School ('The Renewal of Britain'), Trinity College Cambridge, Thatcher Foundation, Cambridge, 6 July.

Thatcher, M. (1980a) Speech to the CBI Welsh Council, Cardiff, 11 December, Thatcher Archive, Speaking Text, Cambridge.

Thatcher, M. (1980b) Speech to the Press Association Annual Lunch, 11 June, Thatcher Archive, Cambridge.

Thompson, C. (1973) *The Industrial Selection Scheme: A Study of Conflicting Objectives in Urban and Regional Planning*, Working Paper 81, Centre for Environmental Studies.

Thornton, P. (2005) 'Brain drain from UK is "worst in the world"', *The Independent*, 25 October.

Thrift, N. (2003) 'Performance and …', *Environment and Planning A*, 35, pp 2019-24.

Thrift, N. (2005) *Knowing Capitalism*, Sage, London.

Tickell, A. and Peck, J. (2003) 'Making global rules: globalization or neoliberalisation?', in J. Peck and H. Wai-Chung (eds) *Remaking the Global Economy*, Sage Publications, London, pp 163-81.

Times, The (1947) 'Churchill's plea', 29 August, p 1.

Times, The (1956) 'Fewer jobs for coloured men', 8 August.

Tiratsoo, N. and Tomlinson, J. (1998) *The Conservatives and Industrial Efficiency, 1951-64: Thirteen Wasted Years?*, Routledge, London.

Toynbee, P. (2002) *Hard Work: Life in Low Pay Britain*, Bloomsbury Press, London.

Tripp, A. (1942) *Town Planning and Road Traffic*, Edward Arnold, London.

Tuan, Y. (1977) *Space and Place*, Edward Arnold, London.

TUC (Trades Union Congress) (2002) *Migrant Workers: A TUC Guide*, TUC, London.

Turner, B. (2000) *Status*, Minnesota University Press, Minnesota.

Turok, I. (1989) *Development Planning and Local Economic Growth: A Study of Process and Policy in Bracknell New Town*, Pergamon Press, London.

Turok, I. and Edge, N. (1999) *The Jobs Gap*, Joseph Rowntree Foundation, York.

UNISON (2005) *Support for Migrant Workers*, Press Release, 6 September.

Urban Task Force (1999) *Towards an Urban Renaissance: The Report of the Urban Task Force Chaired by Lord Rogers of Riverside*, DETR, London.

Urban Task Force (2005) *Don't Fail England's Towns and Cities at This Crucial Time*, Urban Task Force, London, www.urbantaskforce.org/ UTF_final_report.pdf, accessed 22 November 2005.

Urry, J. (2000) *Sociology Beyond Societies: Mobilities for the Twenty-First Century*, Routledge, London.

Urry, J. (2003) *Global Complexity*, Polity Press, Cambridge.

Ward, S. (2004) *Planning and Urban Change* (2nd edition), Sage, London.

Weaver, M. (2001) 'Loans top-up for Starter Homes Initiative', *The Guardian*, 5 September.

Weber, M. (1968) *Economy and Society: An Outline of Interpretive Sociology*, Bedmeister Press, New York.

Weiner, M. (1995) *The Global Migration Crisis: Challenge to States and to Human Rights*, Harper Collins, New York.

While, A., Jonas, A. and Gibbs, D. (2004) 'The environment and the entrepreneurial city: searching for the urban sustainability fix in Manchester and Leeds', *International Journal of Urban and Regional Research*, 28, pp 279-304.

Whitehead, M. (2003) '(Re)analysing the sustainable city: nature, urbanisation, and the regulation of socio-environmental relations in the UK', *Urban Studies*, 40, pp 1183-206.

Willers, W. (1994) 'Sustainable development: a new world deception', *Conservation Biology*, 8, pp 1146-8.

Wills, J. (2001) *Mapping Low Pay in East London*, A Report Written for TELCO's Living Wage Campaign, Department of Geography, Queen Mary, University of London, London.

Wolmar, C. (2004) *The Subterranean Railway: How the London Underground Was Built and How it Changed the City Forever*, Atlantic Books, London.

Workpermit.com (2005) *A Detailed Guide to the HSMP*, www.workpermit.com/uk/highly_skilled_migrant_program3.htm

Workpermit.com (2006) *UK Government Reveals New Immigration Points System*, 7 March, www.workpermit.com/news/

World Bank (1989) *Urban Policy and Economic Development*, World Bank, New York.

World Commission for Environment and Development (1988) *Sustainable Development: Building for the Future*, Oxford University Press, Oxford.

World Conservation Union (1991) *Caring for the Earth: A Strategy for Sustainable Living*, Gland, Geneva.

Wren, C. (1996) *Industrial Subsidies: The UK Experience*, Macmillan, Basingstoke.

Yorkshire Post (1965) 'Union calls for end to colour bar', 8 July.

Index